Prism Nova

Anthology Tales

Copyright © 2024 R. D. L. Nicholas

All rights reserved.

No part of this book may be reproduced, stored in a retrieval system, or transmitted by any means, electronic, mechanical, photocopying, recording, or otherwise, without written permission from the author.

ISBN (Paperback): 979-8-9908442-5-4
ISBN (Hardcover): 979-8-9908442-6-1
ISBN (eBook): 979-8-9908442-4-7

Table of Contents

Chapter 1	My Mother and My Friend	1
Chapter 2	Gifts for the Lovely Lady	9
Chapter 3	Rumors of the Forbidden Mansion	17
Chapter 4	Motherly Conflict	26
Chapter 5	A Friend for the Forbidden Quest	34
Chapter 6	Killy Ri Forest	41
Chapter 7	Guardians of the Ravine	50
Chapter 8	Diavolo Mansion	58
Chapter 9	An Unsuspecting Summon	66
Chapter 10	Fighting for Survival	73
Chapter 11	Blossoming Romance	81
Chapter 12	The Name of the Game	88
Chapter 13	Joker	94
Chapter 14	Sacrificial Mark	102
Chapter 15	King Tuathal	108
Chapter 16	Foolish Knight	118
Chapter 17	Devil Dog Poker	127
Chapter 18	Creeping Pit	135

Chapter 19	Einri's Dagger	143
Chapter 20	Donal & Mairead	149
Chapter 21	The Doorless Room	157
Chapter 22	For Love or Friendship	168
Chapter 23	Through the Tunnel	175
Chapter 24	Motherly Advice	187
Chapter 25	Fire and Pitchforks	201
Chapter 26	The Fifth Floor	210
Chapter 27	The Stakes	220
Chapter 28	The One Girl	237

Let me tell you a story.

A story from another world,

In another galaxy,

Known as Spiritus Phantasia.

It is a world different from ours,

But also familiar in a way.

In a time that may,

Or may not,

Be on par with ours.

I bring you . . .

Myths of Atlast:

The Ram and Ewe's Quest
for the
Lost Lambs

R. D. L. Nicholas

CHAPTER 1

My Mother and My Friend

... To the world known as Atlast, the fourth planet from its yellow star that is in the Arca Cluster. A planet that possesses three rings which the denizens of the continent, where our story takes place, refer to as the Trinity Rings. It is a world that has two moons; a blue moon known as Nacia, and a gray moon named Evana. And like anywhere else in the universe, the people of this world have many myths, and this one takes place sometime in the XXIVth century AS (Anno Salvator).

It is in Atlast's northern hemisphere continent called Mystia, where the archipelago country of Eiral lies, northwest of the mainland. It has five major islands, with the main one named Elosa, where its main capital, Amelon, lies. Southwest of Elosa is the island of Durigh, with Dunban as its capital in the east, where the denizens of Durigh also happen to possess an accent that is similar to our Irish. It is an island that is either covered by a vast forest, or luscious green fields, with a mountain range along its southern and western coast that takes up a small percentage of the land. The forests tend to have large glades within them that contain enough space to possess farmland and towns. One of those glades, in the southwestern part of Durigh, lies the town of Arvann, where our story begins, at a ranch that is west of the town.

The sun has just risen from its dawn as a flock of ducks flies past the housing area of the ranch, which is only a few hundred yards from the main road. Every house in the housing area has the same masonry built with thatching, which inhabits one family each, with a few barns made of wood to the northwest. A young, thin, girl carrying a basket with light freckles on her face, dark brunette hair, dark blue eyes, and wearing a used dress (with a few patches sewed on), and a light handmade winter poncho, walks out of one of the houses. She only takes a few paces before her mother calls out her name, "Iuile", as she happens to be the fifth eldest of her parent's eight children, and the second eldest of their daughters at the age of fifteen.

After rolling her eyes in agitation, Iuile replies to her parent, "What is it, mother?"

After Iuile's response, her mother comes out of their house and appears to be in her early forties. She also shares her daughter's hair color, but with strands of gray due to age, along with stern brown eyes, wearing an older dress that had been patched up several times, and an apron. Her mother becomes annoyed by her daughter's tone as she replies, "Watch your tongue, young lady." This causes Iuile to change her agitated appearance, to a pleasing one when she turns to face her mother who continues, "And where do you think you're going? Surely not to school since it's closed for today."

"We're completely out of spices and sewing material", replied Iuile with a slight hint of sarcasm, while trying to maintain her composure, "and none of our relatives of aunts, cousins, in-laws, and so forth, have any to spare. So I decided to head to town to pick some up since you always tell me to take initiative, and not to just wait for you to tell me what to do."

This has Iuile's mother hesitant due to suspicion for a moment, before remembering that they do need to stock up, and reply, "That you did." Iuile gives a soft grin as she is under the impression that her mother is about to compliment her for her foresight. Only for her mother to say, "But you foolishly left without telling me where you are going!" Iuile's hope for praise vanished as her mother continued to scold her, "Do you want to get kidnapped by bandits? Or worse...."

"I'm sorry!" Replied Iuile who became embarrassed before softly continuing in anger, "But I'm not a child anymore."

"Then act like an adult", replied her mother in her usual strict tone. "The type of woman who does not let her emotions dictate her actions!" She then takes a deep breath to calm herself before continuing, "Anyway, I don't like you walking to town without your horse. But given this morning's circumstances, it couldn't be helped since Gearoid does need a horse more than you to help your father, and the rest of our kin, with the cattle."

This has Iuile's mother pondering and says to herself, "Nor do I think that anyone around here has a mount to spare at the moment, due to their own errands, and Deus forbid that I let you ride that hog!" This gives Iuile a sigh of relief, as she would die from embarrassment if she rides her uncle's mount. After coming to a decision, Iuile's mother said, "I guess I have no choice but to let you go. Just don't dilly dally while walking to town, no window shopping on what we don't need, or visit any family members, and no riding with, or talking to, strangers."

This struck a nerve with Iuile, who was gazing at the ground to her right while listening to her mother's scold, causing her to immediately turn to her mother and yell, "I'M NOT A...." But she quickly realizes that not only is she making the wrong move, but repeating herself. After pausing for a moment, she continues in a calm manner that would please her mother, "I know very well to ignore anyone who is not native in this glade."

Iuile's mother appears to be getting ready to snap her head off due to her outburst. But considers not to, as she knows that her daughter realizes during her pause, that she was treading into dangerous waters, only to turn back to safe land. Iuile's mother replied with a logical voice, "You know, as long as you are living here, you will always be a child." Those words only anger Iuile as her mother continues, "Well, we wasted enough time arguing, I need you to get to town as soon as possible and be back, so that I can knit new clothes for your brother, Cian." She then mumbles to herself, "Boy is growing way too fast compared to his older brothers." She suddenly realized something, and said in a regular voice, "Better yet, just wait in town until one of your kin heads there to sell the milk, eggs, and so forth in the marketplace after lunch, I think it's one of your brothers' turn. Anyway, you should be done by then, so he'll be able to return to work in no time."

Feeling as if her mother is treating her like a child who needs to be constantly looked after, Iuile quickly attempts to rebuke her in anger. Only for her mother to cut her off once more saying, "That's enough! I need you back as soon as possible, as there is too much to do around here with just your sisters." Iuile's mother gestures for her to approach her, which Iuile responds without argument while bottling her frustration. When Iuile is in front of her mother, she pulls out a coin from her apron pocket and says, "Just head to town, and gather only what we need. Now here's a five copper coin, which you forgot to ask, for the groceries and lunch, since whoever turns it is to head for town won't be there till sometime past noon . . . and don't forget the change, including any zinc coins."

This made Iuile blush brightly while saying, "Yes ma'am", as she does not wish to argue with her mother any longer. She takes the coin and leaves while her mother yells to be careful in her travels. Iuile walks away mad not only at her mother for treating her like a child, but at herself, for she is utterly embarrassed that she did forget to bring money. As Iuile travels down to the main road, she mumbles to herself angrily, "She never gives me a chance to do anything, I wish she could just trust me."

Even though the trek to the main road is not long, it gives Iuile plenty of time to calm down with her feud, and skips in a carefree manner while humming a tune to herself. She glances around to see the flowers blooming, with dew on their petals and surrounding grass, for spring is starting in this hemisphere. It is not until Iuile leaves the ranch's entrance gate to the main road, that she sees a familiar face with beautiful blonde hair, walking from the west down the road toward town, in an absent-minded daze. Iuile becomes ecstatic upon seeing the recognizable blonde, who happens to be none other than her best friend as she calls out her name, "Eilis!"

The seventh child in her family, out of twelve, and the third eldest daughter who appears more mature than Iuile, even though they are the same age. Eilis apparently breaks out of her trance upon hearing her name and notices Iuile. She gleefully rushes towards Iuile while holding her skirt up, so that she can run easily. Once Eilis reaches Iuile, wearing a poncho and a dress that is more worn out than Iuile's, she begins to gasp for air while bending over. Iuile decides to squat low enough to where they are both at head level and smile. When Eilis catches her breath, she lifts her head up to stare at her smiling friend with her charming brown eyes, and noticeable mole on her left cheek. The gaze into each other's eyes causes both of them to start giggling.

They both straighten themselves up with Eilis saying with annoyance, "I am so glad to see you! My mom is driving me crazy with her expectation of me in finding a husband."

"Tell me about it", said Iuile sharing a similar annoyance as they both walk together towards town. "By the way, where's your horse?"

"Let's just say that there are none to be spared at the moment", said Eilis who sounds as if she has no care. She follows her reply with a curious question, "What happened to Pixie?"

"My brother's horse kicked the bucket this morning, and needed one immediately for work", said Iuile. She starts to feel depressed for the loss of a horse for a moment, before setting that emotion aside, and going back to their early conversation, "Anyway, my mom keeps bugging me to go on a date with Niall."

Giggling softly, Eilis begins to recall who Niall was before asking, "Isn't he Finbar O'Faolan's son, the one that always runs away from a fight?"

"That's the one", said Iuile who shares her friend's humor. "Though my mom's exact words were", she then mimics her mother in a mocking tone, "'he's a fine strong lad with temperate ways'." They giggle to themselves for a moment before Iuile continues, "She even goes as far as saying that he decked Einri for wrecking his clan's crop, due to his shenanigans."

Disbelief from what Iuile said has caused Eilis to ask, "He decked Einri? Lord O'Ceallachain's heir? I once saw him bring down an orc with one punch! Great Almighty, he at least bruised almost every young man in town. I don't believe it."

"Neither do I", Iuile said in a disinterested tone, "because I don't see how someone of his stature can easily take down Einri. My mom is just trying to impress me. She even went on that it's not like I'm going to marry the guy, and that I'm just dating him so that I get to know him better."

Giving a soft smirk of finding something relatable, Eilis asked her friend, "Did she give her boring speech on how the purpose of dating someone, is to get to know them and see if this is the person that you want to spend the rest of your life with?"

Amuse that they are on the same wavelength of understanding, Iuile giggles before saying, "It's like our mothers are from the same mold! If I want to date someone . . . it should be with someone I really like."

"Not me", said Eilis with confidence. "The first chance I get, I'll leave here to head for Dunban, and make something of myself."

Becoming concerned for her friend has caused Iuile to ask, "That sounds really dangerous. Our moms always said that there are only two types of women who make it in cities."

Knowing full well of where Iuile is going with her words, Eilis cuts her off with disbelief that she would fall into any of those categories, saying, "Yes, I know, the divine sisters, sorvi, and leasing companions. That will never happen to me, because I will be more than any of those, or a housewife!" Eilis turned to face her friend, with a grin that Iuile is familiar with whenever Eilis is going to ask her something crazy. "Why don't you come with me?"

A feeling of dread fills Iuile as she panicky replies, "I can't."

"You can't", Eilis asks, "or you won't?"

"I won't", replied Iuile with heavy doubt before turning to look into her friend's eyes with worry. "You heard the stories from town of young girls who went into cities alone, and without a male escort."

"Again with men", Eilis said with annoyance in her voice. "Why can't we prove that we don't need them?!"

Iuile replies with concern, "Is it really worth proving with our life, or dignity?"

With no acknowledgment of obtaining any consequences, Eilis quickly responds, "Why not? Why can't we seek our fortune like men? Why can't we be more than housewives?"

"Let's see", said Iuile as she quickly pondered. "We're not as strong as men, not as daring as men, we're more of a target, and let's not forget that the two of us have the same fear of mice and roaches."

"Just so you know", replied Eilis with a grin, "I happened to kill a roach by myself."

Doubt is the only thing Iuile has while glancing at Eilis, and casually asking her, "How did you kill it?"

"With a frying pan tied to a broom", said Eilis with a proud voice, and confident appearance.

"First the roaches", said Iuile with a sarcastic tone, "then the world?"

They both come to a stop, where Eilis gives Iuile a threatening glare and says, "You know, that sarcasm is very annoying."

"Oh, so it's all right when you tease", said Iuile who is not intimidated by her friend, "but when I do it, I'm a jerk."

"It's not that", said Eilis, "it's that I'm being serious, and you're being mean."

"Again", said Iuile, "it's all right when you . . . ."

"Alright", said Eilis cutting Iuile off again, and looking in the opposite direction, "you made your point. Can I help it that I like to tease?"

"I'm sorry, Eilis", said Iuile while giggling. "I'm just teasing with you. However, there is a roach crossing the road."

Both girls have become silent as the roach takes its time crossing the road, causing Iuile to slowly take a few steps back, as she is terrified of the bug. She then watches Eilis to see if whether or not she will kill it with her foot, only to see the look of panic in Eilis' eyes as she stares at the creature. It was not until the roach fully crossed the road, did Eilis said nervously, "No reason to kill something, just to prove a point."

"I guess you're not ready to kill them without your broom-pan yet", said Iuile sarcastically. Eilis falls silent due to embarrassment and gazes away from Iuile to where the cows are grazing on the grass. Iuile on the other hand, feels that she should say something, but realizes that she might make things worse, and therefore decides to be quiet. Their silence remained for the rest of the trek towards town, while a zeppelin flew overhead.

CHAPTER 2

Gifts for the Lovely Lady

The town of Arvann is a simple town with dirt roadways, where most of the buildings are at least two stories high. The first floor has a stone foundation where the shopkeepers conduct their businesses, with the second floor normally being made of wood that jetties, and therefore larger than the first floor. It is either where the shopkeepers live with their families, or stores their stock. The only exception is the inn which is four stories high, with the second to fourth made of wood that has a jetty larger than the other at each floor up.

The locals and the travelers are usually busy during the day, as the farmers, ranchers, and so forth, conduct their business with merchants, or at the shops, pubs, inns, etc. With a train station that designates the town as its last stop, before heading back towards the island's capital of Dunban. Technology based on science is new to this world, as some people in towns and villages believe that the trains and zeppelins are fueled by magic when in reality, they are currently running on coal. This is because long ago, technology was once based on magic, and that liquidized magic did fuel the trains, zeppelins, and even ships, for centuries. Causing the delay of science for centuries at the same time, as the people of Atlast found no need for it due to their reliance on magic.

But after the Magi War, the Rozolic Church, along with other forms of religion, or government, had deemed magic as sacrilege, and therefore illegal due to the dangers and damage caused during the war. This brought about the Plague Age, as several disasters came about due to the forbidden use of magic, causing the economy to crash down. With deadly diseases spreading like wildfire, and an uprise of monstrous creatures led by a sorcerer that brought forth the Third Orbis Crusades. Of course, the ban on magic did not stop wizards and wizardesses from practicing the art in secret, in the name of aiding mankind.

One such aid is to fight off warlocks and witches who do not have enough sense, to leave the dark arts alone. Those who study the Wizardcraft, only reveal themselves to those that show no prejudice towards them. Along with a small group of clergy who believed that the pyzer at the time, went too far with the ban on them. But I'm drifting away from things that do not relate to this story, and I apologize.

Iuile and Eilis have already entered the town at a time that is an hour before noon and are passing by the blacksmith's shop. Iuile tries to act casual as she glances at the shop while blushing, only to be disappointed upon seeing that the blacksmith is shoeing a horse by himself. After passing the blacksmith, Eilis ponders aloud, "I wonder if Mrs. Phadraig has acquired new clothes in her store?"

"I don't have time for that", replied Iuile while avoiding a cart that was being pulled by a pygmy woolly mammoth (at a height of six feet). "I only have time to do my errands and eat lunch, before one of my brothers or cousins comes by to pick me up. Of course, I would like to visit my sister, Roisin, at her husband's barber shop, or Aunt Fiadh and my grandpa at their pub, The Selkie's Dance."

After giving a sigh of annoyance, Eilis asked, "I swear, what's the deal with pubs having ridiculous names? Like this one, The Dizzy Raptor."

"I actually talked about that with my dad one night", replied Iuile. "Of course, I made the mistake of questioning him while he was on the bender, anyway, he said something about letting the customers know that they are not leaving the pub sober." While Eilis is shaking her head over a foolish answer, something occurs to Iuile that causes her to ask her friend, "Now that I think about it, do you need a ride back?"

"No thanks", replied Eilis who appears as if she has no interest in returning home any time soon, "I like to take my time, so as to avoid doing chores."

Feeling annoyed by her friend's lack of responsibility has Iuile asking her, "Eilis, even I get upset with my mom's rambling, but that doesn't mean that I should tap the egg close to the edge of the table."

"Oh please", said Eilis as she rolled her eyes, "I got five sisters who give her plenty of help."

"And I recall your eldest, Darcia, is already wed", said Iuile.

"With my mother playing matchmaker with my second eldest, Finola", Eilis said angrily, "and after she deals with her . . . ." She immediately gets distracted upon gazing through the window of a clothing store named Purple Wears, "Oh my, that is a beautiful deep sky blue dress."

Unable to pay no heed, due to her curiosity, Iuile turns and glances through the window, where she begins to be mesmerized by such an exquisite piece of clothing. For she always dreamed of marrying a handsome nobleman, who sweeps her off her feet. Then takes her to exotic places, have romantic dinners, and dance in grand balls, like in the fairy tales that her mother used to tell her. A time Iuile had long forgotten, when her mother was very kind, and caring to her.

"We can easily buy this if we make something of ourselves", said Eilis excitedly.

Her friend's words cause Iuile to immediately break out of her own trance, and reply with disappointment, "I rather that it be a yellow dress. But, it would be nice to wear a new dress for once, along with my sisters who'll end up with the one I'm currently wearing."

"And a grandiose yellow dress you shall have", said someone from behind. They turn to a muscular young man who is two years older than them, well-dressed, and handsome. He is tall enough to have them slightly tilt their heads up to see his dark hair, and light blue eyes while presenting a magnificent smile to them. However, instead of asking the muscular young man what he meant by his words, Iuile and Eilis were instead distracted by his right eye, due to the bruise on it, as it appears as if he was hit by an object.

"Hello, Einri", said Eilis who was giggling.

Trying to control herself by not laughing, while forgetting what Einri said, Iuile managed to ask him, "What happened to your eye?"

"Eh, uh, my . . . ." Einri said hesitantly, as if he was at a loss for words, before finding a proper reply and answer, "Horse kicked me, while I was waiting for the blacksmith to shoe him."

"I recall that Mr. Smyth never lets anyone stand behind a horse that he is shoeing", said Eilis as she gave a mischievous grin that Iuile is familiar with, whenever Eilis finds some way to tease someone for her amusement. "You wouldn't have gotten that from a fight that you actually lost."

"What are you talking about?" Einri replied with a nervous laugh, "I never lost a fair fight in my life."

Those last words have Iuile fully irate and reply, "Fair? I recall my brother, Gearoid, said that you never fight fair if your life depends upon it." She becomes hesitant after finishing her words, and decides to honestly say, "Well, he didn't speak it like that."

This upsets Einri, and yet curious he decides to ask, "And what did he actually say?"

"Well, I can't tell you", said Iuile, "because it is something that a lady should not dare say." Her eyes then begin to wander, for she cannot help but utter her brother's rude comment. But she does not wish to sacrifice her dignity by repeating them, as she knows that she will never hear the end of it from her mother if word gets out on what she blurted out. Her only option is to turn to Eilis and whisper it into her ear. For she knows that her friend would not dare speak it out loud unless she wants to catch some serious fury from her own mother as well. When Iuile finished revealing the comment, Eilis started to break out into a hysterical laughter.

This only enraged Einri as his face became red, causing the girls to prepare themselves to hear a spoiled boy's rant. But to their surprise, Einri quickly regains his proper color before saying, "Well, curiosity does kill the cat, Iuile, and I would not dare force you to speak of something that is unladylike. I would, however, like to give you a proper apology by bringing you to dinner. I'll even buy you a new dress as a gift so that you will have something formal to wear."

The thought of actually receiving a new dress for herself, is very tempting for Iuile, as she cannot lie to herself about wanting to accept such an offer. However, recollections of Einri's misdeeds to those she holds dear, have Iuile reply, "I'm terribly sorry, Einri, but I would never go out with someone who . . . ." She was suddenly cut off by Eilis who elbows her side, causing Iuile to react to the pain before asking her friend in a whisper, "What was that for?"

"You know what that was for", whispered Eilis. "Don't turn down his offer."

This shocked Iuile who replied, "What about the talk we had earlier?"

"It's different when the guy is rich", said Eilis as she gave off a greedy smile.

"No", replied Iuile in her normal voice, "I will not date someone who harasses my kin to the point that my brother, Peadar, was beaten up! Which happened here just yesterday!"

"That little turd was your brother?" Einri mumbles to himself to where Iuile and Eilis can easily hear him.

Iuile takes Einri's words as an offense and asks, "Excuse me?"

Realizing that they heard his muttering, Einri coughs a bit before saying, "What I actually said, was that it must have been a misunderstanding, as I would never beat someone up for no reason."

"You beat him up because he tripped and fell into the mud", Iuile said angrily. "Which some of it splashed onto your, so-called, expensive boots!"

"Well . . . you see . . . ." said Einri who began to trail off as he rubbed the back of his neck. His eyes then begin to wander to the point that he sees something that enrages him, and yells out, "HEY NIALL!!! IS THAT YOU?!" Iuile and Eilis turn to see a shaggy blonde-haired young man, of whom Einri assumes to be Niall, who appears thin and is wearing a beat-up fur coat with what seems to be leather armor underneath. He is also holding the reins of his raptor which he is walking with, which is green with black and brown patches. The shaggy blonde turns towards Einri who continues aloud, "Yeah, I know it's you now, coward!" Niall appears indifferent towards Einri's comment, and glances over at Iuile and Eilis (causing Iuile to blush) for a moment, before turning and walking off with his raptor.

With a mischievous grin, Eilis says to Einri as if she just deduced a mystery, "Oh I see now, the rumors are true that you finally lost a fight . . . and to Niall of all people."

What Eilis had spoken had apparently struck a nerve with Einri, who became furious and embarrassed as he said, "What did you say?!"

"Oh, I'm just teasing you", replied Eilis who began to flirt with him, "I know that there is no way on Atlast that a simple farm boy could ever beat up a mighty noble, such as you."

It seems to work, as Einri begins to calm down for a moment before saying, "Of course you are. You had always been known to be a huge tease when it comes to men."

"You have no idea", Iuile thought to herself as she folded her arms, and casually looked the other way.

"Anyhow", said Einri who was staring in the direction that the shaggy blonde went, "I'll let you think on my offer, Iuile." He then returned his attention to Iuile, and gentlemanly said, "Now, if you will excuse me."

When Einri left a good distance to go after the shaggy blonde, Iuile said to Eilis, "You got a lot of nerve."

"For what?" Replied Eilis who does not believe that she did anything wrong, "Of what I said about Einri? The guy is always hitting on you, I just don't see why you shouldn't take up on his offer. He may stop harassing your brothers and cousins if you do."

"Because he is despicable", said Iuile, "and unforgivable for what he does to people. Besides, you know that I like . . . ."

Their conversation was suddenly interrupted by a group of young men who approached them, with one of them nervously saying to Eilis, "Hello Eilis . . . you're pretty as always." He hands Eilis flowers, that he apparently picked from the ground, while continuing, "I saw these, and thought of you."

He is then knocked over by another young man with a wrapped present, which he hands to Eilis while saying with confidence, "Who you calling pretty? Eilis is more than pretty."

"Yeah", said another young man, with annoyance, who appeared below the second, and handed Eilis his gift while saying with grace, "she's beautiful." Iuile takes a few steps back due to more young men appearing and attempting to get Eilis' attention, as she starts to flirt with every single one of them. With not a single one of them paying any attention to Iuile, who stands there with jealousy, along with other girls who are around their age, who give a sinister glare towards her friend.

CHAPTER 3

Rumors of the Forbidden Mansion

Regardless of where you live, every country, in any world, has its own tales that the natives enjoy talking about. Including the ones involving terrifying places that no one with a sane mind would dare go to. Places that are very taboo, yet, ironically, tempting to go due to a fool's curiosity. Only for that poor fool to never return because of an untimely disappearance, and possibly death. One such tale is about to be known to you as Iuile finally finished her errands, with both her and Eilis' ponchos having been taken off, and placed in their own baskets, due to the weather becoming too warm for them. After Iuile had ordered a sandwich meal as take-out, and placed it in her basket, Eilis, who also ordered out, suggested eating at the northwestern part of town.

This does not please Iuile, for she knows why Eilis would want to eat over there. But she is not in the mood to convince Eilis to eat someplace else, because she is still mad about how her friend gets all the boy's attention. This intense anger has caused her to think to herself, *"Deus forbid that she tells them that she is not interested in them. Otherwise, she will not only lose attention to herself, but all the free stuff that she'll get."* She glances at the bags that Eilis is carrying, for they contain the gifts that she received that only she likes. As with any gift that Eilis does not like, she throws it away with no one, but Iuile, looking.

"I wouldn't have a problem if Bradach wasn't one of her admirers", Iuile continues to ponder. *"Out of all those boys that are interested in her, why does it have to be him? I have half a mind to tell Eilis how selfish she is for robbing not just me, but every other maiden in town from having a date. Oh, how I would like to tell Bradach the truth about Eilis and confess my feelings for him."* Iuile's pondering begins to make her blush upon becoming hopeful, only for the reality that she views to break in, and begins to think, *"But then he'll believe that I was lying about Eilis, turns me down, and hates me for the rest of my life."*

"My, what romantic things are you dreaming about", said Eilis with her mischievous grin on her face. "It wouldn't involve a certain blacksmith's son named Bradach, would it?"

This has Iuile turn to Eilis with a blank look, because she has been taken off guard to where she loses all train of thought, before blushing upon realizing what her friend just said and replied, "It wasn't that, Eilis!"

Eilis only giggled while they left the north edge of town, and begins to walk down a road with a stone wall fence to their left, before saying, "I was just teasing, but sorry about Bradach. It's really hard to keep him away when he's so obsessed with me like every other guy."

"I know", said Iuile, "it's just really frustrating to see him ogle over you, instead of me."

"That wouldn't be a problem if you just confessed to him", replied Eilis.

The thought of confessing to Bradach, has caused Iuile to fluster and say, "It's not that easy. Every time I tried, I panic and chicken out."

"Well you better", said Eilis teasingly, "or I'll just take him for myself."

"That's not funny", replied Iuile angrily, even though she knew that her friend was not serious, and was only trying to motivate her.

They continue to walk down the road while gossiping until there is a gap in the fence, where they walk through it to enter a tall grassy field. From there they approach a tree on a hill and sit under it, facing northwest, with a view of farmlands stretching towards the edge of the glade. Beyond the forest to the west, swarmed by a sea of clouds, is a mountain range known as Gaibroch Mor Mountains. Both girls pull out their meals from their own baskets and begin to eat in silence until the whistle from the train close by, startled them.

"Holy moly", said Eilis who is flustered and annoyed. "That steam engine scared the daylights out of me. Water-fueling racket monsters if you ask me"

"Coal, not water", said Iuile to correct her friend while chewing her food. After she finishes the first bite of her sandwich, she excuses herself for talking with food in her mouth before saying, "They're fueled by coal to boil the water that powers the train."

"Whatever", replied Eilis, "it's all algebra and magic to me." Eilis continues to eat her own sandwich and stare towards the mountains for a moment, while Iuile gazed at a zeppelin drifting north, before saying, "I do wonder if the tales are true?"

Those words cause Iuile to roll her eyes with annoyance, for she knew Eilis was about to bring up that subject because they always have this conversation whenever they are under the same tree. Iuile sighs heavily before replying, "Even if it is, that place is known to be extremely dangerous to the point that it is forbidden to go over there. We even had people travel through town in search of it, not to mention Jevul Jagers, who wished to collect the one platinum coin bounty, venturing forth to that mansion. None of whom ever returned. It'll be safer to catch King Tuathal of the little people, or any other leprechaun for their three wishes than to go to that cursed place."

"Yeah, but it won't be as romantic", said Eilis who gazed towards the sea of clouds in a daze. "Just imagine, a place where every night is a masquerade party, with a Romalia theme, where there is singing and dancing. I'm curious about what type of games they have over there, or what shows they perform. Don't you ever wonder what Marquis Savio DeGallo looks like, and whether or not he can really grant your wish? Just think about it, you could wish for anything you want, your deepest desires, becoming a reality."

"From what I heard, he is a wolf in sheep's clothing", said a mysterious voice that caused both girls to be startled again. They turn to their left to see the young man, whom Einri assumes to be Niall, from earlier who is mounted on his raptor. He appears to be ashamed as he decides to reply while looking at his raptor's head, "Sorry, I was passing by when I overheard."

Iuile attempts to ask the young man a question, only for Eilis to intervene by asking, "Niall, right?"

"Yes", replied Niall with annoyance.

"Sorry", said Eilis", "but I wasn't sure earlier. It's really hard to tell you and your brothers apart, even though none of you were born on the same day."

This appears to make Niall agitated, and respond in a mumble that the girls could barely hear, "Blind as a blasted bat if you can't tell."

Iuile on the other hand, turns to Eilis with confusion when she finishes speaking, and asks her friend during Niall's mumbling, "You seriously could not tell them apart?"

What Iuile said dumbfounded Eilis who asked, "Wait, you knew it was him the whole time?"

"Of course I knew it was him", replied Iuile. "It's no different than telling twins apart. You just need to pay attention to the details of their appearance."

Such reasoning caused Eilis to raise an eyebrow with puzzlement, as she decided to whisper to her friend to where Niall could not hear, "I thought you said you did not like him?"

Blushing like someone with a sunburn, Iuile replies in a whisper, "I don't! I got a few twins in my family, remember!"

This only made Eilis look away, and shake her head while grinning, before saying with doubt, "Of course." She then returns her attention to Niall and asks him, "Anyway, what do you know of Marquis DeGallo?"

This has Niall silent, while slightly turning his head away from the girls, for a moment before saying, "Only that he will grant you one wish if you beat him in a game, and if you in someway do beat him, the wish that he will grant is only equivalent to that of the devil's promise . . . empty."

When Niall finished speaking, Iuile remembered the question that she wanted to inquire with him, before Eilis interfered, and asked Niall, "Why were you in town?" Only for her words to cause Niall to turn his head further away while fidgeting with his rein.

There was only silence from Niall for a moment, before he finally decided to turn in the girls' direction, while not making any eye contact, to say, "It's . . . my turn to hunt. I came by to purchase a new string for my longbow."

Niall's choice of weaponry has perplexed Eilis, causing her to ask, "Wouldn't a rifle be a better weapon?"

"A rifle can easily spook other animals close by", said Niall who sounds nervous, and talking as if he is reading a manual, "and attract dangerous monsters in Killy Ri Forest." He turned his attention to his raptor's head again before continuing, "I can also catch a lot of game if I use a bow, and avoid the monsters easily at the same time. Arrows are also cheaper than bullets, and can be easily reused."

"Is that so", said Eilis who does not appear impressed. She then has a puzzlement occur to her, making her ask him, "Now that I think about it, why do hunters use raptors? Why not horses?"

"Because they're good at hunting", replied Niall. "For they know how to stay quiet, unlike a horse. They can also . . . ." Niall paused for a moment after realizing that he is droning in his response, and decides to cut it short saying, "I'm sorry, but I wasted enough time, as hunting takes time, patience, and luck. Excuse me."

"Wait! I have one more question", said Iuile who quickly stood up, and to her relief, Niall decided to wait for her question. "Did you really punch Einri?"

With his head still facing away from Iuile and Eilis, Niall is once again being silent for a moment, before finally answering, "Yeah."

This shocked the girls to the point that Eilis asked, "How long did the fight last?"

Again, Niall is silent before answering, "I hit him once. And he went down."

"There's no way Einri went down that easily", said Eilis who sounds disbelief, "and since when did a coward have the courage to fight a noble?"

"Your ignorance of what it means to be courageous is pathetic", said Niall who turns to make eye contact with Eilis, while knowing full well that he upset her with his insult. "And just so you know, Lord O'Ceallachain thanked me himself, as he is getting sick and tired of his son harassing the town. I can also care less if you of all people would believe me or not. Now if you excuse me." He pulls his rein saying, "Let's go, Crono". The raptor dashes away silently from the girls and heads west towards the place known as Killy Ri Forest.

Utterly offended by what Niall said, causes Eilis to complain to Iuile who decides to sit back down, "The nerve of him! Can you believe that he called me ignorant!" They both watch Niall silently head west for a moment before Eilis says, "Huh, that explains how he easily snuck up without us noticing. Raptors really are quiet."

When Niall rides off until he is a good distance away, Iuile (whose cheeks are red) realizes that she is in a stupor. She breaks out of her trance to turn to her friend, while choosing her words carefully so as to not start an argument, and ask, "You know, I just realize that he comes off really shy until you stirred his cauldron."

Completely surprised by what Iuile just said, Eilis turned and stared at her friend, as if she just realized that Atlast has two moons, before replying, "Are you telling me that you do not know what Niall's parents are known to have?"

This puzzles Iuile to where she asks, "No, what?'

"They're known to have nothing but sons", said Eilis. "That's why he is being shy, he has trouble talking to girls around his age who are not related to him." She then changes the subject by asking, while looking back at Niall's direction, "Though now that I think about it, isn't it a little early to bring a raptor out from brumation?"

"Well, spring does begin at the start of the new year", replied Iuile. "So he should be fine."

As they continue to watch Niall, who changes direction to travel down the main road, Eilis turns to ask Iuile, "How often have you talked to Niall?"

"Once in a while", replied Iuile causally.

"Interesting", said Eilis with a curious look on her face. After pondering in silence, she decides to ask, "Had you told him that you like Bradach?"

Having Niall, or anyone other than Eilis, and a few female family members, know about her feelings for Bradach, caused Iuile to feel embarrassed and reply, "Of course not! Why would I?"

"Oh, no reason", replied Eilis who sounded coyish. "It just makes sense now on how you knew it was Niall. I just don't know if I should be curious on either why you don't know about him being sisterless, since, you know, you're already acquainted with him. Or that you never told me how well acquainted you are with Niall, and . . . other things, like how shy he is when he is with you."

Before Iuile has a chance to respond, a horse carriage passing by catches their attention, causing them to look behind the tree, and see that it is on the same road that they traversed earlier. They can barely make out the driver, who appears to be looking for someone, or something, when he gazes in their direction and stops. The driver then jumps off his seat and begins to run towards them. It takes Iuile a moment before she recognizes the driver is none other than her third eldest brother. Iuile realizes that something is wrong with the way her brother is moving and begins to dash toward him after grabbing her basket. When they reach each other, Iuile knows for certain that something horrible has happened upon seeing the look on his face, as if he has seen death, causing her to ask, "Peadar! What's wrong?

"It's Dad", said Peadar, with the same color hair and eyes as her, while being covered in bruises as he pants. "He had fallen deadly ill while we were branding the cattle!"

Fear and horror have overcome Iuile before asking, "What happened!?"

"No time to explain", reply Peadar. "I picked Roisin up at Tooth & a Haircut while looking for you in town", his tone then changed to annoyance, "which was frustrating since you were supposed to stay in town!"

This caused Iuile to panic, for she now remembers her mom saying that she should wait in town until one of her kin came by to pick her up. This made Iuile worry about getting into more trouble with her mother, and genuinely said, "I'm so sorry, Peadar! I just got distracted from my conversations with . . . ."

"Don't worry, I won't tell Mom about this since it's not really important", said Peadar intercepting his sister's apology, as he does believe that Iuile might have been absent-minded, due to her friend. "Just don't do it again. Now let's go, Roisin will explain what happened while I drive us to the clinic."

This makes Iuile feel relieved that she is not going to be in trouble with her mother, but it does not give her any real peace of mind, as she is now fully concerned about what happened to her father. Iuile tries to hold back her tears due to her fear of the worse for now is not the time to cry without knowing full well what is going on. Before Iuile and Peadar could head towards the carriage, Eilis yells for them to wait, and wonders what is going on. Iuile turns to her friend, and manages to control herself to say, "My dad is at the clinic due to some illness, I need to go!"

Eilis becomes shocked for a moment before saying, "Well then, go on! You don't need to worry about me, I'll be fine." Iuile thanks her dear friend for her understanding, followed by exchanging a farewell with words and a hug. Iuile then leaves with Peadar towards the carriage, where her brother jumps onto the driver seat, and waits for Iuile to enter the carriage, and closes its door, before driving off.

When Iuile enters the carriage, and secures the door for safety, she sees her eldest sister, Roisin, who possesses the same hair color as her, but has their mother's eyes. She was already crying with a handkerchief in one hand, and cradle-holding her second child, and only daughter, Myrna, who is only a year old, in the other. Iuile noticed that her son was not with her, which she assumed that he was left with her brother-in-law at his barber shop. When Iuile sits next to Roisin, she immediately hugs her for comfort before asking her what happened. Only for Roisin to respond while trying to hold back her tears, "Peadar told me that he was fine at first, while they were branding the cattle, when suddenly, Dad started coughing. They didn't think much about it until he coughed up blood. Next thing they knew, he fell to the ground and passed out!"

CHAPTER 4

Motherly Conflict

Over the past few millennia, the denizens of Atlast's medical problems were either solved by the use of magic, or science. Usually magic. However, the age of science had become a necessity late into the Discovery Age, thanks to the large population relying more on medications, rather than potions. Yet there are still those in Mystia that use the art of Alchemy or Herbology. Arvann is one of the towns that use both a doctor named Dr. Keegan McCleary and a wizardess named Granny Yueng (an old lady who is not related to anyone in town but likes to be called by that name). Which ones they go to, depends on the situation, or their belief. In Iuile's father's case, not to mention the current situation, they decided on a scientific professional.

Now, there is nothing unique about the clinic that Iuile's father is currently at, far southwest of Arvann, as it is not really a clinic. If anything, it is just a house that the natives of Arvann refer to as a clinic, even though there is only Dr. McCleary who lives there with his wife, who works as a midwife and aids him as a nurse. It is also one of the few buildings in and around town where the second-story floor is also made of masonry. The place is surrounded by a stone fence, that is an average adult's waist high, with a barn

The Ram and Ewe's Quest for the Lost Lambs

next to the building where Dr. McCleary keeps his horses, and stagecoach, for house calls.

Peadar parked the carriage outside the fence next to several other carriages, along with their relatives' mounts of horses, pygmy woolly mammoths, donkeys, oxen, and a pig from that weird uncle. Iuile made a mad dash towards the house when the carriage stopped, with Roisin right behind her at a slower pace due to her infant. Peadar managed to catch up and jog beside his eldest sister, in case she needed assistance. Before Iuile passed through the gate, she noticed her father's sister, Aunt Caitriona, with her daughters (Iuile's cousins), Kiera and Sinead (all of whom are blonde), a few yards north of the inner fence, and facing northeast. Iuile ignores them as she is too concerned for her father's condition to wonder what they are doing, and heads straight to the building.

When Iuile enters the clinic, she sees her younger siblings waiting at the bottom of the stairs. With her grandmother, Etna, sitting in a chair, and cradle-holding her youngest brother, Cian, who is blonde and fast asleep. Sitting next to, and being comforted by, her grandmother, are her younger twin sisters, Bidelia and Nessa, who are both brunette with blue eyes. With the rest of her kin in the waiting room, right of the stairs, who are able to make time to come by and give support, as they appear either ill or distressed over the worst-case scenario. When Peadar and Roisin enter the building, Iuile comes into the waiting room where she finds her eldest brother, and elder twin to Roisin. He is sitting on a couch with his redheaded wife, Raicheal, and their twin, brunette, daughters, Lean and Lile, as Iuile approaches him and asks, "Roibeard, why are you all still down here?"

"Dr. McCleary asked us to wait down here", replied Roibeard, "as he doesn't want us to disturb him while he is examining Dad."

While Roibeard is answering Iuile's question, Roisin begins to look around, as if she is searching for someone. When Roibeard finished speaking, Roisin asked her twin brother, "Where's Mom, and how is she doing?"

"She seemed fine when she asked Mrs. McCleary earlier if she could use the kitchen", replied Roibeard, "so that she can make something for everyone. While at the same time making her usual mumbling to herself, mostly about blaming Dad for his carelessness."

This does not surprise Iuile who goes down the end of the hallway, which is left of the stairs, to the kitchen, and sees her mother very calmly making tea and biscuits. Infuriating by how her mother is acting as if nothing horrible had just happened, Iuile approaches her mother and asks, "What are you doing?"

Iuile's mother turns to her with eye contact that says, what a stupid question to ask you foolish child. While breathing heavily, Iuile's mother replies strictly, yet calmly, as she returns her attention to kneading the dough, "I'm making snacks and refreshments for everyone while we wait for Dr. McCleary to finish examining your father."

When Iuile's mother finishes speaking, Roisin enters the kitchen and pauses, as she senses tension, before asking their mother, "Do you need any help, Mom?"

"Like I told to your aunts, sisters, cousins, and such", said their mother, "I like to do this alone, for there is no need to worry over . . . trivial matter."

This strikes a nerve in Iuile who replies, "Trivial matter? Trivial matter? YOUR HUSBAND, OUR FATHER, COULD BE DYING IN AGONIZING PAIN!!! And you consider this trivial matter?!"

"Iuile", said Roisin as she tried to calm Myrna, who was becoming upset from the yelling, while their mother gave the sign of the clover. "That's enough!"

"NO!" Iuile snaps back at her sister, after turning in her direction, with tears in her eyes, "She's always like this! It's one thing that she never shows feelings towards you or me! But not to be heartbroken of her own husband, our father, who could die at any . . . ." Iuile becomes silent when someone forcefully turns her around and is slapped by none other than her own mother. Iuile is shocked by what her mother did, whose slapped cheek is covered in flour, as she slowly turns to stare at her mother's calm face, with rage in her eyes. She also noticed that her mother is breathing more heavily, which Iuile assumes that she is trying to hold her anger back.

After taking a deep breath, Iuile's mother wipes her hands on her apron while saying, "I told you once, and I told you a thousand times, don't let your emotions dictate your actions. Otherwise, you will one day have something horrible happen to you." She grabs a towel, and hands it to Iuile while telling her, "After you clean your face, I want you to go wait outside, and not to come in until I call for you." Iuile grudgingly accepts the towel and cleans the flour off her face before throwing it at her mother, who grabs the towel without it touching her head, and runs out of the kitchen crying.

As Iuile runs down the hallway, Aunt Caitriona and Sinead just enter the clinic while aiding Kiera, who is in the later stages of her pregnancy and appears tired and stressed. When Iuile noticed her relatives entering, she carefully passed by them and exited the building. Iuile continues to run until she passes the gate, and into a grassy field where she falls to her knees. She then begins to sob over her mother's cruelty, followed by crying even more due to her father's condition.

A squirrel and several birds take notice of Iuile's wailing, with the horses and other mounts paying no heed, as she cries for what seems like an eternity for her. When suddenly she feels someone's hand touching her shoulder, causing her to turn and see Roisin bending over her, with a smile on her face. She does not have Myrna in her hands, telling Iuile that Roisin had handed her to a kin, before heading outside to comfort her. Roisin kneels next to Iuile and hugs her saying, "Mom does love Dad, she just doesn't show it openly." Roisin decides to stop hugging Iuile and continues, "The only reason she is hard on us now, is because she doesn't want us to grow up spoiled and weak. Being an adult is not as easy as you think, and I thank Mom for her hardship which made me as strong as I am today. The day will come when you will thank her too."

Iuile finds this hard to believe, and wonders if Roisin is just saying this to make her feel better. She always remembers her as being too kind and optimistic for her own good towards everyone. She also ponders if she heard her sister right when she said, 'hard on us now', but assumes that she misheard her. They both wait outside for an hour and talk before Roibeard calls for them. When they approach him at the front door, Iuile asks if Dr. McCleary is finished seeing their father.

"Yes he did", said Roibeard with a gloomy appearance, and shoulder-holding Lile who appeared upset, "and it's not good."

Those words cause Iuile's heart to skip a beat, with Roisin asking what is on her mind, "What is it?"

"Dr. McCleary said that he has a serious illness called pneumonia", replied Roibeard who suddenly appeared as if he had seen a ghost, "and that he is completely out of the proper medicine that can cure it. He is also not sure if he will last before the medicine from Dunban arrives. Even by train, heading there and back would take almost six days, if it did not make any stops. By then it will be too late due to how severe the illness is. Of course, it would have been quicker by zeppelin, except the only skyport in Durigh is at Dunban. Anyway, we are visiting Dad in groups, with Mom saying not to get you till last, Iuile. But Dad wishes to see you immediately."

"Wait", said Roisin, "what about Granny Yueng?"

"Mom said the wizardess left for her yearly trip to Amelon to see her sister two days ago", replied Roibeard. "Even though she goes by cart and catches a ferry from Durigh to Elosa, it might still be too late to catch up with her and bring her back." Those words cause Roisin to cover her mouth while her brother continues, "Well Iuile, go on, I need to go find Gearoid."

When Roibeard leaves, Roisin begins to have tears filling her eyes, as she now believes in what is to become their father's fate, with no means of any hope. Iuile stands there with a blank stare, due to the harsh reality that has been bestowed upon her. Only for her trance of despair to be interrupted by Roisin, who tells her while trying not to burst out crying, "Go on ahead . . . Iuile . . . I want to . . . calm down before . . . seeing Dad."

When Iuile agrees and dreadfully enters the building, she recalls what Roibeard said about their father wanting to see her immediately, making her very nervous, for she has a feeling that her mother told him of what happened earlier. Iuile slowly walks up the stairs as memories of her father begin to pass by her mind. As she remembers the time when her father comforted her, after she scraped her knee as a child, by cradling her in his arms. Another is the time he made goofy faces, and acted like a fool in order to make her laugh. She then clenched her wooden clover that he carved, just for her, as a necklace. Followed by a recent time when he gave her a head wreath that he made himself.

When Iuile reaches the second floor, she sees her mother down the hall and sitting in a rocking chair while knitting outside of what is obviously her father's room, with Cian sleeping in her lap. Iuile knows that when her mother is knitting in a particular way, means that she is in her own world, and if she is quiet enough, she can pass by her mother without exchanging any words. Iuile tiptoes quietly and manages to reach the door without her mother noticing. When she is about to touch the doorknob, her mother says in a calm and nurturing tone, while not looking away from her knitting, "You really need to control your emotions, sweetie.

"Iuile closes her eyes tight while her mother continues, "Otherwise, you'll ruin your life with irrational decisions . . . . Anyway, where's Roisin?"

Holding back her anger, and her tears, Iuile replies back, "When Roibeard told us of Dad's condition, she lost control and started crying. She said she wanted to calm down before seeing him, and told me to go on ahead."

There is only silence as Iuile's mother sits in her chair knitting, as if pondering over Iuile's words, before replying, "Don't say anything that will upset your father."

Overcome with relief that there is going to be no conflict with her mother, Iuile opens her eyes and replies, "Yes ma'am." When she finishes speaking, she hastefully and quietly enters the room.

After closing the door, Iuile turns towards the bed where she sees her father with his goofy grin that she loves, the blue eyes she inherited, gray hair with a little blonde that he has left, and his short beard. She immediately dashes toward to hug him, causing her father to blurt out, "Slow down there, pumpkin, and not so tight." Iuile's father begins to undergo severe coughing, causing Iuile to immediately stop hugging him, and takes a better look at her father to see that his face is very pale. When he stopped coughing, he said to her, "I need you to be a little gentler until I'm fully rested, pumpkin. Now I need you to listen to what I have to say." Iuile kneel next to his bed as she listens to her father, "Your mother loves us very much, hehe, she's just too stubborn to show it since you started to blossom."

"I really find that hard to believe", said Iuile while holding her tears back. "She's the only woman here who is not upset!"

"Baaaa, she's just trying to be strong for you and your siblings' sake", replied Iuile's father. "Just remember", he places his hand between Iuile's cheek and chin, "no matter what happens, or what you do, your mother will always love you. Always." He begins to cough once more as Iuile is dumbfounded that even her father is defending her mother's actions. It then dawns on Iuile that this may be her very last time to see her father alive, causing tears to fill her eyes.

When Iuile's father finishes his spurt, he notice his daughter is about to cry, and says with a smile, "Don't you worry about me, sweetie, I'm in Dominus Deus' hands now. If it's His will, so be it. I live a good life, and blessed with a good, strong, wife who gave me eight beautiful children. You have your older brothers, Roibeard, Gearoid, Peadar, and the rest of your kin who will help take care of you, your mother, and your younger siblings. So be strong like your mother, and have faith in the will of our Dominus Deus."

Iuile has always been a religious girl, who never gave her parents any issues about going to church. For she always believes in the Almighty, Creator of All, and that His divine will is just. Yet now, for the first time, she doubts that Dominus Deus would spare her father's life. The thought of seeing her father in a casket, fills Iuile with sorrow and despair, as she could not control her emotions any longer, and burst out crying. Iuile buries her face onto her father's chest, who in turn puts his hand on her back for comfort, with patting, while coughing away from her.

As Iuile shed her tears, she thought to herself, *"I can't let this happen! There has to be another way besides relying my faith in Dominus Deus!"* She then recalls her conversation with Niall and Eilis. With her logic and reasoning saying, *"I can't do that! It's too dangerous!"* While her emotions are telling her, *"But it's the only way to save him!"*

CHAPTER 5

A Friend for the Forbidden Quest

For those of you who are curious about what the sign of the clover is, it is a simple practice created by the Rozolians that is similar in principle, to the sign of the cross on Earth. But instead of the crucifix, it is the clovifix that the Holy One, Dominus Yeshua Roze, who was strapped to a wooden human-sized three-leaf clover, during his final hours before his death. Where the Pater is on the Top Leaf, the Filius is on the Left Leaf, and the Spiritus Sanctus is on the Right Leaf. You start with two right fingers (the index and the middle) on the forehead, then diagonally move them to the left shoulder, followed by a horizontal move toward the right shoulder, and finally, diagonally once more to the abdomen with an Amen. As for the Rozolian religion itself, it is a popular religion that is shepherded by a pavus who spread the word of Dominus Deus, and his begotten son, Dominus Yeshua. A religion that is led by the pyzer, with an epipavus being an equivalent to that of a bishop.

Now that I have quenched anyone who was curious, I can return to the story as Eiral's chilly night sky is a marvelous beauty, with both moons shining brilliantly. For Nacia is in its full moon phase, with Evana being directly behind the Trinity Rings for the moment. Though people of Earth only have the moon and the stars to romance the beauty of the night's sky, it is nothing compared to the beauty of Atlast's night sky, where the natives romance both the moons, the rings, and the stars. And in case you do not realize, the moons are not always out together on the same night all the time or on the same day. Even a double lunar eclipse is a rare sight to see. With a double solar eclipse being rarer, however, having two moons means that a single solar eclipse happens more often than that on Earth.

Yet it is this very night, that a double lunar eclipse is about to begin as Iuile rides on her horse, Pixie who is brown with a white face, heading west of the main road at a high speed, in order for her to reach the ranch where Eilis resides. She wears a heavier poncho due to the nights still being cold, from the leftover effects of winter that are slowly leaving for the spring season. Before she has her horse enter the housing area, she slows her steed down for the sake of not waking anyone up, or drawing attention if anyone is up, as she has Pixie move quietly, as a horse can get, past homes.

During Pixie's trek, Iuile notices a couple of Eilis' male cousins passed out on the ground, with an empty jug nearby. With Eilis' aunt on the rooftop with a mug on her face, snoozing. This brings Iuile memories of rare moments when her mother opened the pantry door, where her father was found upside down and asleep. Her mother's only response was to locate her ingredients, followed by closing the door and letting him be, where she then returned to the stove to make breakfast.

Iuile snaps out of her flashback upon noticing some of Eilis' relatives passing by, riding on horses or donkeys, and halts Pixie. They apparently did not notice Iuile, due to her and Pixie's position next to a house, as they passed by and talked loudly. With one of them mentioning about heading to a bar in town for a couple of hours, among them are Eilis' father and older brother. As soon as Eilis' relatives are a good distance away, Iuile heads for her friend's home.

When Iuile reaches Eilis' house, she gets off Pixie and attempts to retrieve the lantern from her horse's saddle. Only to change her mind as the moons are giving off plenty of light to see, and approach the window that resides the room where Eilis sleeps. Iuile then glances through the window to be sure that Eilis is asleep in the room that she shares, along with the bed, with her two younger sisters, Grania, and Riona, both of whom have the same hair color as their sister. While Eilis is asleep with her sisters, Iuile tries to think of a way to wake her friend up without disturbing her siblings.

Not wanting to waste time pondering the situation, or going on alone, Iuile decides to risk it by lightly tapping the window. To Iuile's dismay, the light noise did not wake Eilis up, so she taps harder, and harder, until finally, Eilis wakes up, along with Riona. Iuile's heart leaps as she does not want Riona to know that she is here and quickly hand gestures to Eilis that she does not wish to wake her sister up. Luckily, Eilis sees her first and quickly understands what Iuile is trying to inform her.

Iuile watches as Eilis talks to her sister (what she says, Iuile does not know as Eilis is speaking very softly). It did not take long before Eilis and Riona lie back down, with Eilis glancing out the window that Iuile was behind. Iuile sees that Eilis is staring back at her, causing Iuile to make hand movements once more, while silently moving her lips, letting Eilis know to get dressed and meet her in the barn. Eilis manages to interpret the message and shakes her head, signaling to Iuile that she understands. This makes Iuile feel relieved and heads back to Pixie, grabs her horse's rein, and quickly walks north towards the barn area where she enters the nearest barn. While traveling to the barn, Iuile noticed a stone dome, with a chimney and wooden door, next to one of the barns which made her curious.

Upon entering the barn, Iuile brings Pixie into one of the empty stalls, to drink and rest, and begins to wait for Eilis. Iuile waits anxiously for what seems forever, until Eilis finally shows up, and fully dressed, causing Iuile to say, "What took you so long?"

"Excuse me", said Eilis as she continued furiously from being unnecessarily scolded, "but a certain someone woke one of my sisters up, causing me to wait a long time before she fell back to sleep."

This causes Iuile to blush and apologize for her ignorance before asking, "Is your clan getting raptors?"

"You notice", said Eilis with a grin, while having no concern or worries of why Iuile is visiting at this hour. "My new brother-in-law likes to hunt and wishes to bring over a few raptors from home, after they wake up from their brumation of course. So my family, and the rest of the clan, decides to build him a raptor dome. As for the reason that I didn't ask him why he uses raptors for hunting, is because I figure why wait when I can ask Niall when it occurs to me."

"Lucky you", said Iuile with no hint of jealousy, as she was only curious before saying with anxiety, "anyway, I need you to come with me!"

Eilis begins to stretch her arms and back, due to still being exhausted while saying, "Can it wait till morning?" She then recalls what happened earlier, after attaining comfort in her body, and asks with concern, "But more importantly, is your father alright?"

"No it can't wait", replied Iuile who sounds desperate, "and it's because of his condition that we need to go now!"

This has Eilis puzzle on what Iuile is planning, and reply, "Go where?"

"To Diavolo Mansion", replied Iuile, "and have an audience with Marquis Savio DeGallo!"

"You're out of your mind", said Eilis who sounded like someone who was trying to reason with a lunatic, "Tales of Diavolo Mansion are nothing more than a fairy tale!"

What Eilis said has Iuile confused, for this is not what she expects her friend to say due to her constant yearning to going to such a place. Iuile decides to question this and asks, "What do you mean? You always talk about going there before."

"Yeah, well . . . I was just teasing", replied Eilis who does not sound like even she is convinced. "No, ah, it's just that, I never really thought that we would do this. Are you sure that Dr. McCleary is unable to heal him?"

"Roibeard told me that Dr. McCleary does not have the proper medicine in stock to cure him", Iuile replied. "He also said that it may be too late to receive the medicine from Dunban."

Realizing how desperate her friend is to save her father, Eilis decides to ask Iuile with hopes of convincing her out of a mad quest, "What about Granny Yueng? Surely she should be able to heal him if it's that bad."

"Roibeard said that she already left for Elosa two days ago", replied Iuile.

"Alright then", said Eilis, "say we did head over there, and it turns out it doesn't exist."

"It has to exist", said Iuile with desperation, and forming tears in her eyes, "otherwise people from our town would not be afraid to approach Mt. Gaib. Not to mention the disappearances of travelers and Jevul Jagers who search for it. It wouldn't hurt to at least see if Marquis DeGallo really does exist, and is able to grant wishes."

The thought of actually having her wish come true, and not be just a dream, has Eilis intrigued. But in order to accomplish this, they would have to make a dangerous journey that would place their lives in danger. Not wanting to risk such an ordeal, Eilis asks Iuile about something she said earlier, "What about you saying that it'll be safer to catch King Tuathal, or any other leprechaun for their wishes, than to go there?"

"Because even though it's safer", replied Iuile, "it'll take forever to find a leprechaun. That is of course they do exist since the only people who said that they had seen them are drunks."

This has Eilis giggling, as she begins to remember a past amusement saying, "Like the time your dad said that he almost caught a leprechaun while drunk?"

The nerve of her best friend speaking ill of her father with his current condition, not to mention the danger her father underwent during the ordeal, has Iuile reply with no remorse, "Yeah, and let's not forget about the time your dad said he was almost killed by a banshee, while drunk."

This silence Eilis, who begins to recall such an event when she was a child before replying, with fear, "Don't kid about that. I'd seen the scratches that she gave him on his back." She then realizes why Iuile brought up the horrible memory and says, "Sorry for mocking your dad. But it still doesn't change the fact that we have to travel through Killy Ri Forest, and we all know that anything in there is dangerous, due to the monstrous creatures that lurk within that cursed place."

Such reasoning only has Iuile shrug such nonsense by saying, "There are men around town who hunt in there all the time. It can't be that dangerous."

"Only because they know how not to get killed while hunting in there", replied Eilis with reasoning and fear in her voice. "We don't, therefore it's too much of a risk. And like you said just now, and during lunch, we had people passed through town looking for that place, only to be never be seen again."

"That won't happen because this is for a noble cause", said Iuile whose mindset is absolute, "and it's a risk I am willing to take. With or without you, I am going over there to save my father. I can't sit around and wait for him to die!"

Knowing now that her friend is fully determined to risk her life for her father, Eilis approaches Iuile, and hugs her for comfort while saying, "Alright, I'll go with you." This makes Iuile smile with joy in knowing that she is not alone in her quest. When they stop hugging, Eilis asks her, "Did you at least ride here on Glory?"

"Sadly, I rode here with my horse, Pixie", replied Iuile while sounding disappointed, "who is in one of your stables. Apparently, Glory escaped from the barn again, and I didn't want to waste time searching for him."

"Well, I guess it can't be helped", said Eilis. "But it might be for the better since he is the fastest horse that your ranch has because none of my horses can keep up with him. So we'll make due. Go get Pixie while I get Speedy." Just as Iuile was about to retrieve her horse, Eilis quickly called her back to ask, "Before I forget again, while we were in town earlier today, why didn't you confirm to Einri that it was Niall?"

Such a foolish question to ask has Iuile staring back at her friend with an appearance that says, why are you questioning me whether or not kittens are cats, before finally replying back, "Why in the world would I help that jerk?"

"Ah, right", replied Eilis, who realized that she asked an idiotic question, with an obvious answer, "well then, let's go get our horses." Iuile agrees and goes to retrieve Pixie while wondering how someone so clever, can be so stupid. After retrieving Pixie, Iuile rides her horse back outside to wait for Eilis, who does not take long to come out with Speedy, a white horse with large brown spots around his body. They then ride off together heading west, where they decide to pass through other properties, and towards the part of the forest known as Killy Ri Forest. When they left Eilis' ranch, Eilis said, "Something tells me that by the end of the night, and that we somehow manage to come back alive in one piece, we are going to be in some serious trouble."

The only response Iuile said was, "It is worth my mother's wrath."

CHAPTER 6

Killy Ri Forest

There are many forests on Atlast that are known to be dangerous, due to monstrous creatures that lurk within them. Especially at night, since the most treacherous ones are nocturnal, and Killy Ri Forest is no exception. The people of Arvann know that traveling through there is a fool's errand if you have no combat or survival skills, and merchants gain nothing since there is no road to travel through that leads to profit. The only people that dare travel to such a horrifying place, are experienced hunters, as they know how not to get killed.

That's because oddly enough, a good game can be found in Killy Ri Forest, unlike Dun Mulla Wood. Even though Dun Mulla Wood is not only bigger than Killy Ri Forest, it does not have a vast amount of animals to easily find and hunt. So if any townsfolk wish to save money, or have no money to spend, would courageously enter the forest for the sole purpose of supporting their family. Any other reason is no more than a jester that foolishly walks towards tragedy.

As for the location of Dun Mulla Wood, it covers the eastern, and most of the northern and southern parts around Arvann's glade. It is also a much safer area compared to Killy Ri Forest, as an innocent child can wander around the woods all day, with a low chance of any harm coming to them since the trees are less dense. This allows more sunlight into the forest which prevents certain foul creatures from laying a hair on anyone. As to why, is something that will be explained later, as Iuile and Eilis travel through the forest of wicked inhabitants.

"We're never going to get there at this pace", said Eilis who is holding a lantern in front of her, while riding Speedy.

"Would you rather accidentally run into a tree?" Iuile replied with slight annoyance and holding her own lantern, "I just said that I don't want to risk our horses running into a tree at high speed, we might accidentally injure them."

"Even still", said Eilis who sounds frightened, "at this rate, we won't reach the mansion till midnight."

"If that's the case", said Iuile who sounds terrified herself, "then we should be back no later than four hours past midnight. If everything goes well that is."

Upon hearing the chance of being almost up all night made Eilis reply with an angry tone, "Are you serious! It's my family's turn to get up an hour before sunrise to feed the livestock, by myself since Finola is visiting family in Gallina, while my mom teaches my younger sisters how to sew clothes!" She then mumbles to herself, "Granted that it's actually my punishment for going to town without a horse."

"Remember the time that you had kept a rabbit as a pet several years ago", said Iuile who is purposely changing the subject. "What was her name? That's right, Merry Bell. You loved that rabbit more than life itself, only for her to be accidentally killed by one of your brothers, which caused you to cry all night. I remember because you snuck over to my house to sob and complain about how your brothers are jerks until one hour past midnight. I comforted you even though I had to get up past five to help my mom and aunts cook dinner for Pascha."

The Ram and Ewe's Quest for the Lost Lambs

Such harsh memories made Eilis silent for a moment while giving a pouting appearance, before finally replying, "You made your point, though it doesn't help that the following day . . . they teased me by saying that they had Merry Bell for breakfast. Not to mention that my mom whipped me for worrying her when she found out that I snuck out."

This has Iuile feel relief that she convinced her friend to bear with this ordeal, yet at the same time, feels guilty. Because Eilis is undergoing this experience due to Iuile's fear of traveling alone, causing her to say, "I'm sorry for reliving that painful memory, and dragging you out here. I . . . I just want someone who I can trust to come with me." To their horror, a goblin appears out of the bushes, causing Iuile to screech out, "A poucka goblin!"

This foul goblin that has horrified the girls is a native to the archipelago and rarely leaves the forests or caverns. It stood around three feet tall with green skin, bat-like ears, and no nose, for in its place are two slits for its nostrils, like a snake. Its jaw sticks further past his lips, with its bottom canine teeth being two inches long. But what horrified the girls the most, were the soulless beady black pupils of the monster's yellow eyes. The poucka goblin picks up a rock on the ground, and throws it with his chimpanzee-like arm toward Pixie, causing the steed to panic after being hit on her left shoulder, and stand on her hind legs. This spook the goblin, who hastefully backs away far enough to avoid the horse's front legs. During this whole time, both Iuile and Eilis scream and panic, as they do not know what to do.

The wretched goblin manages to find an opening and attempts to strike the horse again. Only for a loud bang to be heard in the darkness, with Eilis' lantern being completely destroyed at the same time. This causes Eilis more hysteria as pieces of the lantern land on the ground. The destruction of the lantern apparently scared the goblin further, making the creature back away quickly once more before having the chance to strike Pixie. It is at this moment that

Iuile decides to get a grip on herself, and tries to gain control of her horse. With much success as Pixie starts to calm down where Iuile decides to turn to Eilis and yell, "We need to leave at . . . ."

But Eilis cuts her off by yelling back, "Iuile! He's attacking again!"

This causes Iuile's heart to stop as she turns back towards the goblin, who decides to make a leap towards her. Just when the creature is a yard away, an arrow shoots right through the creature's head. The goblin flies off due to the force of the arrow and lands in a bush where it dies. Both Iuile and Eilis turn to see their saviors, only to find Einri reloading his bolt action rifle, which appears to have been fired due to gun smoke, and Niall with his longbow at the ready as they appear before them on their raptors. With Einri's raptor having a similar color as Niall's, except the patches are of a different pattern.

This of course only made Iuile feel dumbstruck by what she is seeing, while at the same time feeling relieved upon seeing Niall, with Eilis asking what is on her mind, "Since when are you two buddies?"

"We're not", replies Niall who sounds annoyed over Eilis' assumption, while giving Einri an evil glare from the corner of his eye.

"We were in the middle of a contest until we found out you two were in trouble", said Einri while sounding heroic.

Those words cause Niall to turn his head towards Einri and say, "You wanted the contest, I was in the middle of tracking my prey, which you spooked and caused me to waste my night looking for that animal again."

"That sounds like something Einri would do", said Eilis who does not seem surprised while staring at Einri's rifle. She then asks with assumption, "He also wouldn't be the one who shot at my lantern with that rifle now, would he?"

The Ram and Ewe's Quest for the Lost Lambs

"Of course not", said Einri while preventing Niall from answering first, "Niall here thought it was a will o' the wisp and shot at it!"

The confession Einri made has Niall silent while glancing at him with a scornful look. With Iuile suspecting that something is not adding up, causing her to intervene, and ask coyly, "Is . . . that true, Niall?"

For some reason to Iuile, Niall looks like he is going to fall off his raptor, only to quickly regain himself with only Einri not noticing, as he seems to be distracted by something. When Niall recovers, he clears his throat before casually saying with mimicry, "I recall Einri's exact words being; 'Hey Niall! Watch me mess with those screaming merchants' heads by shooting at their light source!' To which I reply; 'What idiot of a merchant would travel through here? And at this hour?' I then tried to tell him that he shouldn't fire his rifle while in this forest, only for it to be too late because . . . ."

Past experiences of when it is Eilis' boiling point, cause Iuile to hastefully back her horse away, about two yards, from her friend. Because Eilis' face is turning bright red due to sear anger, and instantly cuts Niall off to yell at Einri who has her full attention, "YOU JERK! What if you missed it and hit me instead?! I have half a mind and do to you what my father does to our stallions that act aggressively! Like the one I'm riding on at this moment!"

Such words begin to run through Einri's imagination where he gives a disturbed look. With the only person that replied was Niall who had his eyes widened, giving Iuile the rare chance to clearly see his green eyes, "Whoa, that escalated quickly." His eyes then went back to their normal appearance before saying with annoyance, mixed with sarcasm, "Anyway, thanks to Einri's gunshot, along with that outburst, it'll be a matter of time before this goblin's friends will find us. If, we're lucky that it's his friends."

Panic has stricken Iuile who realizes what Niall said is true, and says to Eilis in a low voice, "Look what you have done."

"Me?" Reply Eilis, "This little . . . ."

Wanting to end any more bickering as soon as possible, Niall quickly interrupts the girls by saying, "I would like to ask what you two are doing here in the middle of the night. But we should really leave here right now and bring you back home."

Returning home is not an option for Iuile who says to Niall with desperation, "But we need to head to Diavolo Mansion."

"Whoa there", said Niall sounding concerned, "that place is tainted, and damned by the Almighty."

"Hah", laughed Einri, "Dominus Deus, just a couple of days ago I asked the 'Almighty', that I would be more charitable if he filled my goblet back up, and he didn't."

Completely annoyed that Einri is picking this moment to question his faith on an easy answer, caused Niall to reply, "I seem to recall the good book saying that you should not put Dominus Deus to the test."

"Hah", laughed Eilis, "like it really said that."

"My thoughts exactly", said Einri who happily agreed with Eilis.

The only thing that is passing through Niall's mind, as he places his hand on his face, is that he is surrounded by idiots. Iuile however, decides to intervene, as she agrees with Niall by saying, "Um, actually, it did." Both Eilis and Einri turn to her as she continues, "It was in last week's sermon."

"You know what", said Niall, for he no longer cares about who is right or wrong, "it doesn't matter. Because we need to leave here at once and return to the glade due to the common knowledge that goblins don't hunt alone, and it will be a matter of time before more show up, or worse." He then turns to Einri to remind him, "Oh yeah, Black-Eye Dunderhead. The fact that you had a rifle, and I don't, is another dead giveaway that you shot at the lantern, due to the rifle's gun smoke, and its bang."

This struck a nerve with Einri, who pondered on what Niall said for a moment before cursing his own ignorance, followed by replying to Niall with annoyance, "And don't call me a dunderhead again!"

During Niall and Einri's discussion, Iuile begins to panic and reply when Einri finishes his retort, "We can't go back! We need to head towards Mt. Gaib."

Upon hearing Iuile's plea in desperation, has made Einri become more curious and asks, "Why on Atlast for?"

"Whatever it is", said Niall, "it's not worth it."

"How dare you say that my father's life is not worth it", said Iuile's emotions. *"He doesn't mean it like that"*, replied her logic and reasoning. *"He might understand and help us if we tell him of Dad's condition."* Her emotions then question, *"But what if he doesn't, and force us to return home? No, I can't risk it! Regardless of the danger, I will press on!"* Iuile's emotional fear of having her quest coming to a halt has caused her to respond with a desperate tone, "It is completely worth it!"

"What is 'worth it'?" Ask Einri.

"We don't have time for this", said Eilis who decided to cut in before turning to Iuile. "Let's just leave these cowards and just go. I never like guys telling me what to do anyway."

"Who are you calling a coward?" Replied Einri who feels as if he was insulted.

Eilis turns Speedy towards Einri with a mischievous smile, and tauntingly replied, "Are you saying that you are not a coward?" This is not the first time Iuile has seen Eilis use her charm to get her way with men and knows that she is trying to get Einri and Niall to aid them.

"Don't let Eilis' banter fool you", said Niall with indifference. "She's just trying to manipulate you for her own agenda."

For Niall to see through Eilis' deception has Iuile surprised, for she has never seen any man being able to resist her friend's charm, except for Eilis' male kin of course. Iuile turns to Eilis who appears shocked as well, for this has never happened to her before. Though it did not take long for Eilis to regain her composure, and teasingly said, "Oh you're just saying that because you don't want to return to town alone . . . ." She suddenly went silent due to Einri pointing his rifle in their direction, and fires at the monstrous fuath orc behind them.

Both Iuile and Eilis are in complete shock, for they cannot believe that they could have felt the vibration of the rifle, and the force of the bullet. However, the shock quickly changes to terror, once they slowly turn to see a fuath orc lying on the ground, dead. It is a dark greenish creature that appears to be over seven feet high, with his tusk being six inches long, and black long hair around (but bald on top) his head. His ears are pointed like an elf, which all orcs possess, with a nose that is wide. The creature's arms appear to be that of fatty muscles, with most of the body covered in wolf fur while wearing leather boots with a tribe-looking necklace, and wielding a large stone ax with a wooden handle.

As the girls stared at the fuath orc in horror, Niall said casually to Einri while still looking at the corpse, "I was wondering what was sneaking around us."

"I know", replied Einri in a friendly manner. He then turns to Niall and asks him with enthusiasm, "I'd noticed him after bringing up the will o' the wisp. You?"

"Between you firing at the lantern, and meeting up with Iuile and Eilis", replied Niall calmly. He then turned to Einri and said, "Go ahead and reload your rifle."

"Ah, right", said Einri as he began to reload his weapon, by pulling back his rifle's bolt. "The only downfall with these is that you can load only one bullet at a time. Wish there is a way to store more. You know, something that allows you to fire multiple rounds before needing to reload. Though I did hear that a gunsmith did find a way, but it could be a rumor."

The Ram and Ewe's Quest for the Lost Lambs

During Niall and Einri's conversation, Iuile and Eilis slowly turn to them in bewilderment, because the girls cannot believe that they are talking as if they are having a friendly chat in town, in a place of sheer horror. When Einri finished reloading his rifle, Niall smiled at him, and said sarcastically, "Now go ahead and fire another round into the air so that every curse monster knows where we're at. Like, I don't know", his tone suddenly changed to anger in a low voice, "A blasted dullahan!!!"

This apparently dawned on Einri who replied, "Ohhh, I probably should have listened to my butler when he suggested that I bring my bow and arrows, instead of my rifle."

"You think?!" Reply Niall who decides to turn to Iuile and Eilis to say, "Alright, Einri here is going to take both of you back, since he's carrying a Viking horn, as I can't return home until I catch something." When Niall finishes speaking, Einri scratches the back of his head while feeling embarrassed.

Hearing Niall's words of returning home, brings Iuile utter dread, for going back means losing her father. She immediately gathers up her courage, for her father's sake, and says to Niall, "That's too bad because we're not going home until we visit Diavolo Mansion." Iuile then whips the rein to signal her horse to move and leaves with Eilis right behind her. The only thing that she hears, is from Niall who yells for them to wait.

CHAPTER 7

Guardians of the Ravine

There were many attempts to mine Mt. Gaib by those who had no interest in pursuing the myth of Diavolo Mansion. But like those who sought that cursed place, never came back alive. The town of Arvann finds it natural for a new fool to come by, ignore their warnings, and venture off. Never to be seen again to the point that they immediately build a grave for the next dead man walking. Many speculated what killed them off of course, some believed that they stopped by Diavolo Mansion due to curiosity, or to seek shelter, others think it was the poucka goblins or a fuath orc. As for whether or not these types of goblins or orcs attack humans, is yes they do, but it is most likely in the forests or caverns of any of Eiral's islands. As to why, is because poucka goblins are superstitious idiots, and fuath orcs are unorganized morons.

Poucka goblins are native only in Eiral, and nowhere else on Atlast, as they do not have the intellect to build a boat. Yet somehow, someway, they manage to occupy all over the archipelago country, and no one knows how. Though they are well organized, and live in tribes large enough to pillage towns, they rarely do. With the natives of Eiral knowing very well of this, and barely see the goblins as a threat out in the open during the day.

This is because these goblins have this insane belief that any light from the sky, sunlight or moonlight, will curse them for a certain period of time, depending on how long they are exposed to it. With lightning causing them to wet themselves. There are very rare occasions at night when they do attack when there is no moon out, or Nacia is in its new moon phase. But most of the time they would not dare, for in doing so would mean checking the night sky, and risk exposing themselves to any of the moons' light. This is why Dun Mulla Wood is safe compared to Killy Ri Forest, since Killy Ri is denser, and therefore much safer for the goblins compared to Dun Mulla.

As for the fuath orcs, who are smart enough to build boats, are well known and inhabit northern Mystia. Though they have 'some', intelligence, they are very few in numbers, and not well organized as they cannot help but attack and kill those of the same gender for the alpha position. There are times when they try to get along, only to end up attacking each other in the end. They also view other orc species with extreme prejudice, and would not hesitate to murder any of them in a group of less than ten. As for attacking humans by themselves, let's just say, that charging at someone from a distance who possesses a range weapon, is not the best strategy.

The fuath orcs on rare occasions are capable of claiming the alpha position in a goblin tribe, but with great difficulty, and annoyance, when it comes to the poucka goblins. This of course is troublesome if they do succeed in leading a poucka goblin tribe because the orc leader can inform the poucka goblins when there is no light out at night. This is why when anyone finds out that there is a fuath orc leading the poucka goblins, they immediately call forth members of Jevul Jagers who will slay the orc, along with any goblins who decide to follow the orc, before the monsters have a chance to pillage a village. And to answer those who are wondering who Jevul Jagers are, they are merely a guild of hunters who pursue and slay wanted monsters, fairies, dallions, and so forth.

As for the devilish fairies and dallions, they are normally kept at bay by having an iron clover. This is because magical creatures like unicorns, pixies, and such, fear iron in general due to its unusual magnetic properties that absorb their magic, and cause severe harm to them. With the blessings being added to the metal by a pavus, or higher, as a bonus to keep the dallions (monsters that fear sunlight and holy talismans) away due to their fear of Dominus Deus, and his Holy Son. The iron clover is normally hung in a person's dwelling where it is easily accessible when it is needed. For seeing it, while being powered by the user's faith, is enough to cause dallions great dread, and therefore they do not invade a person's home without a good reason. Of course, bearing an ordinary clover (made of wood, metal, and such) can be used to scare weak dallions if it is not blessed, as long as it is fueled with faith.

Anyway, Iuile and Eilis have been riding through the dark forest for some time, when Iuile finally decides to slow her horse down. Followed by Eilis who managed to catch up to her, and said in a whisper, "About blasted time!" This gives Iuile a slight touch of fear due to Eilis sounding upset, "I've been quietly telling you to slow down since we left Einri and Niall. You gave me serious trouble for not wanting to go fast because our horses might get injured, and out of nowhere, you decided to haul off when the boys tried to stop us!"

"Calm down", whispered Iuile, "and stay quiet. We ought to be lucky that nothing else attacked us since that goblin and orc. I'm also sorry. I panicked because I was afraid that they might force us to return home."

"Which I won't", said a familiar voice, causing Iuile and Eilis to turn and see Einri approaching them on his raptor, with his rifle slung to his back. "You naughty girls are curious if the rumors of Diavolo Mansion are true."

"Actually . . . ." Said Iuile who was about to be honest, until Eilis cut her off.

"Why you got us", said Eilis while using her charm, and having Speedy bring her closer to Einri. "We just want to see what the whole deal is about."

"Well lucky for you", said Einri who had apparently forgotten that Eilis was mad at him earlier, "I'd traveled there a few times with my buddies, and therefore know how to get there." While he is speaking, he has his raptor approach Iuile and stops next to her. Upon finishing his words, he quickly takes her lantern away and blows it out.

This anger Iuile to the point of yelling, "WHAT ARE . . . ." Only to be immediately cut off due to Einri covering her mouth, in order to silence her.

"Ssshhh, that lantern is a dead giveaway of where we are", said Einri excitedly. "Along with loud noises which travel further at night." He begins to slowly take his hands off Iuile before calmly saying, "Don't worry, I've done this before to the point of getting in and out without being in any danger. Just stay close to me, as I am used to traveling through here in the dark."

"Wow, Einri", said Eilis, "I never thought you said something intelligent."

"That's because I like to act foolish to amuse people", replied Einri before riding off.

Both Iuile and Eilis give a look that says that they are not convinced by his words and turn to glance at each other before following suit. This is because they both know that what he said was not only stupid, but an outright lie. Regardless, Iuile appreciates Einri's willingness to aid them. However, it also does not change her attitude towards him, but given her desperation to save her father, she is willing to put up with Einri for her father's sake. They travel for what seems like an eternity to Iuile, and just when she is about to ask Einri how much longer till they reach their destination, Einri slows down and raises his hand in a closed fist in order to signal them to stop. He then gets off his raptor and signals them to get off their horses, tie their reins to a low branch, and follow him, all while staying silent.

It was not long before Iuile decided to ask Einri in a whisper, "It doesn't seem like we reached Mt. Gaib?"

"What?" Whisper Einri as he seems confused before saying, "Oh, the mansion isn't actually on the mountain. It is on a huge hill that is at the end of a long valley, and a few miles from Mt. Gaib."

This only baffles Eilis who decides to question Einri, "Then why do we need to leave our mounts when it's still far away?"

"Because we need to walk from here", replied Einri who stopped and turned to the girls, "I'll explain later, just do as I say. You also don't need to worry about any monsters. For some reason, they never pass through the pathway we are now on unless someone is giving off light." He turns to walk off, with both Iuile and Eilis following him while feeling nervous. After walking a good distance, Einri suddenly stops for a moment before turning to them, and whispers, "I should probably tell you that there are a couple of trolls guarding the ravine that we must travel through, in order to enter the valley that leads to the mansion.

This horrifies Iuile who is speechless, with Eilis whispering excitedly, "Trolls!!! Trolls!!! You are now telling us about trolls!!!"

Einri begins to feel horribly guilty for not telling the girls to where he hastefully, and apologetically, replies, "I'm sorry! I'm so sorry! My friends and I normally don't tell any first-timers about this, because we like to poke fun at the looks on their faces when they see the trolls. You're the first girls that I actually bring to Diavolo Mansion."

"Wait a moment", said Iuile who appeared befuddled, "I thought there were no trolls in Durigh, or any of the islands of Eiral?"

"Well, I guess that turns out to be a lie", said Einri, "because there are certainly trolls on Durigh, as you will soon see."

Whether or not there should be trolls on their island is no concern for Eilis, who is not only upset about running into them for the first time, but that Einri tried to pull a terrible prank on her and Iuile. This caused Eilis to reply in an angry whisper, "Still doesn't matter, because you should have told us sooner!"

"He's telling us now, Eilis", said Iuile who is baffled that her friend is still upset over being closely tricked by Einri, of all people. Eilis tries to argue, only for Iuile to cut her off again saying, "No buts!" She then turns to Einri and asks, "I suppose you have a way of getting by these so-called, 'trolls', Einri?"

"As a matter of fact, I do", said Einri. "Just keep your distance, and let me do all the work."

When Einri begins to walk away, his arm is pulled back by someone, causing him to turn with the hope that it is Iuile looking for security from him. Only to be disheartened to find that it is Eilis who asks him, "Please tell me they're not jotnar trolls."

This changes Einri's disappointment to delight, as he can now get back at Eilis for getting his hopes up by pulling his arm away from her, gently grabbing her chin, and replying, "Of course not, my pretty little flower." This gives Iuile and Eilis a sigh of relief as Einri lets go of her chin, and walks off saying, "They're mountain trolls."

This terrifies both of the girls as Eilis dreadfully replies, "Mountain trolls! Not as bad, but still bad!"

"Don't worry", said Einri who stopped and turned to them, "I have everything under control." Einri then presses on as Iuile and Eilis follow from a distance, in case he does not have everything under control, which they assume that he does not.

"I hope that he at least has a piece of iron on him", Eilis whispers to Iuile.

"Trolls aren't fairies", Iuile replies back with a whisper, while not being surprised that her friend is unaware of this since Eilis always had poor grades at school. "They're normal monsters, so iron or holy talismans have no effect on them." Iuile begins to wonder if Eilis remembers to bring a clover and iron with her, due to what her friend just said. Instead of asking, Iuile only assumes that Eilis did, as she could not be that stupid to leave home at night without either one.

They travel further through Killy Ri Forest until they reach a part of the forest where some of the trees appear to have been crushed. When Einri exits the forest, the girls decide to wait inside, behind a fallen tree, as they gaze at the ravine that is across the forest end. The ravine is fifty feet high, with a width of six feet, and is completely dried up. Sitting on either side of the ravine's entrance, like a pair of guards, are two rock-like beings, which Iuile assumes are the 'mountain trolls' that Einri spoke of. They both appear to be deformed, muscular, humans made of sedimentary-type rocks, with yellow glowing, crystal-like, eyes that appear fragile. Their height is fifty-five feet tall, and a shoulder-to-shoulder width of fifteen feet.

When Einri approaches the stone figures with a smile on his face, they begin to stand up after noticing him. The mineral creatures give a small smirk while pounding their fist into their hand as if they are looking forward to a beating. Einri is only a few yards away from them when he decides to stop and says, "I challenge the strongest one among you to a fight." This causes Iuile to roll her eyes, while Eilis places her hand on her face.

The rock monsters glance at each other for a moment, before turning back to Einri with a bigger grin, with one of them saying, "I accept your challenge."

Being filled with pure confidence has Einri glee with joy, as he decides to turn to where the girls are hiding, and wink at them. Their only reaction is that both of their faces have a look of disappointment, as Iuile suspects that this is the end for Einri who turns back towards the stone figure and says, "So you are the stronger one?"

The other mineral creature appears to have taken offense to this, and pushes his friend aside saying, "No! I'm the stronger one!"

This infuriates the other one to where he pushes his friend back saying, "No! I AM!

With everything going according to plan for Einri, he decides to intervene in their argument saying, "Trolls! Trolls!" Both of them turn to Einri with a confused look as he continues, "I said that I will fight the strongest one, not someone who pretends to be the strongest." This only angers them more as one of them sucker punches his comrade, causing both of them to fight each other. Einri hastefully runs back towards the demolished part of the forest, and tells the girls while still feeling confident, "Am I good or what?"

The nerve that Einri believes that he succeeded in something that he only made worse, has Iuile dumbstruck before asking him, "How is getting them to fight each other going to help us?"

"I can't believe you're that naive", said Eilis who is irate by her friend's ignorance. "We can sneak by them while they fight."

"Exactly", said Einri, "and the ruckus they make always causes the horses, or any other mount, to panic, which is the reason why we left them behind. Now let's go before they come this way, as they can easily crush through these trees like a bed of flowers!" Einri begins to run around the battlefield, at a great distance from the stone giants, with Iuile and Eilis following him from behind. The moment they reached the entrance to the ravine, one of the rock monsters threw the other into the trees where they were just at. Iuile turns and stares for a moment in awe, before going into the ravine. Because Einri was right in that they can easily crush the trees, like a bed of flowers.

CHAPTER 8

Diavolo Mansion

Horrors of the unknown have always haunted any sentient being, which is the feeling that Iuile is having right now. For whatever awaits Iuile and her party, could lead to their death as she recalls hearing that anyone who travels to Diavolo Mansion, has never returned. Yet she refuses to go back for her father's sake and with Einri proving himself of knowing his way to the mansion, means that he had been there before, and returned alive. This gives Iuile hope as they travel through the ravine. Though how Einri knows of such things is something that Iuile would like to ask if she was not terrified by the rattle in the ravine. The rumbling surrounding them causes Iuile to forget her question, all the while Einri casually explains that it is only one of the 'trolls', being rammed or pushed onto the ravine during their tussle.

". . . yet oddly enough", said Einri, "on our way back home, they don't seem to bother us. For some reason they only seem to want to keep people from entering, not leaving."

Something occurs to Iuile when she asks Einri, "Now that I think about it, what happened to Niall?"

"That coward didn't want to come, saying that going over there is 'forbidden'", replied Einri. "I questioned if he was going to rat you out, with his only response was that he is getting too exhausted from hunting, and needs to find his game quickly as he hasn't eaten a full meal since lunch."

"That may not have been a problem if you didn't cause him to lose his game", replies Eilis who, along with Iuile, feels bad for Niall's situation.

Hearing this has Einri turn to Eilis, and reply while sounding like he was offended, "Who said that I messed up catching his buck?"

"Niall did", replies Iuile, "remember, you were right next to him when he told us."

"Must of been when I was figuring out where that orc was", Einri mumbles to himself before saying to the girls, "anyway, what he said was a lie. He's just isn't good at hunting. Besides, I happened to show up sometime after he botched his shot. Started to whine about how he'll never catch something, and how pathetic he is."

"Distracted or not, you still didn't object when he told us that you messed up his shot", said Eilis who grins at the loss of Einri's words.

This is followed by Iuile asking, "I would also like to know how you knew it was a male deer if you showed up afterward?"

Realizing that his embellished side of his escapade is falling apart, causes Einri to appear infuriated for a moment, before managing to calm himself down and admits, "Okay, fine, I messed up his game. So let's drop it and head towards the mansion. We still have to finish crossing this ravine, then we need to travel up a hill, after crossing the valley, in order to reach Diavolo Mansion."

"Now that I think about it, Einri", said Iuile upon receiving an epiphany, "are the trolls working for Marquis DeGallo?"

"Probably", replies Einri, "my friends and I once came to the ravine's entrance before the sunset to see if anyone passed through.

Only to find many people who were appropriately dressed walked by them after sunset."

Eilis finds this very unusual and asks, "And they don't attack them?"

"Oddly no", said Einri while sounding befuddled by what he saw. "No asking for any invitation, or who they are. The trolls just let them pass. As if they didn't even notice them."

What Einri is explaining is very bizarre for Iuile to comprehend, as it is very odd for the guests to the masquerade to walk so far, and ask, "They just pass by them on foot? No mounts or carriages?"

This has Einri laughing softly before replying, "Well you see, the strange thing is that they appear out of nowhere. None of us are able to figure out where they came from. Anyway, now that I think about it, another reason we didn't bring our mounts, is because those trolls like to play with horses like they were dolls to the point of accidentally killing them." This shocks the girls speechless, for they both love their horses dearly and imagine the worst-case scenario if those rock monsters got a hold of them. Especially Iuile, who begins to recall aiding Pixie's birth six years ago with her father, who was so pleased with Iuile's assistance, and the bond Pixie quickly had with her, that he decided to let Pixie be Iuile's horse. "It was for the best that we left our mounts further back, and I don't want to test how they react to my raptor, Hunter. But not to worry though, for again, for some reason they won't be attacked by any monsters, as long as they stay at that, exact, spot."

They finally reach the end of the ravine and into a valley with tall grass, and scattered trees. The hills are a few miles apart to the north and south, with more far west across the valley from where they exit the ravine. Both Iuile and Eilis gaze at the top of one particular hill in the west, that is right in front of Mt. Gaib and the rest of Gaibroch Mor Mountains. They notice that there is some light coming from the top of that particular hill which Iuile finds a bit odd, for it appears to be brighter than it should be. Iuile also begins to have doubts of reaching their destination and returning home before daybreak, because she can tell that it is too far to walk or run on foot unless they have their mounts. She then becomes aware that Einri is heading toward several abandoned horse carriages that happen to be near the ravine's entrance.

When Einri opens one of the empty carriages, he bows and says gentlemanly, "Ladies first."

Both Iuile and Eilis are perplexed as they approach the carriages, causing Iuile to ponder whether or not Einri is making a bad joke, with Eilis asking, "Is this supposed to take us to the top of the hill?"

"That is correct, madam", replies Einri sarcastically as he straightens back up. "You didn't think that the marquis' guests would dare trek across the valley, and up the hill, on their own two feet?"

This confuses Iuile further and asks, "But what is going to pull it, or even drive it?"

"Believe it or not", replies Einri in an honest and casual tone, while knocking the carriage, "this thing moves by itself. Takes anyone to the top of the hill and back, and I mean anyone. So we don't need to worry about getting caught while riding towards the mansion."

"Good enough for me", said Eilis as she entered the carriage, with Iuile following her from behind. After Einri enters, closes the door, and takes a seat across from the girls, is the moment that the carriage starts to move on its own. It begins to drive itself across the valley at such an incredible speed, that no animal that could pull it, can match it.

After riding a good distance down the valley, Iuile decides to gaze through the window, on her right, to see if Nacia and Evana are still visible. Only for her heart to rapidly pound itself with excitement, for they appear to be closing in on their alignment with each other. She begins to blush and recalls having fantasies of being with a true love, who confesses his feelings for her during a double lunar eclipse, or even better, kissing at the moment of a sunrise. Iuile then remembers another fancy that involves dancing with her true love in a ball, as it is about to strike midnight. Wonderful dreams that Iuile desperately yearns to experience just once, even if it is just an instant, and possibly with Bradach. Her daydreaming quickly changes to an unusual concern for Niall, and worries if he will be safe by himself.

The woe that Iuile is having is suddenly interrupted, and forgotten, by Eilis who asks Einri, "Now that I think about it, who else knows about this?"

"Only certain young men from Arvann who are capable of traversing Killy Ri Forest", replies Einri, "and not rat on this shenanigan. I learned it from one of my buddies, who knew about it from his cousins, and so forth. We head to the mansion at least once in our life to see what the fuss is all about."

What Einri had confessed made Iuile realize something, causing her to question, "Wait if you knew about it like that, how far does this go? I mean, wouldn't it be possible that our fathers and uncles knew about this? Even our grandfathers?"

Iuile's realization dawns on Einri when he replied with a new awareness, "That's a good point, how far does this go down?"

Wanting to inquire a question herself, has Eilis interrupt Einri's puzzlement and asks, "I'm more curious about why you only bring men. Why not any women?"

"I . . . rather not say", replied Einri with a guilty appearance.

Refusing to answer Eilis' question is a mistake that Iuile knows too well, for it will only make her more curious as she tries to pressure Einri. While Eilis is probing Einri, the carriage reaches the hill's base, and with no hesitation in slowing down, it hastefully goes up the slope, and towards the top of the hill. Iuile and Eilis did not realize this, due to the inside of the carriage still being level, even though the outside is tilted. It is at that moment when Iuile decides to guess what she assumes to be the reason, "Is it because there aren't any women in town who can safely travel through Killy Ri on their own?"

To no surprise, Einri replied, "That, and that women can't keep secrets." Einri immediately covers his mouth, because he realizes the part about secrets would offend Iuile and Eilis. Both of whom are indeed offended, and are upset to where they decide not to speak another word to him until they at least reach the mansion. Which happens to be now as the carriage stops after reaching the front gate. Einri quickly exits out of the carriage first and holds the door open for Iuile and Eilis, with the hope that they will be distracted enough to forget what he said, while saying, "Here it is ladies, Diavolo Mansion."

When Iuile exits the carriage, she becomes awestruck by the ten-foot-high wall covered in various types of beautiful plant life and excitedly dashes towards the open gate to become even more impressed. For the mansion's architect is nothing she had ever seen on any of the islands of Eiral, including the main island of Elosa. It appears to her, from what she recalls from her schooling, to be of a Gothic structure from the country of Romalia in southern Mystia. Meaning that the tales that she heard about its architecture are true, as she is also astonished by the size of the mansion to be larger than any mansion that she had ever seen, yet it appears to be only three stories high. Iuile then notices that the carriage they rode in on is suddenly moving towards the other carriages, that are not too far from the gate, and parking next to them.

This is followed by Einri, who is slightly hunching over upon passing the gate, leading Iuile and Eilis into the front yard that possesses hedges that are six feet high. The hedges themselves are designed to come off like a simple maze that Iuile and her party traverse. While Einri guides them through the maze, they pass by different gardens in which Iuile and Eilis gaze at their beauty with marvel, for their flowers are more magnificent than they can ever imagine. The maze also contains plants that had been topiary into various figures and shapes, such as nymphs frolicking around the garden, along with their woodland friends joining in on their merry.

Upon reaching the center of the maze, lies a stone fountain that is surrounded by dolphin statues that appear to be swimming around it. In the center of the fountain, is a beautiful marble mermaid holding an umbrella with the water coming out of its finial, causing Iuile to stop and be mesmerized. Iuile's trance is only broken by Eilis who tells her that they need to keep following Einri. This causes Iuile to blush due to embarrassment, before continuing to follow Einri with Eilis asking, "Why does a selkie need an umbrella when she's wet all the time?"

What Eilis said is a good point, making Iuile ponder for a moment before replying, "Maybe it is placed there to be cute, and not meant to be taken seriously over an absurd idea. Also, that was a mermaid, not a selkie."

"Sounds like the artist is plain mad", said Eilis while looking ahead. She then turns her head to Iuile and asks, "How do you know it's a mermaid anyway?"

"By their tails", replied Iuile while gazing at the mansion's gargoyle statues that she could not make out, due to the height of the building, and the darkness of the night. "A mermaid's lower half is a fish tail, while a selkie's lower half is a seal's tail. Not to mention the sealskin that a selkie use to fully hide themselves from humans."

Their conversation is suddenly interrupted by Einri who explains, "They got guards in armor at the front doors. But don't worry, as the hedges are blocking their view of us. We are heading to the maze's north exit, where there are more hedges blocking the guards' view. From there, we'll head towards the north side of the building where the ballroom is. Just not the east side, because the windows there are obscured by thick rose bushes that are too much of an annoyance to see through due to their sharp thorns."

When they exit the maze, they continue heading north and pass by more hedges and topiaries before passing by another flower garden that causes Iuile and Eilis to stop, and revere at such beauty. "I hate to say this", said Eilis, "but we can admire them longer when this is all over."

"Right", replied Iuile, "my dad's life is more important than this."

They hurry to catch up with Einri to the north side of Diavolo Mansion. When Iuile and Elise reach him, they find a row of bushes against the building that is high enough to hide from any view from the inside. Einri walked further down before leading his hand towards a bush and said, "Now ladies, witness a world of wonderment."

CHAPTER 9

An Unsuspecting Summon

Iuile's past birthdays normally consist of simple presents (handmade dolls and candy as a child, while as a teen; sewing material, used clothes, and one time a broom, which made her annoyed in secret), simple games with friends, and a simple cake with no frosting. During the holiday festivities, a simple, yet charming, celebration in town. The only excitement she ever saw was her vacation trips to either the island capital of Dunban with her family, or the country's capital of Amelon, while her uncles watched the ranch with their sons. As her family ranch does not consist of just her immediate family, in case you did not know, but her father's entire family (well . . . just the ones that did not pursue other careers). Anyway, she had never seen so many people clustered together in her life at Dunban, with every street looking the same to the point that she wondered how anyone found their way around, with Amelon being even worse in her perspective.

But what she is seeing inside Diavolo Mansion's ballroom has triumph either trip to the country's capitals. Because she has never seen such beauty and wonder in her life, for it has taken her breath away. As Iuile and Eilis stick their head and shoulders in the bushes, she sees that the room itself is enormous. It appears to be at least three stories high (though it seems as if it is higher than that), making her assume that it is the size of Einri's father's manor.

Those who are participating in the festivities wear gowns and suits in colors that she did not know existed, for they are mixed with so many varieties. Iuile also sees that each and every person is wearing a different type of mask, as neither one is the same, while they playfully and happily dance to the music. She turns her attention to the musicians with instruments that she recognizes from her own town's festivities, among others that seem foreign to her. For they sounded very exotic, and hypnotically romantic, as she could not help but to blush and be mesmerized.

Only for Eilis to break her trance by saying, "Are they really doing that with all this noise going on?"

Filled with curiosity, Iuile looks over to the other side of the mansion to see that they are finishing a puppet show, and changing the scenery. This brings Iuile back memories of when she first visited Amelon for the holiday when she was a child. One of the things they did there was visit the Prachorion Theater. She recalls confusion as to why the villain was telling the audience that he was going to cast a spell on the princess, just so that she would forcefully fall in love with him.

When Iuile asks her mother this, she replies that everything is pretend and that nothing bad is really happening. Her mother then explained to her that what the villain is doing, is giving something called internal monologue to the audience, so that they have a better understanding of what is going on. This is followed by Iuile recollecting later in the play when her mother held her and Peadar for comfort during a scary scene, that involved a demon, as she softly says, "Mom." For Iuile had forgotten how caring her mother was to her as a child. Always kind and understanding, but strict and demanding now.

The memories of her mother are then followed by memories of what her father did when a certain actor appeared in the following scene. He got straight up and yelled with anger and seriousness, *"COME OVER HERE YE BUCKING TIGER, AND FIGHT ME LIKE A MAN!!! I know exactly how you won your so-called 'heroic', medals, at the Battle of Zuban!!!"* Iuile's father is aided by other natives of Durigh, who join in on his threats, along with her brothers, Roibeard and Gearoid (who is blonde with blue eyes).

Roisin had her face covered, due to embarrassment, while Iuile's mother folded her arms, sighed, and said with an attitude that says that she accepted what she walked into upon marriage, *"Well, there goes the rest of the evening."* With both Peadar and Iuile looking around in confusion about what their father and brothers are doing.

Realizing that she is daydreaming, and missing out on the action, Iuile shakes off her past memories and notices that they are now beginning a play with live actors. Due to being unable to hear what the actors are saying, Iuile decides to turn her attention to the banquet that is right across the room from them. Even though it is at a far distance, with the guests constantly passing by due to their waltz, Iuile is able to see the variant meats of geese, pork, lamb, and beef, along with some delicacies she has never seen before. She is curious about what else they have, such as desserts, but cannot tell due to the guests blocking her view of the rest of the table. It suddenly occurs to Iuile as she glances towards Eilis, who is under the trance of the marvels of the ball herself, that even if she does receive her wish, she knows deep down that her best friend would want to make a wish herself. A wish Iuile knows too well that the only thing that Eilis would wish for, is to be rich and independent.

"Well ladies", said Einri, causing Iuile and Eilis to come out of the bushes, with twigs and leaves in their hair, and turn to him where he had been standing behind them with a look of satisfaction on his face, "are you pleased from what you had seen?"

The girls glance at each other for a moment, before returning their attention to Einri with Iuile asking, "Which one of them is Marquis Savio DeGallo?"

"He doesn't show up until thirty minutes till midnight", replies Einri. "Not to mention that him showing up is the sign that we need to leave."

This only puzzles the girls, with Eilis asking with a tone of suspicion, "Why's that?"

Einri was about to answer but became silent for a moment before finally saying, "You know what, I don't know. I was told to leave by the time he shows up, and definitely before the stroke of midnight."

There was a sudden silence from the ballroom, causing all three to enter the bushes in order to find out what was going on. Only to see everyone gazing at a large column structure, that is shaped and designed to appear like a four-tier cake. There is no sound coming from any of the guests of the party, or from the musicians, though they appear to be getting ready to perform once more. Iuile decides to turn her attention back to the cake, while the lights begin to dim down somehow.

Suddenly, there was a flash, followed by a loud bang at the top of the cake. The musicians begin their melody, which sounds fast and jingles, as a person dressed in a purple tuxedo with a cape, a cane with an amethyst cap, a matching top hat, and a black and golden Pantalone mask (all of which are covered in glitter), appears at the top of the cake, and starts to sing. The mysterious masked man then jumps off the cake and begins to skip, jump, and frolic around the ballroom while entertaining the guests who supply him with great applause. He then starts to dance with various women and men, telling jokes, and playing tricks, all while singing his melody.

"That's the marquis!" Said Einri with panic. "We need to leave now!"

"But I need to see him", said Iuile with the sound of desperation in her voice.

"Iuile's father has an illness that will kill him", said Eilis who is clarifying her friend's reply. "The real reason why we even came here, is to meet with Marquis DeGallo so that Iuile can wish for him to cure her father."

"Ohhh no", said Einri with terror in his voice as he exited out of the bushes, followed by Iuile and Eilis. "I was told under no circumstances should we meet Marquis DeGallo, or stick around by midnight. It is very dangerous if we do, and therefore too much of a risk."

"Then that is a risk I am willing to take", said Iuile who walked away with the determination to enter through the front doors, with Eilis following suit, then Einri who became upset over what the girls are about to do.

As soon as Iuile is about to go around the corner of the building, a beautiful blonde woman, wearing a pink Columbina mask, runs by them. She was being chased by a hefty man with dark hair and a matching beard, wearing a bronze color medico della peste mask, and holding a large peacock feather that he was using on the Columbina mask lady. The Columbina mask lady gleefully tries to flee from the feathered man, while giggling with excitement and playfulness. They completely stop when they notice Iuile and her party, who are just standing there in shock that they have been found.

As if nothing wrong has occurred, the Medico Mask Man asks, "What are you doing out here?"

"You should be inside and party with the rest of us", said the Columbina Mask Lady while still giggling.

Surprised that they are not in trouble for trespassing, have Iuile, Eilis, and Einri glancing at each other, for they do not know what to say. Only for Eilis to decide to break the silence and ask, "So we can just enter at any time?"

The bellowing laughter of the Medico Mask Man can be heard throughout the night before he finally decides to reply, "But of course!"

Still suspicious that this is too good to be true, has caused Eilis to ask, "But what about the guards?"

"What about them?" Reply the Medico Mask Man, "They're just armor golems whose heads are movable by magic, but always stationary."

Even though luck seems to be on their side, Iuile could not help but feel that something is wrong, and ask, "Are you really sure that someone of our . . . ."

But Iuile is quickly cut off by the Medico Mask Man, "Don't tell us your status! The whole point of a masquerade ball is so that anyone can come and have some fun, regardless of status. So long as they are wearing a mask, that is.

"So if we retrieve a mask", said Iuile with suspicion, while clarifying what she heard, "then we can participate in the fun, and meet Marquis DeGallo?"

"Of course", said the Columbina Mask Lady, "but there's no need for you to return home just to retrieve a mask since Marquis DeGallo possesses many assortments for guests to borrow." She begins to pull some twigs out of Eilis' hair and continues, "Especially since you both need to fix your hair, and be properly dressed." After Iuile and Eilis blush upon realizing that their hair is a mess from the bushes, the Columbina Mask Lady grabs their wrists in order to forcibly drag them around the front of the building and into the mansion.

The girls hear Einri yelling for them to wait, only for the Medico Mask Man to say, "Come along you, we need to dress you up for the ladies." He manages to snatch Einri's rifle, causing him to protest, only for the masked man to push Einri from behind while cutting him off saying, "No weapons are allowed inside, we'll just leave this with the guards."

This befuddled Einri who questions the Medico Mask Man, "But I thought you said that they are stationary?"

"But they are", said the Medico Mask Man who causes Einri to be more confused. When they approach the ten-foot-tall statues in front of the double doors, the masked man sticks the rifle into one of the statue's cuisses, where it absorbs the rifle until it fully disappears. He then drags Einri, who is dumbstruck from what he has seen, into the mansion. All the while the two moons are closer to alignment for their double lunar eclipse.

CHAPTER 10

Fighting for Survival

What has happened to Niall for those of you who are wondering, will now know, and for those that don't, too bad. The fourth son of a farmer who loves to hunt, and teaches all his sons how to hunt a beast in case of harsh winters that come. Niall, who is eighteen, was sent out by himself for the first time to prove to his father that he is capable of taking care of himself. A young man who finds masculinity acts as normal, with feminine acts abnormal due to his constant surrounding of his brothers, male cousins, and a tomboyish mother. He comes off as a wiry and intellectual young man, headstrong, yet cautious, as he rides through Killy Ri Forest on his raptor, Crono, who is already on the scent of his lost prey.

"None of my business on what they are doing", Niall mumbles to himself, "got enough problems as it is thanks to that mule, Einri. My family is looking forward to some meat for tomorrow, and they don't want to waste money at the butcher." He begins to recall his failed attempt to have a conversation under the tree on the hill, followed by anguish due to the impression that he made a fool of himself. "Aargh, I knew that I shouldn't bother to talk to her till after the hunt. Of course, the one time that she allows me to say something involves a question to fulfill her curiosity."

When Crono comes to a complete stop, he begins to softly growl to where only Niall can hear him, telling him that they are close to his target. He examines the darkness of the forest, which he is used to due to many hunts with his kin, where he spots the buck, and readies his bow and arrow. Just when he is about to release his arrow, an image of something horrible happening to a certain girl, appears in his mind, causing his arrow to fly right over the deer, and scare the buck to where it runs off in a random direction.

The disbelief of what just happened has Niall staring at the spot where he missed his shot, where he then shakes his head to clear his mind before muttering, "I haven't missed a target since Dad trained me to shoot an arrow." While Niall is trying to regain his composure, Crono decides to follow the deer, only to trip and fall, with Niall falling off his saddle. After regaining his senses, Niall examines himself to see that he is unharmed, before checking on Crono to see that he is fine also. He then looks up towards the canopy and asks, "You're trying to tell me something, aren't you?" There is only silence as Niall continues to stare up at the canopy, before finally saying, "Fine, I get the message."

When Niall and Crono stand back up, he saddles up on his dino who then attempts to go after the deer. Only for Niall to pull back the rein and say, "Nope, we're going to help some idiots. Could get help first, but they might be dead by then, so let's go." Crono hiss with annoyance. "What? Are you hungry?" The raptor gives what sounds like a mixture of a purr and a growl, telling Niall that he is.

"Fine", said Niall with a grin, "just give me a moment." He digs into his pouch where he pulls out some jerky, and places it near Crono's mouth saying, "It's not much, but eat up." Crono sniffs at the jerky for a moment before eating it. Feeling somewhat satisfied, Crono dashes off towards Diavolo Mansion, all while Niall eats a single piece of jerky, as he does not want to use up all his rations.

It is not long until Crono comes to a sudden halt, due to several poucka goblins dashing out from the bushes and pausing upon seeing Niall before deciding to kill him and his raptor. Only to regret it later as Crono begins to rip and tear one of them apart, while Niall shoots the other three with his arrows, killing each one with only a single shot. After the fight, Niall gets off his raptor in order to reclaim his arrows while saying, "These goblins may have been looking for the one that I slew earlier." After claiming his ammo, he turns to approach Crono, only to halt with disgust upon seeing his dino feasting on one of the goblins and ask, "Really?" Niall's question causes Crono to stop eating and turn to his master with blood on his lips. "You're really going to make a meal from something that foul?" Crono only tilts his head with a confusion of what he did wrong, then gives a whatever attitude before returning to his meal.

This has Niall having nothing but disappointment with Crono, but at the same time, he understands that he is only an animal that is hungry, and following basic instincts. Niall only shook his head before climbing back onto his mount and said, "Anyway, let's . . . ." He falls utterly silent due to a sudden chill, followed by hearing the sound of a horse walking around in the distance. Niall's heart skips a beat as the sound is horrifying, and he now knows that the goblins were not searching, but escaping. Though he cannot see it, Niall knows, for he has heard stories that when you feel a sudden chill, regardless of how warm your outfit is, and hear a horse walking nearby with hoofs that make a horrifying sound, means that you are in the presence of a dullahan. With the lack of a wagon noise, means that it is a bastoir dullahan

This powerful undead creature is a headless horseman that normally carries his head around his arm, and is capable of seeing all around without turning. The body is armor in black with a cape, with his only weapon being a human spine that he uses as a whip. The horse that he rides in on is no beast, but a monster known as capoiann. This creature appears demonic with black hair, a dark purple mane, blood-red eyes, and breathes smoke out of its nostrils. But the most dangerous thing about capoiann, is its hooves, for it is red hot, and burns the surrounding ground that stops an inch from it. But that is nothing compared to the dullahan's head, as it is the most terrifying thing from the duo, for unlike the body that appears that it is still alive, the head is a rot that will continue to decay, for all eternity.

Trying not to panic, and control his breathing, Niall whispers a command to Crono to stop eating and move as silently as possible. The raptor understands by halting his meal and nimbly travels through the forest without making a sound. As Crono treks on, Niall scans his surroundings while praying to Dominus Deus that they will not be found by the horseman. Only to hear the capoiann cry out, and running in their direction.

Knowing full well that the dullahan has figured out their location, Niall gives Crono the command to make a mad dash, in hopes of outrunning the monster. An attempt that may seem pointless as horses are faster than raptors, not to mention that the cold air slows the poor cold-blooded creature down. But Niall has no choice but to hope that Crono can outrun the capoiann. For the fear of death has bestowed upon Niall as he and his raptor try to survive this ordeal they are in, and curses Einri for idiotically bringing a rifle into Killy Ri Forest.

Closer and closer, the bastoir dullahan's horse gets to Niall and his raptor, whose heart is beating more, and more, rapidly. Hoping and praying that he somehow gets out of this horrible predicament. Yet to Niall's surprise, he hears the capoiann cry out once more, and the sound of its hooves starts to fade away. This causes Niall to halt Crono, and listen to his surroundings, only to hear nothing as the dullahan has apparently abandoned him. Niall is completely confused as to why the headless horseman left, only to assume that the undead had found a better prey.

Not wanting to let his guard down, Niall once again inspects his surroundings to see that all is clear. Feeling relief, while still keeping his guard up, he commands Crono to press on, followed by thanking Dominus Deus for protecting him. Niall also plans to inform his family that there is a bastoir dullahan in Killy Ri Forest so that they can acquire a piece of gold to ward off the monster. "Well", Niall said to himself as he tried to find a silver lining, "better a bastoir dullahan, which would have just killed me, than a coiste-bodhar, which would have taken my soul to the afterlife, or worse, a diabas dullahan." Niall continues to ride west for some time until he runs into the area where Iuile and her party left Pixie, Speedy, and Hunter.

This perplexed Niall as to why their mounts were there and decided to scan his area. Only to find that there was no struggle and that they seem to have left their rides willingly, causing Niall to shrug it off, and continue west. The reason Niall is puzzled by the situation is because this is the first time he is visiting the mansion due to him being the type to never poke a sleeping bear. He had, however, heard descriptions of how to get there from his brothers and cousins. Time has passed until Niall finally enters the part of the forest that is destroyed, and eventually the ravine with large boulders on either side of the entrance. When Niall is twenty yards from the boulders, he becomes instantly frightened for a moment due to the boulders moving, and revealing themselves to be the so-called, 'mountain trolls'.

The mineral creatures get up with difficulty as if they were recovering from a battle, and give off a nasty smirk on their faces upon noticing Niall and Crono. Niall on the other hand, examines his surroundings and ponders if he should run off. Only to decide that he will not as he does not want to abandon the girls, and seeing that there are no bodies, or blood, around, tells him that they managed to pass by the rock monsters somehow. However, Niall has no idea how to safely pass the menacing stones as one of them throws its fist toward him, while the other blocks the ravine's entrance. Remarkably, Crono manages to evade its blow, regardless of his handicap to the cold air, and rides off with a screech.

With relief of Crono's determination to persevere, Niall shrugs off his fear and takes aim with his bow to shoot at one of its eyes, since they appear to be the only thing that he could damage. When Niall fires his arrow, the stone figure blocks it with his arm, causing Niall to say, "Dang nappa!" But the rock monster blocking his shot means that it did not want to get hit in the eye, telling him that his hunch is right. Niall readies his bow again as the other one tries to stomp on them, only for Crono to jump gracefully away, and avoid its attack.

After Crono circles around the first one, who turns his head in their direction, Niall takes another shot and hits the monster, who is caught off guard, in the eye. The creature gives off an annoying noise, which Niall assumes is screaming, as it kneels to the ground while the other one tries to punch both Niall and Crono. Only for Crono, out of instinct, to jump onto its fist, and run up the arm. The stone figure stares in confusion while Niall quickly recovers from coming close to death, and is saved thanks to his raptor's quick reflexes, as he then shoots its eye, and succeeds. Crono manages to maintain footing from the rock monster's reaction to being hit in the eye long enough to reach its shoulder, where he decides to jump off towards the top of the ravine.

When Crono lands on top of the ravine, he turns to screech at the newly injured monster they escaped from, while Niall sees the first one that he shot staring at them, with a menacing eye, as it is getting back up. Only for Niall to take out the other eye, causing it to drop down into pieces. "Just as I hope", Niall said to himself, "their glowing eyes are their weakness. Though I don't understand the high-pitched screaming after destroying each one."

The second rock monster, who is now enraged over the death of its friend and losing its eye, reaches out to grab the raptor. The rock monster manages to grab Crono by his tail, because of his distraction by his master finishing the first one, and pulls them down from the ravine. This causes Niall to accidentally drop his bow, by reason of his choice to hold on for dear life onto Crono's saddle horn and dangle by his raptor. The mineral creature takes notice that Niall dropped his weapon (while Crono tries to stay calm, so as not to allow his master to fall off), and begins to grin over its victory as it lifts them up at head level. Only for the stone figure to lose its grin due to Niall smiling right back at it, with a dagger in his hand. Niall quickly, and accurately, throws the blade right into its other eye, and shatters it, resulting in the rock monster to toss both him and Crono into the forest. Out of pure luck, Niall and Crono land into the branches that soften their fall back to the ground, while the creature falls apart like its friend.

Niall slowly gets up with his heart racing like a hummingbird while realizing that twice he came close to getting a visit from the reaper within the same hour. He examines himself to see if he has any serious injuries that he may not notice, only to find minor scratches and bruises. Niall then inspects Crono who appears irate, but fine, as he, too, has minor cuts and bruises from the fall. After seeing that his raptor is fine, Niall exits the forest once more on foot, with Crono following him from behind, and sees that the monsters' bodies have broken apart.

"What in the world were those?" Niall asks himself as he decides to take this opportunity to quickly retrieve his weapons. Only to find one arrow missing, and the other too damaged to be reused, so he breaks off the arrowhead and puts it in his pouch while wondering to himself, "Never heard of any monsters like these. Rather curious on what they are." He turns to Crono who is close by and waiting on him. Niall smiles at his raptor, and pets his head before continuing his search for his dagger while saying, "Oh well, all's well that ends well."

During his search for his dagger, he notices a purple radiant cut jewel implanted on what is left of one of the rock monsters. Niall decides to grab it with the belief that he needs force to remove it, only to find that it comes off very easily as he takes a few steps back while trying to not lose balance. After recovering his balance, Niall examines the jewel and notices that it is almost the size of his hand upon holding it. He gazes into the mysterious jewel and sees what appears to be a cloud-like substance, with glittering effects, swirling in it. Niall immediately assumes that it is valuable and says, "Well, lucky me", before putting it into one of his satchels.

Though Niall did think about searching for more jewels, he decided not to upon realizing that he would only waste time doing so. He also decides to abandon his dagger, which he is having trouble locating, as he cannot help but have a terrible feeling that the girls may be in danger. Though luckily, he is not too concerned about pressing forth without his dagger, because he has another one that one of his cousins loaned him. So he plans on retrieving his spoils, and blade, after finding them as he saddles up on Crono. The raptor immediately dashes into the ravine as Niall braces in what he believes to be a long, and terrible, nightmare that is to come.

CHAPTER 11

Blossoming Romance

The double lunar eclipse is only moments away to begin their eclipsing, and with the night so clear, means that it is becoming the perfect moment for two people to confess their feelings. The natives of Mystia believe that confessing one's love to another, and the same one returning that confession before the eclipse ends, would bring great fortune. For it would bring blessings and happiness upon their wedding unto death do they part. A moment that any young maiden would dream about, for they yearn for that special someone to confess their feelings to them. With the only thing that can match such a passion and blessing, is kissing upon a sunrise.

It is also within this same moment that the maids, who are wearing Columbina butterfly masks, have finished adorning Iuile with a floral white and deep sky blue color dress, with silver earrings and a tiara that each contains sapphire jewels. "There you go", said one of the maids. "That should match your pretty blue eyes, and you look more gorgeous with that makeup on." While gazing into the mirror with makeup on for the first time in her life, has astonished Iuile, for she never realized how makeup can make one so beautiful.

The reason Iuile had never worn makeup before, is because it was expensive, during this era, to the point that only nobles could afford it. She had seen female nobles at Dunban and Amelon wore them, and always thought they were beautiful to begin with. But now she knows, or at least assumes, that it is the magic of makeup that makes a woman truly beautiful. "You sure you don't want to remove that clover?" Ask another maid. "You would look more elegant with something more dignifying for a necklace."

The thought of removing her wooden clover, causes Iuile to grasp it, for removing it outside her home would feel like she is forsaking her faith and family. Such a horrible feeling has Iuile turn to the maid and say, "This is the only thing that stays on me."

"Suit yourself", said the maid.

"Here you go", said another maid as she handed Iuile a purely white mask. Iuile takes and examines it as the same maid continues, "It is a Columbina lamb mask. You and your friend seem to be the type that would wear them."

While adorning the mask, Iuile could not help but feel that she was putting on a second mask on her face. After being told by the maids that they are finished, Iuile turns and sees Eilis in a lemon glacier and lavender blush dress, with golden earrings, necklace, and a tiara that each contains topaz jewels, while wearing a similar Columbina lamb mask, except it is a darker shade of white. They stare at each other as Iuile feels that she is gazing upon a complete stranger, and blushes before deciding to break the silence and say, "You look like a fully mature noblewoman."

Blushing in return, Eilis replies with honesty, "So do you."

"Thanks", said Iuile. "Though I would rather be wearing your dress."

"But that color suits you better", said Eilis.

"Thanks, but still . . . ." Reply Iuile who begins to trail off, for she still prefers Eilis' dress. Only to then worry about how her father is doing.

"Anyway", said Eilis as she picked up what she assumes is bothering Iuile, "since they're done with us, let's head to the ballroom."

"Yes", reply Iuile who is eager to join in on the festivities, and meet Marquis DeGallo, "let's do that." They exit the dressing room, and into the second floor's south wing that has a balcony in front of them, with the foyer down below. While they walk to their left towards the center of the second floor's balcony, where the stairway descending to the foyer is located, Iuile decides to say, "I'm surprised how fast they changed us."

"I know", replied Eilis who appeared slightly discomfort. "Does your dress feel tight?"

"Definitely", reply Iuile who shares the same discomfort. "How could anyone stand this? Though we should be grateful that our moms had us practice walking in heels."

Eilis almost fell down, as if she was jinxed, only to catch herself and quickly say, "Not another word about not taking my lessons seriously."

"I was only going to ask if you were alright", lied Iuile while trying not to giggle.

When Iuile and Eilis reach the stairs, they see Einri at the bottom of the steps wearing a tuxedo and a gray Columbina mask, with the double door entrance across the stairway. They feel a slight chill, due to their attire not being made to trap heat, while walking down the stairs. When they reach the ground floor, Eilis asks him, "Is that supposed to be a rat mask?"

This made Einri utterly annoyed by Eilis' comment, causing him to quickly reply to her, "They told me it is a weasel mask! I was about to demand something more dignifying, only to be shoved over here to wait for you ladies." He then turns his attention to Iuile, bows, and asks her, "You look magnificently beautiful, milady. May I escort you . . . ." He becomes silent when he notices Iuile walking past by him, and paying no attention to what he said, for she is starting to get impatient of waiting any longer from being inside the ballroom. This causes Einri to feel foolish and humiliate while Eilis gracefully walks by him, and giggles at his failure.

Upon entering the ballroom to the north of the foyer, Iuile gasped with excitement as she saw that everyone, except for the orchestra, was waltzing to the magnificent melody. She can hear Marquis DeGallo singing, though it seems that he is making up the lyrics, as he goes along in perfect rhyme and rhythm while dancing around by himself. Iuile managed to get close enough to see his angelic blonde hair and sparkling blue eyes like the heavens. The sight of him causes Iuile to be stunned and trance from his beauty, as she wishes to dance with him for only one time, for she has become lost in a dream.

As Marquis DeGallo parades around the ballroom, he manages to make eye contact with Iuile, causing him to be completely motionless. This has Iuile become flush with embarrassment to the point that she hastefully breaks eye contact first, and turns her head away to look at the ground. *"Was he looking at me?"* Iuile ponders to herself. *"No, of course not. He's on the other side of the room, and was gazing at someone more appealing than me, like Eilis."*

While Iuile tries to regain her composure, she decides to search for her friend. Only to see that Eilis is not too far off, and dancing with a gentleman wearing a purple bauta mask. Once more, Iuile could not help but be jealous of Eilis who had a pleasing smile on her face, while trying not to falter, which is making Iuile giggle to herself. Iuile begins to look around to see if she can locate where Einri is and found him dancing with a large lady, who is wearing a black and white volto mask with red lipstick. Though the large lady is very pleased with her partner, Einri on the other hand tries to break away from her.

After knowing that her companions are nearby, Iuile decides to gather up her courage to face Marquis DeGallo and turns in the direction that she last saw him. Only to have her wrist grab, and pull towards someone as the side of her face is slam right into that same person's chest, where they then begin to waltz. Iuile blushes even redder while wondering why this person decides to dance with her without asking. She decides to slowly look up to see who it is, only to find that it is none other than Marquis DeGallo.

"My apologies, milady", said Marquis DeGallo in an accent that Iuile has never heard of, but finds very exotic to her liking, "I could not help but to be breathtakingly amazed by your beauty, and feel greatly insulted that no one had asked to dance with such grace. A grace that matches an angelic princess from Heaven!"

No words could come out of Iuile's lips when she attempts to speak, for she is in complete awe of what Marquis DeGallo said. *"My appearance matches that of a princess?"* Iuile thought to herself, *"Me?! No one ever commented on me like that. I mean, I'd seen men flirt with Eilis. But not me . . . . That of royalty!"*

They continue to move in a rhythm of elegance and awe as if their harmony is of a prince who found his true love. The guests of the marquis begin to one by one halt their own frolicking rhythm and slowly move aside to marvel at the magnificent pair who are dancing as if they are in a fairy tale. With Iuile herself feeling as if she is on the boundary between fantasy and reality, a surreal feeling which she has never experienced before in her life. For they now have the dance floor to themselves, like the bride and groom's first dance at a wedding reception. Marquis DeGallo begins to slowly waltz Iuile towards the east side of the ballroom. As they draw close to the window, both Evana and Nacia are only seconds away from starting their eclipsing while hovering over the duo, causing the guests to become mesmerized by the dancing couple.

"I normally don't do this", said Marquis DeGallo in a tone that says that his heart is under the spell of love, "but your physique taunts me as if Heaven is denying me access through their gates. Yet they allow me to gaze upon the most magnificent angel that the Almighty had ever created! For look out the window!" They both gaze through the window and see that the double lunar eclipse has now begun. For now is the moment for two lovers, under its benevolent grace, to confess their feelings toward each other.

Marquis DeGallo returns his attention back to Iuile, and continues his confession, "Yes! You are too special, and an insult to you if I don't under these conditions. For I am feeling something that I had never felt before, or ever. A feeling of true love! I normally grant someone a wish if they win my game, but for you, my love, I will do it for free. Tell me, tell me, won't you tell me! I've just got to know! What is your heart's deepest desire, and please don't keep me waiting, for it torments me if you keep me waiting to grant your wish."

"I can't believe this!" Iuile thought to herself as she broke from the trance of the eclipse, only to be slowly hypnotized again upon gazing through the marquis' magnificent eyes, *"The marquis has fallen for me? Me . . . a rancher's . . . daughter . . . ? This is truly . . . a dream . . . come true!"* She then realizes her true purpose for making her dangerous journey, and thinks while trying to resist Marquis DeGallo's beauty, *"Wait! Finding my true love isn't important . . . right . . . now . . . . Focus Iuile! For Dad's sake, FOCUS! He's allowing me one wish for free, though I wonder what the game would have been. Oh, it doesn't matter, he is giving me a free wish. Come on Iuile, ask him, don't get lost . . . in . . . his . . . eyes . . . . No! Stop it!"* Iuile tries to fight off her shyness, and resist the marquis' charm, as she attempts to say, "My . . . father is . . . deadly ill . . . and . . . ."

As if knowing what Iuile is about to say, Marquis DeGallo cuts in with the pleasure of granting her wish, "You want to end his suffering. That is your wish? Are you sure?"

"Yes", replies Iuile, "I am sure. I travel far from my hometown to meet with you, just so you can aid my father." The bell begins to ring, signaling that midnight has arrived. This has Iuile's heart leaping for joy, because her romantic dream of dancing at the stroke of midnight during a festive party, has come true, and during a double lunar eclipse! Such an occasion has her glee, for who knew that traveling to a forsaken place would bring her great joy.

"Granted, my love", replied Marquis DeGallo with a smile that almost caused Iuile to squeal. "Once you and everyone else reveal yourselves, I will send someone to kill your father."

CHAPTER 12

The Name of the Game

Horribly shocked due to the reality of what Marquis DeGallo just said, has Iuile feeling betrayed and confused. For how can he assume such a terrible thing to someone whom he truly love? It was then that fear has overcome Iuile of her father being killed, rather than die from an illness. Such dread has caused her to panicky reply, "What? No! That wasn't what I meant!"

"It's rude not to take off your mask when the clock strikes twelve", replied Marquis DeGallo, as if he did not acknowledge Iuile's question. "For everyone, except myself, needs to remove their mask at midnight, due to custom."

Completely irate over the marquis' lack of emotions than he did before, has Iuile taking off her mask and cries out, "I said that what you assumed from what I had wanted to wish for, wasn't right!"

"Oh my", replied Marquis DeGallo in a subtle, yet fake, surprise voice, "you're human."

Those words have Iuile perplexed, only for a different type of fear to befall her when she realized why he said that. She turns to examine the guests of the mansion and finds herself surrounded by monsters, fairies, and dallions. It did not take her long to understand that the horde were disguising themselves as humans, until now, as she searched around in order to pinpoint Eilis' location. When Iuile manages to find her friend, she sees that Eilis was dancing with a hairless gorilla known as a gorigo, who has covered her mouth. This type of monster has an average height of five feet, with no head, but a large mouth with shark's teeth where the neck should be, and an eye on each shoulder.

This is then followed by trying to find Einri and seeing that he was apparently pinned down, with his mouth covered also, by the large woman he was dancing with, who turns out to be a female fuath orc. This creature is muscular in a husky manner compared to her male counterpart, and shorter in height, as she appears to be less than six feet. Her tusk is only two inches long, and in clear view due to her grinning. Both of her ears are covered in rings, hair tied to a bun, and is only wearing a two-piece leather clothing that is not pleasant to look at with her stomach dangling, regardless of one's gender.

A fat anthropomorphic brown rat known as a far darrig, is a fairy that is two feet long (not including the tail), dressed in a red vest and short pants. He approaches Marquis DeGallo on his hind legs and asks him, "Sir, mind if I take her pretty little friend home?" He begins to snicker, "I like to have some fun terrifying her." Eilis becomes even more horrified from what the far darrig requested and begins to pointlessly struggle herself free due to panic.

"If he gets the girl", said the beathair, a dallion that has the body of a woman, with scales of a snake that is dark green with dark brown spots. Her hair questionably appears to be that of shed snake skin, with human green eyes, and gowned in a black robe. "Then I want the man, I can spawn interesting creatures with his blood." This causes the other monsters to lay claim to Iuile and her friends.

With no idea of what to do, Iuile turns to Marquis DeGallo with hopes of salvation, only to see that he is getting agitated and yells out, "ENOUGH!!! None of you will have any of them!"

This calms Iuile as she begins to believe that Marquis DeGallo is going to protect them, and asks him with enthusiasm, "So you won't kill my father?"

Marquis DeGallo turns to Iuile, and gives a smile that says that everything will be all right as he replies, "But that is what you wished for, my Angelic Princess."

"That was NOT what I wished for", Iuile said in a hysteric tone, for she could not believe that her fairy tale dream was shattering into a nightmare like no other. "My wish is for you to cure his illness, not to murder him!"

"I'm so sorry, Angelic Princess", said Marquis DeGallo with regret, "but I seem to recall saying, 'You want to end his suffering.' To which you agree without further clarification. You had made your wish, now I must follow through, for it is the only way for me to show my love for you."

The marquis' dedication to Iuile's love has her in awe, with her emotions telling her, *"There is good in him if he is that devoted in his love for me."* Only for the faint sound of, *"Dad"*, to pop up into her head, causing her to utterly panic, and be fully desperate to fix her mistake in saving her father by saying, "Then I want another wish, Marquis DeGallo!"

"Please, call me Savio, my Angelic Princess", said Marquis DeGallo as he bowed. "However", he then straightened himself up, twiddled his fingers, and continued in a remorseful tone, "that was your only freebie."

Apparently having enough of Iuile not handling the situation well, Eilis decides to stop struggling and stamp on the gorigo's foot, causing the monster to release her due to the pain, and hop on one foot. After freeing herself, Eilis runs up to Marquis DeGallo, wraps her arms around his right arm, and flirtatiously asks, "Oh come now Savio, I'm sure a great, and amazing, man such as you, can easily heal him."

The Ram and Ewe's Quest for the Lost Lambs

"I'm sorry", said Marquis DeGallo with disgust, while pulling his arm from Eilis, "but you don't impress me, and don't you dare call me by my surname alone again!"

First Niall being unaffected by Eilis' charm, then being turned down by Marquis DeGallo, is making Eilis irate and offended to the point that she begins to retort harshly. Only for Iuile to cut her off to ask him, "Then let me play your game! You said that you normally give wishes to those who beat you in a game, did you not?"

"Interesting", said Marquis DeGallo who began to give a sinister smile. "If that's the case, would your friends like to join in as well? And if so, what will they wish for?"

Anxiety has overcome Iuile as she begins to fear of what her friend will wish for. She turns to Eilis who decides to reply, "The same thing Iuile wish for if she loses, and if she does win, then I want the both of us to return to our hometown in one piece." Eilis then slowly turns to Iuile with a grin on her face, and says to her friend, "I'm not going to abandon you in your hour of need."

Fill with joy that she can count on Eilis, has Iuile smiling back to her best friend with relief. Except Eilis is forgetting a certain someone, causing Iuile to ask, "Aren't you forgetting about Einri?"

The concern for Einri has surprised Eilis, who then turns to Marquis DeGallo, smiles at him, and asks, "Will you excuse us for a moment?"

"Why certainly, Sunflower", replied Marquis DeGallo with a smile as well, while twiddling his fingers on his cane which he did not possess before dancing with Iuile, till now.

Being called 'Sunflower' by the marquis, has Eilis blush from such a lovely nickname while taking Iuile's arm, and pulling her aside. After taking a few steps away with her friend, Eilis whispers to Iuile, "You know, considering what he did to Peadar, among other things, do we really want to bring him back?"

This shocked Iuile, for she could not believe what she was hearing, and replied to Eilis in a whisper, "Are you serious, Eilis? We got here safely because of him!"

"Only so that he can manipulate you into dating him", replies Eilis. "You seriously don't think that he is doing this out of the kindness of his heart?"

"Of course, I know that, Pot", replies Iuile angrily.

Being called 'Pot' has confused Eilis, who is unaware that Iuile is referring to the idiom; 'The pot calling the kettle black.' This has Eilis pause for a moment before asking, "What is that supposed to mean?"

"Never mind", said Iuile. "Regardless of Einri's intention, he still helped us, so we shouldn't desert him. Now include the kettle, Pot!"

That last sentence finally dawns on Eilis of the idiom but does not understand why she is being called that. Instead of questioning this, Eilis decides to drop it, for now, and agrees with her friend. After making their decision, they approach Marquis DeGallo, who has an amused appearance while still twiddling with his cane, where Eilis says to him, "I like to include kettlehead . . . ." She was immediately interrupted by Iuile elbowing her, "Ow! I mean that I like to include Einri, with our return home that is, if Iuile wins."

"Kettlehead", mumbles Marquis DeGallo to where the girls can hear him, "Interesting, I think I can come up with something more appropriate. He turns his attention to the orcess who is on top of Einri, and tells her, "Release Dunderhead!"

While trying not to laugh, both Iuile and Eilis turn to Einri as he is released by the orcess, who is greatly disappointed in letting him go. Upon being released, Einri gets up and stretches his back before heading towards Marquis DeGallo while asking him, "I guess that I have no choice but to play along for a wish of my own." When Einri is in front of Marquise DeGallo, he continues to say to the host, "If you don't mind, I would like to keep it to myself until I win. I would also appreciate it if you don't call me Dunderhead."

"Not at all", replied Marquis DeGallo, followed by, "and I'll think about it." This annoyed Einri, who decided not to respond for now, as the marquis said to his human guests, "Now all of you gather around me." When all three are close to Marquis DeGallo, they are immediately transported to another room. One that is dark, with the only source of light, is coming from the fireplace with its mantle shaped like a demonic creature's head. But unlike normal fire that is warm and bright, the flames within the firebox give off an eerie faint light of green and black flames. The demonic fireplace itself has a width of five feet, with a height of ten, and thirty feet in front of the fireplace, is a blackjack-type table where Marquis DeGallo suddenly appears in his chair that is on the dealer side. His back is towards the fireplace as he shuffles a deck of cards saying, "The name of the game . . . is Joker."

CHAPTER 13

Joker

"The game is similar to Weld'em", said Marquis DeGallo. "I'm sure that at least one of you knows the rules to Weld'em?"

"That's where we each receive two cards facing down", said Iuile with confidence, "with five shared cards facing up."

"We then have to match whatever hand that is dealt to us with the shared cards", said Einri who intervened, "in order to create a combination for the best hand."

"Ah, good", said Marquis DeGallo with pleasure, "that will save us some time. This game, Joker, is played similarly to Weld'em, except that you play with four joker cards. Making it a total of fifty-six cards, with a one-fourteenth chance of receiving one. Anyone in possession of at least one of these joker cards when we put our hands down, will automatically lose.

"You will also be dealt with three cards instead of two, the shared cards laid down by the dealer, me, will be three, instead of five. If one of the cards that is dealt into the shared cards by the dealer is a joker, then it will be discarded and replaced by the next card. You can also switch your cards with the shared cards that are laid down when your turn is up. Doing so, however, will cause you to lose your chance of receiving any cards from the dealer for that same turn. Now, all you have to do is beat my hand, and do not worry if you lose, as you can still win and have your wish, if, any of your friends beat me."

"Sounds like you're being cocky", said Eilis.

"Maybe", said Marquis DeGallo as he examined his nails before returning his attention to his guests, "it's just that, I never lose. But I like to be generous with my players by giving them some leverage, and increasing their chance of winning."

"Alright then", said Iuile with a grin on her face, "we'll play Joker." For this is too good to be true for Iuile, because she and Eilis are excellent poker players. This is all thanks to Iuile's mother who taught them how to play different card games because her mother enjoys playing poker with friends and relatives with chump change, or her children, nieces, nephews, and their friends with seeds. As far as Marquis DeGallo is aware, they are naive little girls who are not good players and will therefore go easy on them. Giving Iuile and Eilis an easy win.

While Iuile is holding back her glee, words of what Niall said earlier cross her mind, "... *if you in someway do beat him, the wish that he will grant is only equivalent to that of the devil's promise ... empty.*" Iuile shakes off her doubt and regains some hope that even though her last wish was botched, her next one would surely be successful, for she now knows that she needs to be careful in her wish.

Iuile decides to sit down across the table from Marquis DeGallo on his left side, with Einri on his right, and Eilis in the middle. The marquis continues to explain the rules while shuffling the cards, "I like to further explain that after I lay a card down, I will inquire from each of you if you would like to either have your cards replaced by the dealer or swap only one of the shared cards. When I lay the third one down, we each have one last chance to gain a better hand before showing our cards." When he finishes shuffling the cards, he lays the deck down and asks Eilis to cut the cards. When she did, Marquis DeGallo took the cards and said to them, "I will start passing the cards now.

"But do not pick them up until we clarify something, unless, of course, you want to wager blindly." While the marquis passes the cards, Einri decides to look into his hand. After Marquis DeGallo finishes delivering their cards, he says to them, "Now I would like to inform you, that since I'm betting on one wish to each one of you . . . then you shall equal that wager, with your soul." This shocks Iuile, Eilis, and Einri as the marquis ask Iuile, "Now, Angelic Princess, you bet your soul, for your wish to be for me to spare your father's life, and to heal his sickness?"

The price for Iuile to save her father's life by betting her soul, has her heart pounding rapidly, and her head confused. *"Why is he doing this?"* Iuile thought to herself while staring at the cards that were dealt to her, *"He said that he has feelings for me, and now he is placing me in this cruel position?"* The logic and reasoning part of her is telling her, *"Don't do it! He would never want me to endanger my soul for him!"* Her emotions on the other hand tell her, *"HE IS GOING TO DIE, AND I WILL NEVER SEE HIM AGAIN!"*

When Iuile finally came to a decision, with dread, she lifts her head up slowly, while shivering, in order to make eye contact with Marquis DeGallo, and said, "Yes. I will bet my soul, to wish for you to spare my father's life, and cure his pneumonia." The logic and reasoning says, *"No!!! What have I done!"* While her emotions yell out, *"THERE IS NO OTHER WAY!!!"* Iuile shed a tear over what she had done but is confident in her wish which she finds no fault in.

"Then it is a bet", said Marquis DeGallo. The marquis then turns to Eilis, and says to her, "Given the changes in the situation in that at least one of you beat me, means that Angelic Princess will still get her wish. So Sunflower, you bet your soul, for you, Angelic Princess, and Dunderhead's safe return home to Arvann?"

This surprised Iuile, Einri, and Eilis who asked, "How did you know where we came from?"

"I have my ways", said Marquis DeGallo with a sinister smile. "Now is it a bet . . . or not?"

Giving a smirk of confidence, Eilis replies, "Obviously I bet my soul for Iuile's, Einri's, and my safe return home to Arvann." This does not bode well for Iuile, as she cannot help but feel that Eilis is unaware of what is at stake, given that she has little faith in Dominus Deus. Iuile therefore wonders if Eilis even believes in souls, and if not, then Eilis is under the impression that the marquis betted a diamond for air.

The sinister grin of Marquis DeGallo has become something disturbingly savory for a moment, before going back to a careless attitude as he turns to Einri to say, "And you bet your soul for a wish-now let's play."

Before Marquis DeGallo could grab his cards, Einri gets up to say, "I'm not agreeing to that!" For not only is Einri furious that the marquis did not verify his anticipation to play, but he is also furious at the marquis' attitude towards him, like he is a useless trash.

This is followed by Marquis DeGallo laughing before saying, "You fool, it's far too late when you picked up your hand!" Einri instantly feels a force pulling him back down, followed by his chair immediately moving towards the table. Marquis DeGallo then said with a sinister appearance, "Now . . . play."

Due to the freight that her soul is now at stake, has Iuile hesitant for a moment before taking her hand with dread. Only to find that she has a queen of hearts, three of diamonds, and four of clubs, nothing. She begins to remember her mother saying that she should always keep what is called a poker face, as any movement you give, or appearance you make, will give away what type of hand you have. She glances around and sees that Eilis is giving off a good poker face, as she can't tell if her hand is good or not. Einri on the other hand, is showing that he has a terrible hand, due to the disgruntled look that he is giving.

While appearing bored with the situation, Marquis DeGallo decides to glance at his hand before placing them back down on the table, lays the first card down, and turns to Iuile saying that she is first. The marquis' handsomeness is making Iuile blush, and having her recall what he said to her earlier, *"For I am feeling something that I had never felt before, or ever."*

This causes Iuile's face to become red as a cardinal, making her hide behind her cards while only having her eyes visible. With her emotions saying in a way that is in full display, *"Oh he does love me!"* While her logic and reasoning tell her in a faint that she can barely notice, *"Then why does he want to kill my father?"*

Upon seeing that the first shared card is an eight of diamonds, has Iuile intrigued if she is making a flush with the three, except the odds of getting that are low. So Iuile decides to give up her three of diamonds and four of clubs, since they are useless anyway, for two new cards. After receiving new cards, Iuile's bashfulness fades as she examines them and finds that she is in possession of the ten of spades, and a two of hearts, still nothing. Eilis passes on the eight and asks for two cards, followed by Einri who passes on the eight also, and requests for two cards which changes his expression to deep concern upon seeing what is dealt to him. Marquis DeGallo himself only takes a single card.

The second shared card that Marquis DeGallo lays down is the queen of diamonds . This makes Iuile trade the queen of diamonds with the ten of spades without a second thought, ensuring her a pair of queens, but regrets not swapping the two of hearts instead. Eilis asks for two cards again while subconsciously shaking her left leg, telling Iuile that she is getting anxious, and is hoping for a good hand. Einri trades the ten of spades for a queen of clubs, which Iuile thinks was an unusual decision, only to realize that she might have ruined Einri's pair of queens, and is changing tactics. Marquis DeGallo passes both laid cards and deals without taking another card for himself.

The third shared card that Marquis DeGallo lays down, is the eight of clubs. Eilis slowly stops shaking her leg, telling Iuile that she has something. Einri on the other hand, is getting nervous, making Iuile feel guilty and wondering if she interfered with his original hand. This has caused her to decide to not do any more trading with the shared cards, as it may decrease their chance of success in beating the marquis' hand. It suddenly dawned on Iuile that Marquis DeGallo was acting perfectly calm, so calm that he showed no concern of possibly losing.

Worrying over the worst-case scenario has Iuile pondering to herself, *"Does he have a winning hand? But what choice do I have? I already messed things up, and if we don't beat him, then my father will die and we lose our souls!"*

Recollections of Marquis DeGallo's words have once more passed through Iuile's mind, *"A feeling of true love!"*

This has caused Iuile to hold her tears back because she cannot understand what is going on. For how can he commit something so horrible, such as tricking them into betting their souls, after confessing his feelings towards her? *"Because he truly loves me, and obviously has a good reason for this madness"*, answers her emotions noticeably, while drowning out her logic and reasoning.

"Well, my princess", said Marquis DeGallo in a tranquil voice, "what will you do?"

Realizing that now is not the time to ponder such madness, Iuile tries to put such confusion aside in order to grasp what she currently has in her hand, and what her odds are. With a full house, queens high, Iuile sees that taking a card is pointless. Unless, someone decides to take the queen, which she knows that Eilis, and hopefully Einri, will not attempt such a thing after she traded the queen of diamonds. There is also the possibility that Marquis DeGallo might take the queen.

But Iuile knows that Marquis DeGallo will do no such thing, since he did not take any new cards from his last turn, meaning that he is confident with his current hand, which is not good. She ponders on taking a chance to gain another queen, and get a Four-of-a-Kind, which will increase her chance of winning. Iuile decides to risk it, as the two of hearts is worthless anyway, and asks for another card. She abandons the two of hearts for an ace of hearts, which she curses in her head, but remains calm since she can still win with a full house, as long as no one trades out the shared cards.

After requesting for two cards, Eilis gives a soft smirk from seeing the first card but shrieks upon the second card. Both Iuile and Einri turn to Eilis as Marquis DeGallo asks her with glee in his voice, "Did you get it? The joker?" Tears begin to fill Eilis' eyes as she quickly puts the cards on the table, facing down, and lays her head down while wrapping her arms around it as if to hide her shame. "That is fine, for you will have to show me your hand after my turn." He then inquires Einri on how many cards he wants, only for him to nervously desire one card. After Einri receives his card, Marquis DeGallo confidently tells Iuile to reveal what she has.

The time has come for Iuile to brace for what is to come, and lays her cards down saying with confidence, "I have a full house, queens high."

"How marvelous", said Marquis DeGallo who is impressed, "that'll be a tough one to beat." He casually turns to Eilis and asks, "Now, do you have what I think you have, Sunflower?"

"Just go to Einri next", replies Eilis with humility, while still having her head down with her arms crossed.

"I rather see your cards next", said Marquis DeGallo who gently swift his hand, as if he were swatting a fly. This causes Eilis' cards to fly out from under her arms, and land face up on the table, showing two eights (giving her a four-of-a-kind, and beating Iuile's hand), followed by a joker. "You poor thing", he says in a subtle mocking tone that he feels really bad. The marquis' words only make Eilis clench her fists in anger while looking down at the table, and biting her bottom lip. "An automatic loss." He turns to Einri who immediately puts his hand down with a disappointing face.

"I got the jack of spades", said Einri with annoyance, "and a pair of tens. Making it trash compared to what Iuile has in her hand." Einri continues, with charm, after turning to Iuile, "Though I'm glad that I was able to help you with that full house when I noticed you taking the queen earlier."

This has Iuile impressed by Einri's tact where she begins to blush, followed by saying, "Really? That's very kind of . . . ." She was quickly cut off by Eilis who kicked her leg, followed by giving her a particular look while controlling her frustration. Realizing why Eilis did what she did, while reacting to the pain, has Iuile turning her attention back to Einri, smiled, and said, "Thanks Einri."

"Tsk, tsk", is the sound that Marquis DeGallo is making, for he is amused by Einri's failure. "That's too bad." While Einri gives a frustrating appearance from Eilis' interference, Marquis DeGallo smiles at him and says, "Well, you can still win if Angelic Princess beats what I have. Now let's see what my hand is." He begins to turn his cards one at a time, one by one. ace of spades, Iuile starts to feel extreme dread, for there is only one thing that can beat her hand, considering the given hand. ace of clubs, and . . . .

CHAPTER 14

Sacrificial Mark

"A full house, aces high", said Marquis DeGallo after revealing his ace of diamonds, followed by giving a demonic grin while he scanned through the trash pile. "I see that one of you had a joker earlier."

"That would be me", said Einri with anger, and is puzzled because he did not believe that he did anything wrong. "Was I not allowed to do that?"

"You were allowed to discard it", said Marquis DeGallo. "You just shouldn't have it in your hand when the game is up."

The frustration and anger have finally reached a boiling point for Eilis who immediately gets up and yelled, "I SHOULD HAVE WON!!!"

"But you had the joker, Sunflower", said Marquis DeGallo while sounding bored. "Those were the rules. It was just bad luck that the last card you received was a joker."

During Eilis' argument with Marquis DeGallo, Einri begins to ponder how they could have lost. Only to come up with a single conclusion as he is now fueled with rage, and instantly slams his hands on the table to protest by saying, "It's now obvious that you cheated you . . . ." With the hope of the element of surprise, Einri immediately crawls on top of the table in order to strike Marquis DeGallo. Only for the marquis to avoid Einri's punch, and whacked him in the head with his cane. The moment he hits Einri in the head is the moment that they appear back in the ballroom, and are surrounded once more by monsters, who appear to be socializing, before becoming terrifying.

"How dare you accuse me of cheating", said Marquis DeGallo who appears to have taken great offense of Einri's claim, "when I never cheated in my life! I will admit, however, that my plan to lure you three in here and trick you all into playing my game, by giving Angelic Princess a free wish, was a success."

"Wait a moment", said Eilis. "You mean this whole time you had been toying with us since we got here?"

During all that had transpired after losing at Joker, Iuile had been sitting in her chair in utter trauma. Upon returning to the ballroom, Iuile's chair had disappeared which caused her to fall down, and be unfazed by it. After Marquis DeGallo reveals his true motives, Iuile begins to undergo a mixture of new emotions, making her utterly confounded as it feels like her heart is spinning like a top. As she cannot help but feel that she is in a nightmare that she cannot wake up from. For the sake of clarification that this is happening, Iuile asks the marquis, "You mean that you purposefully botched my wish, just to ensure that you can enslave us?"

"Guilty as charged", said Marquis DeGallo with a playful smile, and bowed with his arms spread.

Realizing that there is no hope for escape, Einri quickly changes his attitude as he gets on his knees, and pleads with the marquis, "I am a son of a nobleman. My father can easily pay you for our debt."

This only has Marquis DeGallo burst into laughter, along with all the devilish beings in the ballroom. Their outburst last for a moment before the host of the mansion immediately halts his amusement, and quickly replies with pure intimidation, "Does it look like I do this for the money?! I do this so that I can have some fun! Now let's etch my master's ownership upon you."

When Marquis DeGallo finishes speaking, Iuile began to feel a severe burning pain in the back of her neck and noticed that Eilis and Einri were reacting in the same manner with their necks. When the pain vanishes, Iuile asks her friend to check each other, only to find that they both possess cursed symbols on the back of their necks, including Einri (yet his looks different from the girls). "You now bear the Sacrificial Mark, my rag dolls", said Marquis DeGallo in a mad tone. "It ensures of your inevitable fate, once I get bored with you."

Terror filled their souls from Marquis DeGallo's words as Einri dared ask, "And what happens when you have grown tired of us?"

Giving a demonic appearance that frightens the three lost souls, Marquis DeGallo replies with pleasure, "I toss you into the flames like worn-out rag dolls. The same flames you saw earlier when we played Joker." He begins a maniacal laugh before saying, "Why do you think I call those symbols on the back of your necks, 'Sacrificial Marks'?" This causes both Iuile and Eilis to scream in horror, while Marquis DeGallo himself continues to laugh, and tells the horde to grab them with the following orders, "I want the females to change Angelic Princess and Sunflower, while the males change Dunderhead. They won't be any fun unless they have, 'some', dignity."

A vivozello approaches Iuile and Eilis with a rovarda. The vivozello is a twelve foot, four-legged bat-like dallion with a head of a visored bat, and teeth of a hypsugo dolichodon. Her arms are like a fox bat, which she uses for flying (as well as walking), with three raptor-like claws on her hands, and talon-like feet. The rovarda is an eight-foot, two-legged dallion that has a head and fur like a wolf, with saber-tooth tiger fangs, whose arms are like a gorilla, and legs like a frog.

When the dallions are close to the girls, the vivozello resist the urge to drain their fluids, while the rovarda defies her need to devour their flesh, and gnaw on their bones. Before the vivozello can grab Iuile, while the rovarda aims for her friend, she quickly raises her wooden clover that is still around her neck, causing the dallions to back away in fear. As the wicked beasts keep their distance from the girls, Iuile becomes aware that a couple of beathairs are approaching her and Eilis from behind. This has Iuile turn her wooden clover to them, causing the creatures to back away from the girls in fear also, and making the other monsters laugh at the dallions.

Eilis clutches onto Iuile as they watch Einri being swarmed by the male monsters, only to notice that they are being approached by three female far darrigs, and a half-dozen female maru elves. These grey-skin elves have blood-red eyes, with yellow pupils, and a nose that is long and pointed. With a height of three feet, they appear very thin with sharp nails, and teeth of a crocodile that drools red saliva. They are not the typical fairies you are familiar with that are wise or friendly, they are the types that take pleasure in the suffering of others, which the elves will not dare do, due to their fear of the host of Diavolo Mansion. When Iuile sees them approaching, she pulls out a piece of iron that she secretly took with her while changing, causing the fairies to dash away, like a rabbit running from a wolf.

This has Eilis feel relieved while saying to Iuile, "Thank goodness that you brought iron on this journey."

Those words had dumbstruck Iuile who replies to her friend, "On this journey? Are you telling me that you left your house without your clover or even a scrap of iron? You cannot be that stupid!"

The insult Iuile had said, has offended Elise who retorted in anger, "Because I had no idea that you would drag me into a den of wolves!"

"Don't you blame me on that!" Retort Iuile who is getting angrier as her friend. "You should always bring protection whenever you step out at night!" When Iuile finishes speaking, a fuath orcess grabs Iuile's iron during her argument with her friend. When Iuile takes notice of the orcess thief, another fuath orcess snatched her wooden clover. Horrified most from having her clover taken away, Iuile yells out, "No! Anything but that!"

Before Iuile has the chance to go after the orcesses, who are bringing her protections to the marquis, the horde immediately swarmed the girls. Iuile tries to break free but is unable to as they huddle around them from prying eyes, and begin to tear their beautiful dresses apart. Iuile shed tears as she feels like a maiden whose ball gown is torn apart by her wicked step-sisters, while they apply who knows what new clothing, and makeup, that they are placing on her and Eilis. Yet the humiliation is nothing compared to the horrible emotions that she is feeling. As if her soul is being slowly torn apart due to Marquis DeGallo's confession, being tricked into betting her, Eilis', and Einri's souls (which resulted in losing their souls), and that her father is now going to be murdered.

When the horde finishes, they back away from the girls, who both cry in shame. Because the only thing Iuile and Eilis are wearing, are ugly color rag dresses, aprons, and worn-out shoes, clothes that poor girls wear in cities. Iuile looks up with tears on her face as the horrible monsters taunt them by placing a mirror in front of her and Eilis. Showing that they changed their appearance to make them appear like rag dolls. The harsh reality that both Iuile and Eilis are in, has caused them to clutch each other in sorrow.

As Iuile cries, she hears Marquis DeGallo mumbling aloud, "What a clever girl my Angelic Princess is." This has Iuile and Eilis turn and see the two orcesses standing in front of the marquis, with their hands clenched with joy. When Marquis DeGallo finishes examining the clover and iron, he stuffs them in his inside coat pocket, and says to the orcesses, "And you two were beautifully brave to snatch these from those naughty little girls, who rudely did not want to play nice." This causes the orcesses to giggle and run off a good distance before fighting to the death, as only the alpha female truly deserves the marquis' praise. The orcesses killing each other causes Marquis DeGallo to give a sadistic smile, before turning away and calling out, "Gatto! Where is that cait sith?!"

A black cat with a white spot on his chest, with boots and gloves on his paws, appears on Marquis DeGallo's right shoulder and says, "You rang, m'lord?"

While polishing the jewel on his cane, Marquis DeGallo says to Gatto, "I want you to go to Angelic Princess' town, and find her father. When you do, I want you to kill him."

As if pleased with his orders, Gatto snickers before saying, "As you command." The marquis' orders cause Iuile to panic enough to immediately attempt to get up, only for Eilis to hold her back. Desperate to do something to prevent her father's death, Iuile forcefully breaks away from Eilis' hold and runs towards Marquis DeGallo and his feline guest. When Iuile reaches them, she gets on her knees and begs him not to, only for the fairy to jump down next to her. This causes Iuile to stare into Gatto's eyes as the fairy takes off his boots and gloves, and after a moment of gazing, the cait sith mutters aloud, "Arvann, and he is last seen in what they call a clinic that is southwest from town. Hehe, shouldn't be too difficult. Much obliged for the information." He hastily runs off as Iuile tries to grab him, only to fail.

When Gatto left, Marquis DeGallo once more gave a sadistic smile as he began to say to his monstrous guests, "Now what game shall we play first? We got all night."

One of the north windows suddenly becomes smashed due to a raptor jumping through, with his master, and attacking any monster that is close by after landing. The creatures frantically backed away from the lizard as Niall said to Marquis DeGallo, "Mind if I crash the party, you ugly, one-horn, mule?"

CHAPTER 15

King Tuathal

Domesticating an animal is a long process that takes several generations to accomplish. Domesticating a raptor, however, (or to be more specific with Crono's species: venaraptor), is a fool's errand, as it is no different than domesticating a crocodile or shark. Yet somehow, someone, somewhere, manages to make it possible. There are many theories of how venaraptors were domesticated to not harm and befriend humans. One is the use of magic to force obedience onto these creatures, another suggests that someone learn the language of the dino and made a deal with their ancestors which is passed down to each generation, and then there is the one involving fairies. All of which is incorrect, for truth is stranger than fiction, and revolves around a dark history involving several idiots which I cannot tell my young audience.

The point being is that venaraptors are now fully domesticated here on Atlast, would not harm the hand that feeds them, and are loyal creatures to their master that they find worthy. At an average height of five feet, with an average length of eight feet, they prove to be cunning and stealthy in hunting, and fierce and agile in battle. But they lack the speed that a horse has, along with their strength to carry heavy loads, or pulling a wagon. Not to mention that they are cold-blooded, meaning that they cannot survive during the times of winter.

Because of this, they develop the ability to go into brumation in a man-made raptor dome. It is inside this dome where their owners can ensure their safe winter sleep, with a fire that is burning at all times. A venaraptor can also act on pure instinct, where they will perform in an appropriate manner for the sake of survival. They also possess night vision which further makes them superior mounts when it comes to hunting.

In Niall's case, Crono is the perfect mount that he is glad to have as they travel down the ravine. Wondering with dread of what new madness and horror will await him. With the only thing for him to hold onto, is the hope and faith that all will end well for him and the others. As to why I am backtracking to Niall before his breaking through the window, is because I did not want to interrupt the suspense of Iuile and the others' predicament. Nor was I able to explain that Weld'em is basically Atlast's version of Texas Hold'em.

While Niall is pondering what trouble he is about to endure in his mad quest, a voice he is familiar with says, "Now where do you think you're going, lad?"

Feeling a sudden weight on his left shoulder cause Niall to turn, and see that sitting there is a redheaded, and bearded, leprechaun that is ten inches high, dressed in a dark green with a purple cape, and a golden crown. After Niall looks ahead while removing his ring on his right index finger, and placing it in his rear right pouch, he says to the fairy with annoyance, "To save some foolish acquaintances of mine, King Tuathal of Gleannasi."

"That's very noble of you", said King Tuathal in a friendly manner, "I thought for a moment that you were doing it for your own interest.... Now, which lass do you have a crush on?"

This causes Niall to sigh, for he knows that he cannot lie to the leprechaun king, and admits, "Okay, I like one of them, but that's not the reason I'm doing this. I'm doing this because unlike the others who travel to that cursed mansion, who are capable of defending themselves and are only doing it to show off, Eilis and Iuile, from what I assume, are doing it out of desperation over something."

The response given has amused King Tuathal, for he, too, looks ahead while casually asking Niall, "So, you had not heard about Iuile's father being deadly ill?"

This surprised Niall who turned to King Tuathal for a moment before looking ahead again saying, "No I didn't, and it explains their desire to recklessly see Marquis DeGallo."

"Yet you did not go after to stop them earlier", said King Tuathal.

This has Niall feeling guilty and confesses, "I fear to disappoint my father if I don't return by dawn with some meat. It's bad enough as it is that Einri keeps scaring them off just to get back at me." It suddenly occurs to Niall who says to himself, "Wait just a second", he then turns to the king and asks, "did you mess up my shot with that deer?"

"What are you talking about?" Said King Tuathal with a tone that sounded as if he was insulted, before continuing with a concerned voice, "I just found out by one of my servants that you are heading into dangerous waters, and came quickly to you. I promised your great-grandfather that I would look after his descendants, but only if they are good folk such as himself." The King of Gleannasi grins as he begins to recall precious memories saying, "Oh how he gave me such a sport during his life. I was so impressed with his cunning, that I tried to have him rest his remaining days with me and my people."

Knowing how the tale ends, Niall cuts him off and says, "But he turned it down because he wanted to be with his family."

"That's right", said King Tuathal, "of course I warned your elder brothers, cousins, and so forth, not to go to that cursed mansion.

The Ram and Ewe's Quest for the Lost Lambs

Only to ignore me, with some of them never returning home . . . . Like your third eldest brother, Caolan. Fool followed a dare where he snuck into the mansion to grab a dessert, only to be found and . . . well, I don't think you want me to finish that."

"I rather you didn't", said Niall with an irate tone, as memories of that horrible night came flooding back. "I still remember that night, Mom and Dad were overcome with fury when they found out to the point where Dad whipped Adhanh and Slaine in the rod shed, while Mom cried all night, and the following day. With me and my younger brothers sitting in our room while being terrified by Dad's anger, and what happened to Caolan. Never had I seen him so angry considering how kind and patient he normally is." Niall gives a deep sigh before continuing, "My clan decided to tell everyone that he was killed by wolves while hunting, because orcs, or any other monster, would have caused them to demand revenge."

"Yes, I recall hearing the news that same day", said King Tuathal with grief. "We held a day of mourning for him." He then eyes Niall, without facing him, with a smile, and speaks with enthusiasm, "But you however, you knew better as you were the only one in your family's generation that has enough sense to stay away from there . . . until now."

Curious of where this is going, Niall asks the king, "So you are going to warn me now?"

"I normally would", said King Tuathal as they left the ravine, and entered the valley with Niall taking notice of the empty carriages, "if you were doing it for the shenanigans like the others. Except you're doing it to save a girl you like, so I'm here personally to aid you. But I got to do it in secret." When Niall decides to inspect the carriages, King Tuathal halts him while saying, "Whoa there, lad", this causes Niall to turn to the king who continues, "that monstrous host will know you are coming if you take a ride in there, even if you were only going to look inside. Just ignore them.

I would also like to note that they pull themselves towards Diavolo Mansion, without any type of mounts I might add, as I know that would be your next question."

"Thanks for the warning, King Tuathal", said Niall who went ahead and traveled through the valley. After a good distance, Niall again shows his gratitude for the king's warning by saying, "Thanks again for saving me from that trap, the last thing I want is to alert that demon of my presence, and for explaining to me what the deal is with those carriages." After King Tuathal returns his gratitude, Niall begins to recall what the king spoke in that he must only aid him in secret, making him feel uncomfortable by the king's response. Because the King of the Leprechauns of Gleannasi is a powerful fairy, and him wanting to hide from someone who had not been around as long as five millennia, is not a good sign. Deciding to just laugh at the reaper, Niall asks sarcastically, "So, you don't like the type of shenanigans that Marquis DeGallo does?"

The king gives a mockingly fake laugh before saying, "The shenanigans that we do are all fun and games, while his shenanigans are sick and sadistic."

"Basically what you are saying", said Niall who is even more worried about what he is getting himself into while continuing his sarcasm, "is that he does tragic shenanigans."

"And don't you forget it", said King Tuathal. "That Marquis DeGallo is pure evil, as he sold his soul to the devil for not only to be granted immortality, and access to wicked powers that would class him as a sorcerer, but to never lose in a game. In return, he will offer his victims' souls to his dark master, after he is through playing with them as his personal toys of course. As is to why that raving lunatic moved from Romalia to the mountains of Durigh, is because of fear of a man that is no longer in the living. But even after his passing, that cruel gambler is too comfortable in his new home and therefor doesn't care about returning. So whatever you do, don't challenge him in a game. No matter what he offers, don't do it.

Something occurs to Niall, who shows little interest in the mystery man King Tuathal speaks of, and asks the king, "Can he really grant wishes like you?"

"That he does", said King Tuathal, "but the only time he grants them is when he gives them away for free, in order to attract more victims. That guy is very good at finding loopholes in his victim's wish."

"Let me guess", said Niall as he switched between serious and sarcastic tones, "the loopholes in the wishes that you give are all fun and games, whereas his loopholes are sick and sadistic. Because they're not comedic loopholes, but tragic loopholes."

"You got a mouth on you", said King Tuathal in an angry tone, only to change it to a pleasing voice, "just like your great-grandpappy."

"Now that I think about it", said Niall who is purposely changing the subject. "You wouldn't know what those giant rock things were, or what they were doing before I got there? Because it looks like they were in a fight."

"Actually, they were Marquis DeGallo's stone golems", said King Tuathal while stroking his beard. "Course the others thought they were mountain trolls."

Memories of Niall's schooling passed through his mind, while giving a perplexed look, after hearing what King Tuathal said before replying, "Wait. I recall my teacher saying that there are no trolls on any of the islands of Eiral because they can't cross the ocean or swim, except for ericius trolls."

"That is true", said King Tuathal. "But those fools from Arvann thought they were mountain trolls for some reason, and refer to them as such. Even though they are created with magic, they are immune to the effects of iron, and yet they cannot be made by any iron. Anyway, the boys from your town would trick the golems into fighting each other and snuck by as they fought. Dang fools never figured out that all they needed to do was to wear masquerade masks, and the golems would just let them pass. Still, I'm impressed that you were able to take them down, though you could have avoided that fight if you followed with the rest of the fools when you had the chance."

"Ironic, I know", said Niall with no regret for staying out of trouble. "How much of the fight did you see?"

"I didn't", replied King Tuathal, "otherwise I would have assisted you during that battle. I only know about it from Mr. Wrinklebottom, he's a gnome, who lives close by to keep tabs for me on who comes and goes through the ravine."

"Interesting to know", said Niall. "Well, it was also good to know that using my iron ring on the golems would have been pointless anyway."

"Pretty much", said King Tuathal, "and I do appreciate you taking it off and hiding it."

"You're welcome, Your Majesty", replied Niall. "Last thing that I want is to accidentally harm you with it."

Feeling pleased with Niall's consideration for his well-being, King Tuathal replies, "I once again appreciate it. Though I'm glad to see that you are smart enough to carry iron on you when traveling." He then glanced at Niall's chest before continuing, "I also assume that you have your clover inside your leather armor?"

"Pretty much", reply Niall who continues on what he was saying earlier, "anyway, what's done is done with those stone golems, both me and my dino are still alive, and . . . . Wait a minute. If Marquis DeGallo makes sacrifices, why does he place golem guards to prevent easy prey from coming to him?"

The epiphany that Niall passes to King Tuathal has him speechless for a second, before deciding to reply, "That's a good question . . . . I have no idea."

The Ram and Ewe's Quest for the Lost Lambs

There was only silence between King Tuathal and Niall as they traversed through the rest of the valley. The mute only ends when Crono reaches the base of the hill, and King Tuathal looks behind him and says, "Huh, just notice that a double lunar eclipse has already started. A very romantic moment for a pair of lovers."

Realizing that Crono is getting exhausted due to the long travel through the valley, and climbing up the hill, Niall decides to halt his raptor, and allow him to rest. Niall then decides to examine the eclipse for a while before saying, "I don't understand why girls get so excited over anything romantic."

"Boys will be boys, and girls will be girls", replies King Tuathal while staring at the eclipse. "A wise one would accept it, while a foolish one complains about it."

"I guess", said Niall who believes the king's words. There was silence once more for a moment between King Tuathal and Niall, with the only sound coming from Crono's breathing, until Niall decided to ask the king, "Now that I think about it, how big can golems get?"

"Oh, they can range from very small to colossal, or just plain huge like the ones back at the ravine", said King Tuathal. "I would also like to point out, in case you are also wondering, that the reason the ones in the ravine are called stone golems, is because of the material they are made from, not the size."

The king's words have Niall pondering for a moment before responding, "So you're saying that a stone golem can be two inches high?"

"Pretty much", replied King Tuathal, "though making something at that size is extremely difficult." After feeling satisfied with the king's answer, and that Crono appears well rested, Niall has his dino continue the climb up the hill at a slow pace.

When they finally reach the top of the hill and enter through the gate, King Tuathal asks Niall to dismount Crono and leads him around the north side of the mansion saying, "There are stationary armor golems at the front doors. Their only purpose is to alert anyone they see to that evil loon, therefore it is best to avoid their gaze." When they reach the spot where Iuile, Eilis, and Einri were spying in the ballroom earlier, they see that one of King Tuathal's servants is waiting for them. King Tuathal jumps off Niall's shoulder to speak to his servant, who appears frightened, and they begin to whisper to each other.

Niall decides to mount onto Crono in order to peer through the window, so that he can easily see over the bushes while on his raptor. From there he sees a group of monsters gathering around in a circle with, whom he assumes with hate, Marquis DeGallo in the center. When the servant finished informing his majesty, King Tuathal turned to Niall and said, "Dang nappa." I was informed that Marquis DeGallo tricked them into playing a card game, that he personally made in order to create a challenge, and lost. I'm sorry Niall, but there is nothing we can do."

While staring at the man he assumes is the host of the manor, Niall asks the king, "Is that guy in the center of the horde, who is wearing a mask and a purple top hat, Marquis DeGallo?" King Tuathal hops on top of the bushes in order to peer through the window and inform him that it is. Feeling guilty upon hearing what happened to Iuile and them due to his own fear, and ignorance of priority, has him wanting to take responsibility, and do something. But when he sees Marquis DeGallo, his guilt vanishes, and is replaced by anger and hate.

Anger and hate that Niall tries to put aside as rescuing the girls, and maybe an idiot, are more important than defeating a foe that he knows he cannot defeat. Niall decides to pull Crono away from the window as he can only think of one way for him to redeem his actions. He then said to himself while putting on his iron ring,

"Well . . . sink or swim, I'm diving in." Niall whips Crono's reins to make him rush towards the window, while ignoring the leprechaun king who tries to stop him, as the raptor jumps over the bushes, and through the window.

CHAPTER 16

Foolish Knight

Marquis DeGallo had many victims visit his mansion for many reasons over the centuries. But those that came for vengeance, or to rescue a loved one, were always his favorites. For they always fall for the same trap of losing to one of his games as he would normally ponder, with glee, of what his trespasser's relationship is with the others. But instead, he gives a frustrated appearance as he stares at his damaged window, before turning to his trespasser with disgust, and mysteriously vanishes.

During this time, Niall pulls out his clover from under his armor, causing any dallions to back away in fear, along with the fairies who sense iron on him. Leaving him to fight off, with Crono, the remaining monsters who are not fazed by the metal or talisman, with the same creatures laughing at the ones that are afraid. All the while, Iuile herself begins to be filled with a spring of hope in her soul and screams out Niall's name. Only for him to glance in her direction with a confused look, before turning away to focus on fighting off the horde of monsters with his short sword and raptor ally. As only the weaker monsters are trying to stop Niall, while the stronger ones stand by, with the scared dallions and fairies

The Ram and Ewe's Quest for the Lost Lambs

whom they still mock, to watch and bet on who will take down the intruder first.

Refusing to give up, Iuile tries once more to call out Niall's name, only to receive the same result. It was only when Eilis and Einri (who was wearing a ragged shirt with holes, pants with a rope for a belt, and face covered with soot) managed to reach her when she asked her friend, "He's here to rescue us, right? Why does he not respond when I call for him?"

"Probably because we're dressed like run-down dolls waiting to be leased", replies Eilis as she, and the others, avoid the monsters running around them since they have no interest in them, due to Niall's arrival. "With Einri looking like someone who fell in, and climbed out of, an outhouse." Einri begins to examine himself while Eilis continues, "For all Niall knows, we're just hired attendants. Of course, we could just sneak out while they're distracted by him."

It then dawned on Einri who said, "I do look like I fell in an outhouse!"

"But they have monsters we have never seen before guarding the broken window that Niall had made", said Iuile while she and Eilis ignored Einri, "with maru elves guarding the doors. It seems like Niall's raptor is the only way to pass through the elves to the foyer with ease."

"Well then", replies Eilis, "we need to say something that no one else would normally know, in order for him to believe who we are."

This panicked Iuile who asks, "But what? We don't know him that well!"

"Come to think of it", said Eilis, "this seems rather ironic that you didn't listen to your mother, and go out with him, otherwise . . . ." She falls silent upon noticing the wrath in Iuile's eyes for even remotely saying that her mother was right on something. "Sorry, I just can't help it due to the irony in this . . . . Wait a moment, you mentioned that you had more than one conversation with him." The idea of Niall being well acquainted with Iuile, has Einri appear worried while Eilis asks her, "What in the world had you two been talking about?"

Such a question has Iuile flustered saying, "Well, I, huh", for she does not feel comfortable telling her friend about her conversations with Niall.

Even though Einri fears losing Iuile to Niall, he fears even more of losing her life and soul. With his only option is to gain Niall's aid, Einri decides to yell out, "Niall!" After getting Niall's attention, Einri continues to cry out, "It's us! On your second eldest brother's birthday! Slate? Or something? Slaine, that's it! Anyway, I lost a bet, forcing me to allow you to spank me with your father's wooden paddle!"

Both Iuile and Eilis stare at Einri, and blush, because they cannot believe what they just heard from him. It was not long before Eilis replied in a seductive, and sarcastic, voice, "Well, you must have been a really naughty boy."

"Can it, Eilis", replies Einri as he begins to blush due to his embarrassing confession.

Upon hearing Einri's words, Niall stares at Einri and the girls while saying to himself, "Good Dominus, almighty. That is them dressed as run-down dolls and a jackass that fell in an outhouse." As soon as Niall finishes talking to himself, something hits him in the face. When he pulls it off, he sees that it is a Columbina ram mask that was thrown, or flew, into his face. Seeing the mask as a pointless trinket, Niall tosses it aside where it falls into a gorigo's mouth, where it choked to death.

After finishing a monster without realizing it, Niall quickly has Crono swoops by and grabs both girls, with Iuile riding in front of him, while Eilis is behind him. Upon retrieving the girls, Niall slightly blushes while saying to Einri, "Sorry Einri, but I got no room for you. You'll need to stay close as Crono clears a path for you!" He then mumbles to himself, "Fairy wasn't kidding when he said that weasel will make you his playthings by dressing you up as dolls."

Feeling insulted for having to run behind an animal to escape, but not wanting to be left behind, Einri frantically chases after them with no difficulty, due to the extra weight on Crono, while saying, "Are you kidding me?! I manage to get your attention, and this is the thanks I get?"

Niall attempts to leave the same way he came in, while ignoring Einri's complaint, when he quickly halts his dino upon finding it to be blocked by powerful monsters. This makes Iuile point towards the doors to the foyer, and inform Niall that it leads to the front entrance. Niall tells Iuile and Eilis to brace themselves before having Crono head toward the ballroom's exit while blushing even redder. With poor Einri slipping and falling down while trying to turn around with them. He quickly stands back up in a mad panic in order to catch up with Niall and the girls, while also evading capture from some orcesses who wish to smooch him.

They manage to escape the horde due to Crono bulldozing through the maru elves, with Einri following close behind. When they enter the foyer, they immediately head towards the front doors that are, for some reason, wide open. Only for Eilis to fly off Crono, with Iuile feeling a mysterious force pulling her back, and pushing Niall off his raptor at the same time. When all three of them fell off Crono, with Einri somehow tripping over something as if it is invisible, the raptor begins to immediately be dragged back into the ballroom where the doors closed by themselves. With the front doors closing also, followed by making a locking sound.

They then hear the sound of clapping caused by Marquis DeGallo, who is sitting on the balcony's handrail of the second floor, next to the stairway, saying, "Well, well, well. If it isn't the Knight and Dimming Armor who has come to save the princess." His attitude then changes to a menacing tone, "Who rudely damaged one of my beautiful windows." His appearance begins to switch between a friendly host, to a threatening one, "But I can put that aside . . . for now . . . . So tell me, who is this fairy you speak of?"

"The fairy ugly enough to spawn a murderous dastard such as you", replied Niall angrily.

Bellowing out a sarcastic laugh, Marquis DeGallo quickly calms down to say with an amused grin, "A funny knight. Never seen one of those, very new. Shining Knights would normally retort", he continues mockingly while moving his arms, "'You won't get away with this', or 'You'll pay for this', et cetera, et cetera." He then places his hand on his chin, with his elbow on his knee, before continuing casually, "I'll take back the dimming then . . . hmmm, you're funny, like a fool, so Foolish Knight will do . . . . Yes, yes . . . and the fact that you call me a murderer, that tells me plenty. So tell you what, you beat me in a game . . . ."

Marquis DeGallo was instantly cut off by Niall with a threatening tone, "How about you lick your coward of a master's rear pants!" For even though he wants to desperately save Iuile and Eilis, and Einri while he is at it, he knows full well that it would be a trap if he accepts Marquis DeGallo's challenge. Not because of King Tuathal's warning, but due to his abuse by his brothers and cousins being boys with their false promises. However, he will not in no way abandon the others after getting this far.

Both Iuile and Eilis blush at Niall's words, which they actually heard uncensored, with Eilis saying, "Wow, I didn't expect you to utter such dirty words . . . ." Iuile becomes confused by Eilis' sudden silence, causing her to turn and find that her friend cannot speak. She then realized that she could not talk as well, along with Einri.

"Oh, such potty words", said Marquis DeGallo with an amused, and a hint of surprised, tone. "No matter, I'll just let you leave here in peace since you don't want to play." Marquis DeGallo continues as the front doors become unlock, "But these three", Iuile, Eilis, and Einri suddenly rise up, and float towards Marquis DeGallo, "are cursed by a spell to stay with me until I get bored with them. You can try to save them, but doing so would mean that the ballroom doors will be unlocked and you will be forced to fight my guests. So, you can either escape, unscratched, through the front doors or head up these stairs and force the ballroom doors to open. If you do decide to fight the horde and survive, then you can try to find me. It'll be like hide and go seek."

Recalling a conversation with King Tuathal, Niall asks Marquis DeGallo with the hope that he would be interested in what he would inquire, "Wait! Can you humor me with at least one question?"

As if amused, Marquis DeGallo replies, "Curious . . . I'll oblige."

Relieved that the marquis would humor him, Niall asks, "Why have golems guard the ravine if you need to make sacrifices?"

Niall's question has Iuile, Eilis, and Einri intrigued, too, (while at the same time confused on the word golem) as they turn to Marquis DeGallo who replies, "Interesting that you would know about the sacrifice, when none of us had ever said such a thing in your presence." He begins mumbling to himself to where no one can hear, "I wonder if he learned it from this 'fairy' he spoke of? Oh well, I'll figure it out sooner or later." After the marquis finishes pondering, he decides to answer Niall with, "As for the question you ask, you could say that I did it as part of making an alluring trap, by creating a forbidden fruit, and spreading word about how delicious that fruit is . . . . Or you can say that I'm just plain mad. Either way, I always manage to gain what I need without leaving my home." Within a split second, Marquis DeGallo disappears with a maniacal laugh echoing through the building with Iuile, Eilis, and Einri.

After Marquis DeGallo disappears with his captives, Niall whispers for King Tuathal, only to hear, "Be quieter than that", said the king who is hiding in Niall's left side pouch. "I hid in here sometime after you decided to idiotically break in, as I don't want that cur of a host to know that I am involved, otherwise he'll attack my kingdom! I just cast a spell that allows us to communicate with each other so that no one else, including Marquis DeGallo, to be able to hear me speak to you. Now let's get out of here before you get yourself slaughtered."

"I'm sorry, King Tuathal", whispers Niall with sincerity in his voice while trying to hold back his aggression, "but I cannot abandon them. With or without your help, I'm going on ahead. For as Paladin Beowulf said, 'The only two allies for which I can always depend upon, is Dominus Deus, and Dominus Yeshua.'"

Those words only annoy King Tuathal who replies with frustration, "Aaargh, cursed the promise that I made on his death bed, cursed your mother's stubborn nature that you inherited, and cursed your father's determination to get the job done, regardless of the obstacles that befall him!" He magically makes a key appear in front of him, and lifts it out of the pouch while saying, "Use this key on the ballroom doors. It'll create a magical lock that will prevent the doors from opening, allowing you to go up the stairs without the need for unnecessary conflict." When Niall receives the key, he immediately goes and locks the ballroom doors.

"The only one that can break this spell", said King Tuathal while Niall was locking the doors, "besides me of course, is the host of this manor. There is also no need to worry about them going through the windows, as they won't dare smash them to get out unless they want to incur Marquis DeGallo's wrath for damaging his property. As for the damaged window you made, I had my servant quickly repair it after I entered through, while everyone was distracted by you. Now be careful when talking to me, keep that blasted ring on you, as I don't want you to accidentally put it in here with me, and don't let what happened to Caolan cloud you of why you are really here!"

"I know", whispered Niall while trying to calm down. "It's just very difficult to push what he did aside." After Niall takes a few deep breaths to tranquil himself, he realizes a puzzlement that he cannot shake as the oddity causes him to ask, "Now that I think about it, how are you able to fit into my pouch?"

"I cast an incantation that invokes hammerspace into your bag", replied King Tuathal. This only confuses Niall even further as he attempts to ask, but is interrupted by the king, "Your bag now has unlimited space! Now focus!"

"Sorry, Your Majesty", whispered Niall who was now concerned about his mount, "but now that I think about it, what about Crono?"

"He'll be fine", said King Tuathal. "Marquis DeGallo likes keeping his victims' property for himself. They'll just tie him down and cage him up in the stables around back once they get out of there. Now hurry, for Dominus Deus only knows what twisted game he has plans for them. You focus on finding them, while I think of a way of freeing them."

Mix with curiosity and hope, Niall asks in a whisper, "Can you break the curse that Marquis DeGallo placed upon them?"

"Maybe", said King Tuathal. "The problem is that his curses are powered by one of the twelve princes of darkness, the Prince of Dolus. So it won't be easy. But you don't need to worry about that, so go on, lad! Focus on finding them first!" Niall obeys as he decides to check the first floor's south wing. "What are you doing? They're in the upper floors, why else would he forbid you from going up the stairs."

"Makes sense", whispers Niall who heads towards the stairway. Before taking the first step, he stops, and whispers to the ruler in his pouch, "King Tuathal."

"What is it?" Reply King Tuathal

"Thank you for continuing to aid me", whispers Niall.

This has King Tuathal give off a heavy sigh before replying, "You're welcome, lad." Followed by mumbling to himself, "What have I gotten myself into?"

CHAPTER 17

Devil Dog Poker

It is during this time that Niall begins to ponder why he is really doing this. Love? Guilt? Revenge? Sense of duty? Even if he does save them, will she even go out with him? Wondering about his reasons as he explores the mansion, causes him to realize that this is extremely mad, as he can be slaughtered at any moment.

Yet here he is, risking his life for a bunch of fools who do not have enough sense to stay away from things that can kill them. The only conclusion that Niall has come to is that he is here anyway, therefore there is no reason to cry like a pansy. It also helps that he feels calmness in his own soul, not his body of course as it is extremely tense and scared senseless, even though he does not show it. Knowing that his soul is calm, means that everything is going to be all right, for him at least, regardless of what happens.

For Niall's faith is strong in Dominus Deus, and having the free will to leave at any time, is enough to give him some peace of mind as he checks each and every door. One after another on the second floor's south wing. With each valley he opens, is a possible evil that he hopes to not fear. When he opens the fifth door, and peers inside, he sees a group of devil dogs playing poker, with a fireplace to the right of him.

One of them has a body and fur like a giant schnauzer, with a vampire bat-shaped head whose body is swarming with some sort of green gas while, not related, smoking a cigar known as a barghest. Another is a cu sith that is the size and shape like a bull with dark green shaggy fur (like a bergamasco sheepdog), but has a head of a mastiff. The next is an ash color elkhound that is the size of a grizzly bear, with four eyes that glow bloody red, known as the garmr. The two-headed dog, orthrus, resembles a rottweiler, with a mixture of black and tan short fur. With the last one being a miniature cerberus that appears like a pit bull with trimmed ears and has a gray short fur. They simply glance at Niall before returning to their game, as if he does not exist.

Niall decides to slowly close the door, and walks off saying to himself, "Just keep walking, just keep walking . . . ." As to why Niall is walking away and not using his clover, is because even though they are called devil dogs, they are not actually demons. They are just normal monsters that had been given that name due to them being canines with monstrous appearances, and Niall knows this, which is why he does not bother raising his talisman.

Before Niall has a chance to open the next door, the following door suddenly opens, and a beautiful woman sticks her head out to look around and sees him. Niall freezes in place due to her magnificent face, light red hair, and yellow eyes with slit pupils as the woman beguilingly said to him, "Well, aren't you a handsome little man. Why don't you come on in and keep me company."

"Don't be a fool, lad", King Tuathal said with concern.

This causes Niall to break out of his trance, and realize something is wrong as he decides to ask her, "Why is only your head sticking out?"

"Oh, it's because I want to surprise you, darling", replied the woman with a seductive tone.

"Yeah", said Niall as he pulled out his bow, and drew his arrow, "you're obviously a hideous trap." The woman takes offense to

Niall's words and bursts the rest of her body out to reveal that she is the half-woman, half-serpent, lamia. However, this creature is known as Romalian lamia, due to this species being native to the country of Romalia. She is wearing only a toga on her upper human body from the waist, with her lower half being that of a snake whose scales are a pink, orange, and yellow crossband pattern with a purple underbelly.

When the Romalian lamia fully reveals herself, Niall fires his arrow at her chest, only for her to catch it with her bare hand, and toss it aside. "Oh snap", was Niall's only response as he was weighing his options on how to retaliate. Only for Niall to realize that he will not be able to draw another arrow, and aim, in time. Because the lamia is coiling herself up for an instant kill, and from Niall's past experiences with snakes, means that she will strike first. Even the thought of using any of his blades to slash her, will not be of any good, as he knows that her thrust will be powerful enough to pin him to the ground, which will allow her to finish him off with ease.

While Niall is debating in his head on how to triumph over his foe, the Romalian lamia springs her deadly strike. This causes Niall to panic and react, without thinking, by opening the door right next to him and bracing himself. Seeing Niall using the door as a shield has caught the lamia off guard, with no means of changing directions in the air, and leaving her no choice but to slam her face into the door. After the successful block, Niall immediately turns and runs away into a random door behind him as the lamia recovers herself, slams the door shut, and licks the blood dripping from her forehead.

Upon entering and locking the door, Niall realizes that he just entered the room with the devil dogs, who only glanced at him once more, before returning to their game with garmr saying, "That boy's back again."

"Waweeweewee, Waweewawa", said cerberus's left head which sounded like he was wheezing at a high pitch.

"I agree, Curly", said cerberus's right head who sounds like a professor from a university, "I think we should tear him limb from limb. Why don't we hold the game off and have some fun with him, Moe?"

Cerberus's middle head, known as Moe, replies with an irate voice, "Are you mad, Larry?! The moment we put our hand down and turn our back is the moment that one of these curs will cheat by looking at our hand!"

"How dare you accuse us of cheating", said cu sith who resents such an accusation.

"Waweewawee Wawoowee Wee", said Curly sarcastically.

"You know that's really offensive, Curly", said Orthrus's Right Head.

Moe chuckled saying, "Why, when it's true, Abbott."

Barghest asks with curiosity, "What rude remark did Curly say this time, Moe?"

"None of your business", said Moe offensively.

"Weeweewoo", said Curly naturally.

"Oh shut up", said Moe who sounded annoyed.

"Good Hato, Curly", said Larry with concern. "Think of poor mother."

"Weewawawee", said Curly with no remorse.

"Now that's just nasty", said Orthrus's Left Head with a thick accent that is foreign to the other devil dogs.

"Enough!!!" Yell Moe, "We finish this game up, then we kill the boy!"

This causes Abbott to be concerned as he questions, "What about counting the chips? If we leave them as is, Chaplin will steal them."

The cu sith, who is named Chaplin, replies with an offensive tone, "Steal my tail, you can go . . . ."

"Weewawoo", said Curly cutting Chaplin off.

"Knock it off, Curly!" Said Moe who was getting angrily annoyed. "Know what, forget the boy. Let's just play this game."

They all agree and continue with their game in silence, only for garmr to ask Abbott, "With all seriousness, where did Costello pick up that weird accent?"

Such a query causes Abbott to sigh before replying, "I ask myself that every day, Mel."

During the devil dogs' conversation, Niall stood dumbstruck in front of the door from what he just witness. They acted like a bunch of guys who get together at a bar after getting done with a hard day's work, and play poker, except none of them are speaking in any of the islands' native accents. Niall then realizes that the Romalian lamia has been banging on the door to get in, only to succeed and slam the door against the wall, with Niall between the door and the wall. The Romalian lamia slithers into the room and asks the barghest, "Where's the boy, Groucho?"

Glancing around the room, while tapping some of the ashes off his cigar, Groucho faces the lamia before replying in a sarcastic tone, "Good question, Maria, maybe he vamoose from your smelly perfume."

This infuriates Maria who yells at them, "WHERE DID HE GO!!!"

"HEY NOW!", said Moe with anger and intimidation. "Don't you take that tone with us! Don't forget that we outnumber you five to one, and we don't mind having you for dinner either."

"Breakfast", said Larry who decided to correct the lead head. "It's past midnight, so I believe it's more appropriate to say that it's breakfast."

Larry being technical is only infuriating Moe, who replies to Larry with saliva flying out, "WHATEVER!!!" He then calms down, slightly, before turning his attention to Maria, and continues his conversation with her with a mixture of politeness and anger,

"As I was saying", he then slowly turns to Larry with pure anger, "before being rudely interrupted . . . ."

While whimpering, Larry says quietly, "I was only trying to help."

"Weewaawee Wowoowee", said Curly who, along with Larry, caused Moe to give off a menacing growl. The threatening sound has caused the left and right heads to lower their ears and heads, in order to show their submissiveness.

After Moe placed his alpha position on his neighboring heads, he turned back to Maria and said while controlling his anger, "He was in here a moment ago, and now we don't know, or care, where he is. Now leave us alone to finish our game so that we, me, Larry, and Curly that is, can meet up with", he hesitates for a second before continuing in a low voice, "a mad wizard."

Immediately curious about Moe's choice of words, Abbot asks him, "You're still bound to that heroic nutbag?"

This angers Maria even further with her only response being to hiss at them, causing none of the devil dogs to flinch, and examines the room while Moe answers Abbot's question. During Maria's interrogation with the devil dogs, Niall tries to recover from the damage he received from being slammed between the door and wall. While recouping, Niall tries to think of a way to either defeat, or at least get away from, Maria. He thought about King Tuathal helping him, but chances are that if his majesty wanted to help, he would have already done so. Not to mention that Niall does not wish to reveal the king's presence, and loses his help over dealing with a monster weaker than Marquis DeGallo, or even the devil dogs who have no interest in him.

After pondering for a moment, Niall has come up with a risky strategy. He begins by putting his left hand in his left satchel, in order to hand gesture to King Tuathal that he can take care of the matter at hand. From there he did the sign of the clover, while asking Dominus Deus for strength, before stepping out in the open while drawing his sword. When Maria notices Niall stepping out from behind the door, she begins to coil herself with satisfaction. The distance between Niall and Maria is further than before as he holds his sword in an ochs stance. When the lamia springs towards Niall with her mouth wide open, and baring her fangs, he hastefully shifts his position so that he stabs his blade into her mouth.

Like a player that rolls a twenty, Niall's plan was a critical success with his back slamming against the wall, due to the force of Maria's attack. It also causes his sword's pommel to slam against the wall for a moment until Niall manages to push Maria back with his arms outstretched. The lamia lands the snake part of her body on the floor after the pommel hits the wall, only to start struggling in fury and pain after being pushed back. Maria tries to claw with her nails at Niall, who resists, before finally dying off and leaving Niall with minor injuries to his arms, thanks to his leather armor.

While holding the hilt of his sword that still has its blade inside Maria, Niall swings the weapon so that the corpse is lying at an angle. He then puts his foot on her shoulder and pulls his sword out of her. It then occurs to him that the devil dogs might want revenge for killing Maria, and quickly looks in their direction with his heart racing. Only to see that they are still sitting in the same chairs, and watching him with interest.

"The boy has brains and guts", said Mel.

"Wawee Wawoo", said Curly.

"Shut up, Curly!" Said Moe, "Didn't I just say we forget about killing him? We're not even supposed to be here, to begin with, so shut it!"

"Good enough for me", said Chaplin, "I owe her money anyway."

Puzzle from what Chaplin said has Abbott asking him, "For what?"

Chaplin only gives a sinister smile, causing Costello to say, "That's nasty dog."

"What can I say", said Chaplin, "I like having my back scratch while licking peanut butter off the floor."

"Yeah, sure", replied Mel who did not believe him.

With no desire to hear the rest of their conversation, Niall quickly leaves the room and notices a table nearby while King Tuathal says, "Well done, my boy! I was afraid that I may have to risk revealing myself to help you."

"I wouldn't want you to unnecessarily aid me unless I absolutely need it", said Niall quietly while using the nearby tablecloth to clean the blood from his sword, and continued with sarcasm, "otherwise, you'll leave me all alone in a scary place, and miss out on all this horrifying, and joyous, fun." Niall manages to finish cleaning his sword upon ending his sentence and walks off while sheathing the blade.

"You are as wise, and smart aleck, as your great-grandfather", said King Tuathal with amusement.

Niall takes appreciation of the king's compliment before saying, "Still doesn't change the fact that this is going to be one, long, night." When Niall reaches the door that he was originally going to inspect, before Maria intervenes, he opens it and sees a middle-aged witch in black clothing, and red hair, belly rubbing a wereboar which is making him shake his leg. The wereboar only halts his leg when the witch stops rubbing his belly upon noticing Niall. "A, very, long night."

CHAPTER 18

Creeping Pit

There are horrors in this universe that one cannot possibly fathom. With sentient beings performing cruelty to others due to desire, ignorance, or against their will. One of these is where Marquis DeGallo falls in, for it is the reason why he committed atrocious actions against his so-called, rag dolls. Acts of wickedness that I cannot tell to my young audience, except for what is to come to poor Iuile as she lies unconscious in a stone room. As what is going to befall her, will be minor compared to what he did to others in the past.

When Iuile awakens, she finds that the room she is in is dark, with little light. She begins to quickly look around and sees that Marquis DeGallo is close by where he is sitting in a chair next to a small table, with a teakettle, while sipping out of a teacup. The emotions that Iuile is feeling right now, have gotten worse, as if a thousand fish hooks snag her heart, and pulling it in different directions. With great difficulty, Iuile tries to contain herself before sitting up, looks around, and notices that the only light she sees is coming from a distance, with what sounds to her, a scurrying of noises filling the room. Iuile begins to feel frightened of where Eilis and Einri are while getting up, as she also dreads to ask about her father's condition. When the marquis notices that she is rising up, he quickly puts his teacup down and stands up.

"Where are Eilis and Einri?" Iuile asks, followed by putting her hand on her throat, as she begins to recall what happened earlier, and says to herself, "I can talk again!"

"I placed a spell on you and your friends for a short time, as I didn't want any interruptions from lowly peasants while us gentlemen speak, my Angelic Princess", said Marquis DeGallo while starting to walk around her. "Dunderhead is somewhere safe, for now, as I haven't played with pretty little flowers in a long time. For I'm so curious about your own desperation for your own life, or the life of another." He stops on Iuile's left side as he continues, "You know that light in the distance?"

Glancing at the light again with curiosity, along with the dread of what Marquis DeGallo is planning, causes Iuile to fearfully ask, "What about it?"

"It is the same flames from the fireplace you saw when we played Joker", said Marquis DeGallo who suddenly moved behind Iuile's right side with his hands on her shoulders. He continues to say to Iuile while slowly shifting to her left, "You see, I make my offering to one of the Princes of Darkness with it, for it is the very flames of Hell! Flames that lie in a large firepot, and above it tied to rope and chain", he gives a sinister grin as he whispers in her left ear, "is your friend, Sunflower."

This gives Iuile a blank stare, as her heart now feels like it has fallen to her feet where it shatters into millions of pieces, before imploding itself due to what she heard. Tears begin to fill her eyes, which she tries to hold back, as she turns to Marquis DeGallo, causing him to take a few steps back, and ask, "Why? Why are you doing this?"

"For entertainment, my Angelic Princess", said Marquis DeGallo with a sneer. He then continues with a friendly tone, "Now where was I, ah yes, if she falls into the pot, not only will she die, but her soul will be dragged . . . well, you get the picture. All you have to do, is walk across and push the fire pot out of the way. And don't you worry about your physical condition. You'll be strong enough to push it", his tone then changes to a mockery of innocence before saying, "I tell no lie."

Knowing that there is more to this than what Marquis DeGallo is letting on, is causing Iuile to breathe heavily. For this is no different to her than when she was a little girl, and her brother, Peadar, told her that she could have his brownie on the table. When she goes to get it with joy, she screams with terror from a snake, which turns out to be a fake, that was placed on top of it. "Turn on the lights", she asked after managing to calm down, "so that I can see what I am walking across."

"Ohhh, this is why I love you", said Marquis DeGallo with glee, while making Iuile's heart leap with joy, "for you are such a clever girl." He snaps his fingers, causing the torches on the walls to flare up. To Iuile's horror, she sees thousands, and thousands, of cockroaches that are in a pit that is wall to wall, and three feet deep. Every one of them crawls over each other, yet for some reason, they do not leave the pit. "I'm just curious if you are willing to walk through these bugs to save your friend. Of course, you don't have to as you can just abandon her, and let her die."

"Never", Iuile said immediately as she turned to Marquis DeGallo when he finished speaking. She then turns back with her whole body shaking as she is completely terrified, which does not help with the other emotions she is also undergoing. But she could not let her best friend die because of her. So Iuile forces herself, with difficulty, to slowly walk towards the pit, and look down at the filthy pests. While breathing even more heavily, she gets on her knees and takes her time lowering her foot into the pit.

When Iuile's foot touches the first cockroach, several of the bugs crawl up her leg, and under her skirt. This makes her panic, and immediately pulls herself out where she rolls away from the pit. When Iuile finally halts, she quickly begins to slap her body in order to kill the roaches. Only for the cockroaches to crawl off her, and return to their domain. After the last roach left Iuile's body, she assumes the fetal position and cries to herself.

Only to be slightly amused by Iuile's failed attempt, Marquis DeGallo decides to pull out his pocket watch and glance at it. He then pulls out a handkerchief, and wipes the watch with it as he asks her causally, "Giving up already?" Iuile stops crying and quickly looks up towards the marquis, "I guess I'll just let Sunflower burn . . . ."

The thought of Eilis dying due to her own cowardliness strikes a nerve in Iuile. But not as much as realizing that her father is still in danger of being murdered by the cait sith if she does not escape to save him. Such a horrifying dilemma causes her to scream out, "NOOOO!" Iuile then forces herself up to run towards the pit and jumps several feet out before falling into it.

The cockroaches swarm all over Iuile when she dives in, causing her to frantically panic, and move as fast as she can across the pool of roaches. The insects crawl all over her legs, to her arms, and around her head, even getting into her hair. Though she tries to move as fast as she can, she finds it difficult because of her shedding tears due to the sheer horror of what is happening, and what she is doing. The only thing that is keeping her sanity together, is that she is asking Dominus Deus for strength for this cruel ordeal that she brought upon herself, and her friend. All while walking, closer, and closer to the other side of the pit, trying her best in keeping herself together. Eventually, she reaches the other side of the pit where she hastefully climbs out of it, rolls a few feet away, and once more goes into the fetal position as the roaches decide to crawl off her and return to their domain.

Knowing that it is still not over, Iuile gathers her courage once more, and forces herself up. When she is on her feet, she finds that Eilis is tied and gagged above the firepot that is five feet in

The Ram and Ewe's Quest for the Lost Lambs

diameter, with its green and black flames giving off a maleficent glow, instead of a red and yellow warm light. Eilis herself is tied to a rope that is hooked on a chain, that is on a pulley above her, with the other end of the link wrapped around an eye bolt, and secured on a hook, which is bolted on a wall nearby. Iuile also sees a wooden handle on the firepot which she grabs hold of, and pushes. Only to find that it moves slightly before halting in place. Baffle by the lack of movement, even though it does not feel heavy, Iuile examines the pot to find that there is a lock on tie rings that is on the jar, and to the floor.

"Oh dear, I'm so sorry", said Marquis DeGallo in a poor attempt to apologize. Iuile turns to find that the marquis is a few feet behind her as he continues, "I forgot to tell you about the key that was on the table near the tea kettle."

Dread has befallen Iuile due to the idea that she has to cross the pool of roaches not twice, but thrice to save her dear friend. Before Marquis DeGallo has the chance to say another word, Iuile immediately jumps, without hesitation, back into the pit. As Iuile travels back to where she started, she begins to recall Marquis DeGallo words, *"Ohhh, this is why I love you."*

This only causes Iuile to hold her tears back while asking herself, "Why then . . . just why?" After reaching the original starting point, while trying not to wail due to immense fear, Iuile dashes towards the small table with determination. Upon seeing the key, Iuile grabs it and jumps back into the pit while continuing to question why the marquis is doing this to her and her friend. When Iuile reaches back to where Eilis is kept hanging, she madly crawls on her hands and knees to the firepot and uses the key to free it from its hold. Only to find that it does not work.

Feeling incredibly frustrated, Iuile said with her eyes closed and full of tears, "You lied!"

"Like I was saying before you rudely, and hastefully, made a mad dash", said Marquis DeGallo. "I brought the key with me so that I can give it to you." Marquis DeGallo then presents the key in question to Iuile, who is stupefied by not only that she pointlessly went back for the wrong key, but that she never needed to cross the pit two more times in the first place. The marquis continues with fabricated pity, "I'm sorry to tell you that the key you went back to acquire, is not the key to this lock." When Marquis DeGallo finishes speaking, Iuile manages to break out of her stupor and tosses the key in her hand away before taking the key from the marquis, and using it to free the pot from its lock.

After freeing the pot, Iuile quickly grabs hold of the handle and pushes the pot out of the way. Once the pot is at a safe distance from Eilis, Iuile heads towards the other end of the chain that is snared by a hook. Only to find another lock, that she was sure was not there before, on the chain and eye bolt, with the hook vacant. Iuile tries to recall if the lock had always been there, but is not sure as she panicky turns to Marquis DeGallo. The marquis has his hand near his mouth and replies like he is in trouble, "The key you tossed aside was to that lock", this has Iuile become stupefy once more as the marquis continues with the look of someone who is the bearer of bad news, "and it flew right into the pit."

Despair is the only thing that Iuile is feeling, as there seems to be no end to the madness that has unfolded upon her. This is followed by her emotions finally overwhelming her as she begins to burst out crying while falling on her knees, and saying, "I'm sorry, Eilis! I'm so sorry! I'm just too confused with all this chaos!" Tears begin to fill Eilis' eyes also, not because of her own safety, but by the cruelty that has befallen her friend in order to save her, with Iuile saying to herself, "Please save your foolish servants, Dominus Deus."

During Iuile's torment of despair and madness, Marquis DeGallo stands behind her while twiddling his fingers with delight, and saying to himself, "How amusing, asking Him for help when he never does a thing, but let you suffer." Marquis DeGallo continues

The Ram and Ewe's Quest for the Lost Lambs

his pleasantry that does not last long before the door close to them bursts open, revealing to be Niall with malice in his eyes. This surprises Marquis DeGallo who questions him, "How did you get up here so fast with all the traps that I set up for you?!"

The sight of Niall restores not only Iuile's hope but her sanity as well as her emotions transforming into one single emotion of joy. Iuile begins to smile and yells out Niall's name, who himself uses this opportunity of Marquis DeGallo's puzzlement by shooting an arrow at him, causing the marquis to walk backward due to the force of the arrow, and fall into the pit of roaches. Niall hesitates if he should make sure that the fiendish host is finished. But knows what is truly important, and runs towards Iuile in order to grab her arm. Only for Iuile to pull her arm away, and say while pointing at her friend, "We can't leave until we save Eilis!"

When Niall sees Eilis' situation, he says, "What in the world is going . . . . You know what. I don't want to know right now." He then follows the chain to the wall, approaches it with Iuile, examines it, and calmly says, "Holy Mackerel. It's a normal, simple, lock. I can easily pick this with the right tools."

As Niall opens his satchel where King Tuathal resides in, who magically summons a lockpick kit, Iuile asks him with puzzlement, "Wait, how do you know how to pick a lock?"

"I have a cousin-in-law that was raised in Dunban", replied Niall while picking the lock. "Though I would normally use this skill with the owner's permission to open their doors or chests."

Upon successfully opening the lock, Iuile notices that Marquis DeGallo is slowly climbing out of the pit unharmed, and completely irate. Iuile then says to Niall with a mix of calmness and panic, "He's coming out of the pit!"

After glancing to see that Marquis DeGallo is almost out of the pit, Niall says to Iuile while handing her the chain, "I'll deal with him while you bring Eilis down." Iuile agrees and takes the chain where she lowers Eilis down while Niall takes another shot, with a grin, at the marquis' head who twirls around with annoyance, before falling back into the pit. When Eilis' feet touch the ground, Niall approaches her and pulls out his dagger to cut the ropes. After freeing Eilis, the three of them quickly head out the door with the hope of escaping this horrible mansion.

CHAPTER 19

Einri's Dagger

As the three of them run down the north wing, with Niall leading, Eilis asks him, "What took you so long?"

"Don't start with me, Eilis", Niall replied angrily. "Before finding you two on the fourth floor, I had to deal with five devil dogs playing poker, eight if you count the heads, a man-hungry lamia, a witch with a slave wereboar, an insecure centaur, a psychotic harpy, a pair of panzer orcs, things that will give me nightmares for the rest of my life, things that will make a pavus blush, among other nonsense. Then there were the ones I dealt with before getting into this cursed mansion. It also doesn't help that I hadn't eaten a full meal since lunch!"

"Sorry about this, Niall", Iuile replies apologetically. For she feels horrible for what Niall had gone through, because of her, while at the same time wiping away tears of joy from being rescued. She also wonders if she heard Niall right when he said, 'fourth floor', but assumes that he meant to say third floor while her emotions are telling her, *"I can't leave yet! He confessed that he loves me! I can't just abandon someone who truly loves me."* This only makes Iuile confused in what to do, regardless of what Marquis DeGallo had done to her and Eilis, as she cannot think logically due to her emotions overwhelming her on what is the right thing to do. For Iuile could not help but feel that Marquis DeGallo's actions were not of his free will.

"Now that I think about it", said Eilis, "where's Einri?"

"That's a good question", replied Niall with a hint of sarcasm, "because I recall that he was with you last."

"Well he's not with us now, is he", Eilis replies back with annoyance from Niall's sarcasm.

"Marquis DeGallo said that he kept him somewhere safe", replied Iuile while trying to push her emotions aside, "as he doesn't want to 'play' with him yet. We need to find him before escaping, and save my father who is now in danger!"

"Ah snackerpuss", said Niall who knows full well that things are going to get worse. "I don't know why your father's life is in danger, but I can at least lead you two out of here so that you can get help while I head back in to get Einri. Since what's really important is making sure you two escape this madness."

"Oh", said Eilis sounding upset as they reached the stairs in the south wing, "so it's important to save us, defenseless girls!"

Utterly peevish in the subject has Niall reply, "You're really not going to make that argument at THIS very moment, are you? Because now is not the time for the, 'I need no man to save me', attitude."

"He's got a point, Eilis", said Iuile who is now fully calm down, and continues with the knowledge that she might upset her friend further, "I really don't think you should look a gift horse in the mouth, or would you rather have Marquis DeGallo force us into another 'game'."

As they reach the second floor of the south wing, Eilis thinks about what Iuile said for a split second before replying sarcastically, "Oh how I am truly living the dream of being the damsel in distress."

They come to a complete stop when a door on their left opens revealing to be Einri saying, "In here where it's safe!" Without any hesitation, Iuile, Niall, and Eilis follow Einri inside, where he locks the door with a key.

"What?" Niall asks suddenly, causing Iuile and Elise to turn to him where they see him looking at his pouch as he continues, "I can't hear you, a what? A thrap?"

Becoming concerned with Niall's sanity has Iuile asking him, "Who are you talking to?"

Realizing the situation of what he just did, and that no one knows about the King of Gleannasi, has Niall turning to them with an embarrassed look and replies, "Uhhh . . . no one."

Annoyed by Niall acting unusual, along with caring less of why that is, has Eilis shaking her head before saying, "Oh, whatever, it's not really important right now." She then turns to Einri and asks him, "What's really important, is what happened to you when we got separated?"

"Well", replies Einri, "I was teleported to a dark, and empty, room where I decided to feel around for a while, before finding the door to the hallway. I then searched all over the mansion when I found Niall, who apparently didn't notice me, opened the door where you two ladies were in. Rather than inform him of my presence, I decided to find a hiding place for our escape, so as to elude Marquis DeGallo into thinking that we will just head out the front doors." He starts to look around while saying, "We should be safe in here for a while."

"I don't think that is a good idea", said Niall, "because in case you had forgotten, he has a legion of monsters inside the ballroom who, if released out of that room, will search for us inside and out. Even though I was lucky in the ballroom that all of them didn't attack me at once, doesn't mean that we will be lucky this time. Nor will it matter if the four of us are fully armed, as it won't be enough to fight against an entire horde. It also seems rather random that you chose this room to hide us in now that I think about it."

"Not to mention", said Iuile after she and the others got a good look at Einri's attire, "when did you have time to change into your original clothes?"

This is followed by Eilis asking him, "And where did you get that key?"

Einri gives a suspicious chuckle before replying, "What key?"

"The key you hid in your pocket that you used to lock them in here until I arrived", said Marquis DeGallo, whose words caused Iuile, Niall, and Eilis to turn in shock from seeing him in a corner that they knew was vacant. With Iuile having flashbacks of the marquis' confession upon seeing him, causing her emotions to stir up once more, and become flutter while blushing.

During that same time, Niall realizes what is going on, and breaks from the silence of shock where he mumbles, "Oh . . . you said trap." He then immediately turns his attention to say to Einri with malice, "You sold us out you . . . ." The next thing Niall knew, he was flung against the wall by an invisible force as Marquis DeGallo gave a maniacal laugh.

When Marquis DeGallo finished laughing, he said, "I made a contingency plan in case you showed up. Before I had my Angelic Princess wake up, so that I could see whether or not she would trek through the pool of roaches, I paid Dunderhead a visit, and made a deal with him in which I would allow him to be free, if he delayed your escape."

While slowly getting up, and in pain from the invisible blow, Niall mumbles to himself, "Pool of roaches . . . really . . . ? Why are girls always afraid of those bugs?"

"You mind not calling me that", said Einri while appearing nervous.

"Not a chance, Dunderhead", said Marquis DeGallo. "Now to hold up my end of the bargain." Marquis DeGallo waves his hand to make the Sacrificial Mark disappear from Einri, who inspects his neck with his hand to feel that it is gone. This puzzles Niall into wondering what Einri is doing, after fully getting back up, while Marquis DeGallo continues with a sinister grin, "Now I will set you free . . . at Ogre Street in Amelon."

In complete dread upon hearing his true reward, Einri replies, "But that is in the most dangerous place on Elosa! If any of those scoundrels see me and recognize me as a noble, they'll beat me to a pulp after robbing me of everything, including my clothes! And that's if I'm lucky!"

"That sounds like a personal problem for not specifying your freebie of a wish", said Marquis DeGallo. The dire host decides to follow up with optimistic sarcasm, "Of course, you could consider this as a bright side of not being a gift to my master."

It finally dawned on Einri that he truly made a horrible mistake. For he hoped that he could double-cross Marquis DeGallo in order to save everyone and win Iuile's heart. But instead, he dooms his companions and is getting his just punishment for making a deal with the devil as he begins to remember his mother. The memory of his mother has him recall something, and quickly pulls out his silver-bladed dagger, with a blue hilt, and yells, "Niall! This wasn't what I planned!" He then tosses his dagger in Niall's direction while saying, "Take this to . . . ."

Only to be cut short by Marquis DeGallo who gleefully snaps his fingers, causing Einri to vanish from thin air during mid-throw, and making Iuile and Eilis gasp from his disappearance. The dagger did not get far due to the throw not being complete, causing the blade to fall between Marquis DeGallo and Niall. The marquis softly laughs as he mumbles to himself, "Can't really sacrifice him anyway, since he didn't place a proper bet by telling me his wish. Though I am curious if he'll survive and return here to save the girls, or whether or not he'll bring others along to aid him. Ohhh, the possibility of playing with him again or not."

While Marquis DeGallo amuses himself with his back turn, Niall draws his sword with a vengeance while ignoring Einri's parting gift. "Don't you do it, Niall", whispered King Tuathal. "Attacking him head-on is pointless! Even if you do land a hit, he'll only heal himself like he did when you shot him with your arrows!"

"I don't care", said Niall who is enrage of the situation. Between Marquis DeGallo's lack of empathy, to Einri's betrayal, Niall has about enough as he says quietly, "Any wound you healed from, to any fatal injury you survived", he then dashes to strike Marquis DeGallo who left himself wide open, "will not halt me from accomplishing my goal!!!" But Marquis DeGallo turns to smirk at Niall's bravery, and sways his hand, causing a hole to appear on the floor within Niall's pathway, where he falls in it. Along with Einri's dagger which Niall noticed due to him accidentally kicking it into the hole with him.

Iuile and Eilis are momentarily shocked after witnessing Einri's fate, only for Iuile to break out of it upon noticing Niall's plight, and rush towards the hole with the hope of saving him. When Iuile takes the initiative, Eilis snaps out of her own stupor and decides to aid Iuile in saving Niall. Only for Iuile to grab him first, and be pulled down with him as she did not count on him weighing more than she could handle. Eilis on the other hand, slows down too late at the edge of the hole where she tries to maintain balance, saying, "Oh crud, oh crud, oh crud!" She manages to fall backward on her rear, rolls back, and bangs her head on the floor yelling, "Son-of-a-monkey's uncle!"

As the hole slowly closes, while Iuile and Niall are falling, Iuile is able to hear Marquis DeGallo say, "Not my love!!!"

CHAPTER 20

Donal & Mairead

During the madness that transpires in Diavolo Mansion, Marquis DeGallo's servant, the cait sith known as Gatto, is out to murder Iuile's father. It is long past midnight when the night has gotten colder due to a strong northern breeze, and the double lunar eclipse is still in motion. In the room where Iuile's father rests in the clinic, is Iuile's mother sitting in a chair, next to her husband, while knitting something that she has no idea what it is that she is making. Her mind is all over the place while an old woman, in green robes, tends to him.

"Stubborn child is way more foolish than her sister, Roisin", murmurs Iuile's mother to herself. "If she had paid more attention and controlled those emotions of hers like I'd been telling her, she would have known how devastated I am about his condition. Keeping busy is the only way to prevent me from getting upset, and if I get upset, then the rest will panic due to a domino effect. Took every strength that I had in so that I would not break into tears after I slapped Iuile when she thought that I was not heartbroken, when in reality I was. Probably didn't even realize that I never went home with them."

"She's still young, Mairead", said Iuile's father while laying in his bed, and gazing at his wife with admiration.

This surprised Mairead as she gave a glare at her husband and said, "You should be sleeping, Donal."

"How can I with you clucking", said Donal before giving a soft laugh.

If it was any other man, Mairead would snap him in two for such words. The only reason she allows her husband to say such remarks is because she knows that he is only teasing her for a reaction. It also informs Mairead, since Donal is talking to her that way, that he is feeling better to the point where she no longer has the need to knit, due to her stress beginning to drop down. "Looks like your herbs are working, Granny Yueng", Mairead said to the old woman who appeared to have a gray balding head, a long crooked nose, and only a few teeth left in her mouth.

"Obviously", said Granny Yueng in a crackling voice, and an accent that is not native to this archipelago. She approaches her bag that is on top of a dresser, that is not too far from the window, while saying, "Of course, you could of learned it yourself if you let me train you to be a wizardess when you were young, before sending you to the wizardry school, Hyvane. But you chose to be a barmaid instead due to your bad habit of playing poker with the customers."

"If I did become a wizardess, then I wouldn't have married this numbskull", reply Mairead teasingly with a smirk.

"Ha", said Donal, "I'll never forget the look on your face when I got you to go out with me! And I'm glad that you didn't go to that warlock school, on the account that I wouldn't want you to learn Witchcraft anyway."

"Only witches and warlocks learn one of the many dark arts such as Witchcraft, you imbecile", said Granny Yueng with annoyance, while standing in front of the dresser with her back against it. She then continues with reasoning and harshness, "I'm a wizardess! A female wizard! Whom, I might add, specialize in Herbology,

Alchemy, Kataralysis, and some Elemtarus such as Igntarus and Caltarus. The good book also says nothing about wizardry being bad, just Witchcraft, Nekromancy . . . ." She pauses due to the irritation of explaining how not all magic is evil, before yelling angrily, "Everything that involves in the dark arts, you blind fool!"

"Potato, Patato, you vile witch", said Donal with fake disgust towards the wizardess. He then grins as he turns to his wife to say, "You on the other hand . . . will always be my naughty little witch, haha!"

This causes Mairead to gently slap his shoulder while replying with a grin, "That's enough, you idiot." They begin to smile at each other for a moment of appreciation before Mairead decides to say, "It's a good thing your best friend, Garvan, decided to foolishly chase after Granny Yueng with his boys and Gearoid. Though I wish Gearoid would have said something before running off so that Roibeard didn't waste his time searching for him before assuming that he ran off in anger." The three of them become suddenly startled when Gatto appears on the window sill and pretends to be a normal cat by licking his paws. He then jumps down on the ground and frolics past Granny Yueng, around the bed, and towards Mairead where he purrs against her ankles.

"Aaawww", said Donal, "isn't that sweet." He then turns to Granny Yueng and asks her, "Is that your cat?"

"I'm a dog person", said Granny Yueng while closing, and locking, the window. "Own a terrier that is bred to chase rats. Call him, Rat Catcher."

"Ah, good", said Donal in a tone that tells Mairead that he is no longer pretending to care, before saying, with censor, "Honey, throw that fooladandy thing as hard as you can through the blasbury window!"

"Fool", said Granny Yueng, "I just closed the window."

Irk from what the wizardess said has Donal reply with irritation, "I'm fully aware that it's closed! That'll make it more painful when she throws that blasted thing out!"

"That won't be necessary", said Mairead as she knows that Gatto is no ordinary cat, due to how Granny Yueng is acting, and kicks the cait sith across the room. She then grabs Donal's cane and walks towards the cat. When she reaches him, she whacks him with the cane.

"Hey!" Said Donal, "I always wanted to do that! How come you get to do that?"

"Because that's a cait sith", said Granny Yueng.

"Kraggling fraggling", mumbles Donal with annoyance and anger before saying, "bring me my iron ax, Mairy, that danglewangle cat is after my life, and I ain't going down without a fight."

Knowing full well that if Donal gets too worked up, he will fall ill again, causing Mairead to say in a strict tone to him, "Lay back in bed, Donal!"

While staring at the fairy with utter malice, Donal decides to settle down and lay in his bed while mumbling, "Little dung ought to be lucky that I trust my better half, or else I . . . ."

"Now then", said Mairead after giving another whack at Gatto, while ignoring her husband's rambling, "why are you here?" Gatto only meows, causing Mairead to strike him again saying, "Stop playing games, we know what you are, and you don't normally show yourself without a reason, so come on. Spill it, or I'll let our town's wizardess, Granny Yueng, have you."

With a sinister crackle, Granny Yueng rubs her hands together while pretending to be malevolent saying, "He's certainly brave, or stupid, to enter a person's dwelling when they normally possess iron somewhere in the building. Either way, it's been a while since I skin a live one. Just give me a moment to find my iron horseshoe to torture him with for answers." She then breaks out into laughter before digging into her bag.

The wizardess words have Gatto horrified to where he says, "Oh bonkers! I didn't notice her in here before jumping in! Most humans would never think twice that I was a fairy unless they have magical powers." He begins to mumble while whimpering, "It's also not fair that she is able to hide her magical presence either." He then says to Mairead and Granny Yueng, "All right, you win. I'll confess. Skinning me is one thing, but anything but the iron!"

Getting frustrated with the fairy's whine, and not instantly answering her question, causes Mairead to pick the cait sith up by the fur, so that she can lift him up to her face, and say, "I'll ask one more time. Why-are-you-here?"

"Like he said", replied Gatto while pointing at Donal for a moment before continuing, "I was sent here to kill him, by order of Marquis DeGallo."

Never a man to go down without a fight, Donal hastefully sits up and yells out while shaking his fist, "I knew he was watangling after me! As for that tallynoogin from that cursed mansion! He can kiss . . . ."

This irates Mairead due to her husband getting excited again, and reply to him, "Donal! Lay-Back-Down!" Donal would normally at this point tell his wife to let him handle it, while still eyeing at Gatto with malice, but understands why she wants to deal with the cait sith herself and lays back down while mumbling more curses.

With attention fully back to Gatto, Mairead asks the fairy, "Why in the world would that demon want my husband . . . ?" Something occurs to her that someone's shenanigans are involved, and immediately turns to her spouse to question him, "What did you, your friends, your brothers including our in-laws, our nephews, and/or the boys do this time?!"

"We didn't do a dang thing", replied Donal while still eyeing Gatto with a nasty stink-eye.

"Actually", said Gatto who brought Mairead's attention back to him, while at the same time feeling extreme fear of Donal, "Marquis DeGallo sent me here to kill him because your daughter, who came with friends by the way, didn't clarify with the wish she made."

What Gatto said has fueled Donal with pure rage as he immediately sits up with a knee on the bed, like he is ready to get up, and softly says with anger, "That tallynoogin has one of my baby girls?! I'll farfastic kill him! He's a DEAD MAN!!!"

Now Mairead is infuriated over both what had happened to one of her daughters, and her husband getting excited again, causing her to turn to him and say, "Donal! BED!" She then returns her attention to Gatto, "And you! Which one of my daughters is over there?"

This has Gatto terrified even more because he has now unleashed a mother's fury, before replying, "Well, she's a brunette."

After squeezing the fairy's fur, and digging her nails into his skin, Mairead replies with a soft rage, "All my daughters are brunettes!"

"Ow, ow, uncle, uncle", replies Gatto as he continues to hastefully say in one word, "Inherteenswithblueeyes!"

Upon hearing the fairy's answer, Donal, who was still kneeling in the same position on his bed and staying quiet as Mairead has her back towards him, begins to speak like a raving lunatic of fury, "Iuile! That son-of-a-donkey-of-a-mule-haven has my baby girl, IUILE!!" He then gets off his bed and paces around the room as he riles himself up for a fight, and says while slowly raising his voice, "He's a meagle Feagle DEAD MAN!!! I'LL WRING HIS BLOOMING LITTLE NECK AND . . . ." Donal stopped mid-sentence due to Granny Yueng blowing some pollen-like substance towards him, causing him to faint with Granny Yueng nudging him to fall on his bed.

"Thank you, Granny Yueng", said Mairead as she tossed Gatto towards her saying, "he's all yours."

Granny Yueng catches Gatto (who is both shocked and horrified) with her right hand as the fairy yells, "WHAT? I told you everything!"

"And she has no further use for you", said Granny Yueng with giggles while showing Gatto the horseshoe in her left hand, which happens to have a glove on. "Rat Catcher will have some fun with you. Granny Yueng turns to Donal while ignoring Gatto's pleas, and trying to avoid contact with the iron, as she says to Mairead, "Seems that the illness had caused Donal to be more emotional than usual." She then turns towards the door to the hallway and assumes, "It also appears that Mrs. McCleary really is going deaf." She returns her attention to Mairead, who is shifting and tucking Donal in bed, to conclude, "Otherwise she would have come in here and wondered what all this ruckus is about."

"It also would've been easier to restrain Donal if Dr. McCleary wasn't out on an emergency call", said Mairead after giving Donal a kiss. "I also agree about the illness affecting Donal, because in a situation such as this, he would have just quietly fumed out the door. Usually runs his mouth when his opponent is weak, and not worth bruising his fist. She then gets up to head towards the door, stops in front of it, and ask, "I trust that you can watch over Donal?"

"I certainly can", replied Granny Yueng. She then becomes concerned as she asks, "But you're not actually thinking of going to Diavolo Mansion by yourself, are you? It is a very dangerous place, even for me."

"Nothing a mob with fire and pitchforks wouldn't fix", said Mairead who is still facing the door while being filled with fear of walking towards death, "with the help of Lord O'Ceallachain to gather everyone of course . . . . Will you aid us with your magic once Donal is taken care of?"

"Never fought in a mage duel", said Granny Yueng, "or any combat in general, other than self-defense like what happened the other day. I mostly heal people from injury or disease, aid in birthing in humans and animals, remove nasty spells, and so forth. Even if I did, my magic is incredibly weak compared to his. Shoot, even the king of the local leprechaun clan, Gleannasi, is weaker than him. I'm better off staying here, especially since I need to tend to Donal more than ever after that tantrum. Otherwise, the illness will kill him.

"Either way, my presence there will only cause more trouble for you to even have the slightest chance of success. I'll only get in the way of getting someone, or myself, killed. Just like you if you plan to go there yourself, with or without a mob." Granny Yueng's last words cause Mairead to clench her fists in anguish. "Marquis DeGallo is a powerful, dangerous, and evil man . . . ."

Mairead instantly turns to face Granny Yueng with tears in her eyes, and replies with a vengeful tone, "Who has cross between me and my child!"

CHAPTER 21

The Doorless Room

Niall wakes up in a dark room, with only a single candle stick holder to give off a faint light on a table nearby, and Iuile on top of him. Her softness causes him to blush as he tries to awaken her saying, "Iuile . . . Iuile, wake up!" Iuile slowly opens her eyes with a slight disorientation before realizing where she is, and that she is on top of Niall. Iuile stares at Niall, while slowly glowing red, long enough to make him feel uneasy, with his only response is to crack a nervous smile and say, "Um . . . Iuile, you're on top of me."

When Niall finishes speaking, Iuile's face became brightly red when she finally decided to get off of him, and stand up, while saying, "I'm so sorry."

"It's alright", replies Niall while sitting up. He then takes a deep breath before getting up, and asks with concern, "Are you okay?"

"Yes", said Iuile while trying to calm down. "Are you okay as well?"

"Yeah", replies Niall as he stretches his muscles. He then checks his pouch to see if King Tuathal is unharmed, and to ask him, "What about you?"

"I said that I was fine", replies Iuile who was befuddled by Niall's question.

This confuses Niall for a moment, before realizing that she does not know that King Tuathal is aiding them. Niall looks into his pouch again and signals the king if he would allow him to tell her of his presence. King Tuathal understands his signals and says, "Of course not! She might accidentally give me away! I also want to remind you that she can't hear me. Just sit tight while I think of something." He then peers through a hole in the pouch that he made earlier and asks Niall to move around, so that he can get a full view of the room.

While walking around the room, as if he is inspecting, Niall notices Iuile picking up the candle holder on the table, causing him to ask her with sarcasm, "Spook by the dark are we?"

This causes Iuile to blush once more, and turns to Niall to reply, "Of course not! If I was, I wouldn't be able to cross Killy Ri Forest now, would I."

"That's good to know", said Niall who then mumbled, "though I recall you carrying a lantern in the forest. But I ought to be grateful that it ended there." His grin dies down as he looks into his satchel, and asks King Tuathal in a low voice, "Any ideas yet?"

While attempting to see through the darkness with the candle holder, Iuile turns to Niall, as she is under the impression that he is speaking to her, and replies, "No, but I may find something if I can find the wall."

The idea that Iuile was able to hear Niall in such a low voice from where she is at impresses him. But at the same time, Niall is also dumbstruck that she does not question why he is talking in a low voice to begin with, and glances at her before replying with a hint of sarcasm, "Yeah, you do that while I think of something."

When Niall finishes replying to Iuile, who does not pick up on the sarcasm, he turns his attention to King Tuathal who says, "It's too dark to see in here." He then notices something, "Ah, a fireplace. How convenient." He claps his hands, causing the flames from the fireplace to ignite, and reveal that they are in a doorless room with furniture and a bearskin rug.

The fire suddenly flaring up catches Iuile by surprise, as she slightly jumps from fright, and looks around with curiosity of what just happened. At the same time, the king takes a peak through the satchel's hole and says, "There appears to be no way to exit this room. I need a moment to think of something. In the meantime, you should talk to Iuile and calm her down, as she appears to be shaken up."

It suddenly dawns on Niall while noticing, with the newly lit room, his sword that he dropped earlier where he decides to pick it up and sheath it. He then begins to look for Einri's dagger, while whispering to the king with hope that Iuile would not hear him, "This is not the time to play matchmaker! Nor do I need her to talk her head off with how annoying and unfair her mother is, or how much of a pain her aunts and female cousins are, with some of them being conniving. And Deus forbids that she complains about Eilis', or any other girls', drama." Niall begins to sigh, and tries to calm down before continuing, "I just want to have a normal conversation where we can get to know each other better, without her chattering nonstop about pointless drivel."

"It can't be that bad", said King Tuathal. "Besides, talking about each other's problems is part of having a healthy relationship."

"True", said Niall with an agreement, "true, but it's not healthy when one does all the talking, while the other barely have a say in the conversation."

"Now that is a problem", replies King Tuathal.

During Niall's private chat with King Tuathal, Iuile decides to put the candle holder down. While she is doing this, she is able to hear Niall murmuring, which makes her curious about what he is saying as she is unable to make out his words. So Iuile approaches him while asking, "What are you mumbling about?"

This causes Niall to be fully irate, as he begins to question how on Atlast is Iuile still able to hear him before turning to her and noticing that she is a few feet from him. He becomes silent and realizes that he is alone, besides King Tuathal who is still hiding, with Iuile in a room with a fireplace. It was not until King Tuathal whispered what to ask her, which Niall repeated, "What's on your mind?"

Asking such a question has Iuile anxious before replying, "Well . . . I'm worried about Eilis, and what Marquis DeGallo might do to her. I'm also worried if Einri is going to be all right. I mean, I know he's a jerk, but even he doesn't deserve to be where Marquis DeGallo sent him. That is, of course, what Einri stated about Ogre Street is true. Now that I think about it, Marquis DeGallo said that he gave Einri a free wish, like he did with me. So why didn't Einri wish us all free?"

The query that Iuile asked is a good one, with Niall pondering about it before replying, "Einri only gets the wish if he made sure we didn't escape, so if that scoundrel did want to help, then it might be because that mask mule wouldn't grant him that wish."

"That makes sense", said Iuile who believes that to be the just answer. She then continues with her other worries, "Anyway, I also feel bad for seeing a vicious side of you whenever you attack Marquis DeGallo while saving me and Eilis." Niall scratches the back of his neck due the real reason that he acts like that, when he sees Marquis DeGallo, is because he realizes of Caolan's possible fate while searching for Iuile and the others. That knowledge, however, is something he likes to keep to himself. As it is a personal matter that Iuile should not worry about while she finishes with her worries with, "Then there's what Marquis DeGallo . . . ." Iuile pauses for a moment before turning away and saying, "Never mind."

"I don't like where this is going", said King Tuathal while looking through the hole, before gazing up at Niall. "You can now whisper to me without her hearing you. While you two were talking, I cast a temporary spell where she cannot hear low voices."

"Good to know", whispered Niall with relief, "and I agree. Normally she would not stop or pause like that, or even give a break for me to cut in for an hour. Except when she expects me to answer her question, which normally does not last long."

"I normally wouldn't do this", said King Tuathal, "but I'm going to cast a temporary charm spell that will make her honest." When the king casts his magic on Iuile, he asks Niall to question her on what she is about to say.

The spell did work, as Iuile turns to Niall to honestly say, "Marquis DeGallo . . . said that he loved me when we fell into this room. Then there were the compliments of my appearance that he gave me in the ballroom, along with his confession of his feelings towards me during the start of the double lunar eclipse at midnight. Yet despite all that, he did all these horrible things to us. How can he confess his love for me and be so cruel?"

Already knowing the answer to this is something Niall is fully aware of, due to his own kin, male or female, among others, to commit similar acts. But never at this level as he replies, "Because he is a manipulative liar who only tells you what you want to hear, in order to easily gain your trust, just so that he can misuse your trust for his own selfish gain. Actions speak louder than words, and he obviously does not love you."

Tears begin to fill Iuile's eyes as she asks with a glint of hope, "But maybe . . . maybe he really does love me . . . and that maybe . . . just maybe, there is more to this than we know. For all we know, he might be forced to do these horrible things to us."

It now occurs to Niall who recalls something that Iuile said earlier but decides to play dumb for an answer he already knows. Because he cannot explain how he already knew of her father's illness, due to him keeping knowledge about King Tuathal a secret, and decides to reply, "Didn't you say that your father is in need of being saved? Why?"

The question Niall asked shocked Iuile, who became ashamed that she had once again forgotten about her father's situation due to the madness that they were in. She begins to confess everything that had happened before Niall's first attempt to rescue them in the ballroom. When Iuile finished explaining, she said, "It's my fault that he is going to be . . . ." She begins to shed tears, making Niall feel uncomfortable because he does not know how to deal with a situation such as this. Iuile tries to hold back her feelings to say, "But after all Marquis DeGallo has done, there may still be hope that there is good in him, why else would he declare his love for me."

Having enough of Iuile's perspective of reasoning, Niall replies with complete seriousness, "Now you're just deluding yourself. I had a cousin who thought the same thing, only for her to ruin her entire life, along with her parents who paid some of the price. Let's also not forget about whatever cruelty he put you and Eilis through when I found you the second time. He's nothing more than a cold-hearted, pathological liar, who does not love you."

The thought of Niall's harsh words being true has caused Iuile to show signs of denial and reply, "No! That can't be! How can anyone lie about love like that?! It's too cruel!"

The only thing Niall did was stare at Iuile with pity while feeling guilty for laying reality on her. But he does not want her to suffer like the others he had seen, and while having a bad feeling that he is going to upset her further, he asks her, "What about all those times when Eilis was flirting with the guys around town?"

This has Iuile confused about why Niall brought this up before replying, "What about it?"

Niall asks, "Was she at least interested in any of them?"

"No . . . not even when they confessed their feelings for her", Iuile replies.

"Yet she pretends to be interested in them", said Niall. "Giving them false hope that she might love one of them."

"No", Iuile said doubtfully, "she's never that cruel."

"Don't get the wrong idea", said Niall as he realized that he did upset her further. He tries to reapply the bandage on the wound while turning toward the fireplace saying, "What she does is a slap on the wrist compared to what Marquis DeGallo has done to you. I mean come on, if he really loved you, he wouldn't send that cait sith to kill Mr. McBannon." Niall turns back to face Iuile, only to see her bursting into tears, which is making him feel guilty upon believing that he did make things worse. "I'm sorry that I upset you. I . . . just didn't want you to get hurt due to his trickery."

Iuile manages to calm herself down before replying, "I appreciate that. But you're right. I'd been aware of what Eilis had been doing, I just never realized that she was being so cruel on their end. It also doesn't help that I couldn't think clearly on what a horrible person that man truly is." She then bites her bottom lip, and squeezes her skirt, before looking at Niall and asks, "Can I ask you something?"

"What is it", said Niall calmly.

While blushing, Iuile gazes at the ground and asks, "What changed your mind to come after me and Eilis?" She then looks back at Niall, while hoping for a positive response.

Whereas Niall has become extremely nervous, for he does not know how to properly respond. Memories of his older brothers and cousins teasing him, when he was little, from any weakness, begin to flash over his mind. From times that he cried when they scared him, to times when he gets upset when they call him names. Yet his brothers and cousins being boys will be boys, is what made him stronger. Therefore, he holds no grudge toward them, otherwise, he would not have succeeded where he is now in this house of chaos.

After Niall hardens himself, he calmly replies with honesty, "I couldn't focus while hunting due to a guilty conscience, and that something might happen to . . . ." He breaks eye contact for a moment, before repairing the eye contact and continues, "I just feel bad for not stopping you and Eilis when I had the chance."

As if being hypnotized, Iuile begins to approach Niall while asking with curiosity, "What were you about to say?"

Niall replies with uncertainty, "Say about what?"

Recalling what Niall uttered, Iuile continues to approach him while replying, "You said 'and that something might happen to . . . .' Happen to what . . . or who?"

While slowly backing away, Niall begins to feel tempting, yet awkward, with Iuile's advance until he decides to stop, and let her get close to his face. They gaze into each other's eyes for a moment before Iuile closes hers, and waits as Niall decides to move his eyes to her lips with allure. The passion is only interrupted when they hear a door creaking behind Iuile, causing both of them to look at the source, and see an open door that was never there before. At that same moment, King Tuathal cursed to himself before saying, "Blasted fool almost had her!"

Wishing to slap his satchel in order to silence King Tuathal, Niall decides to resist the urge, as he knows that it is a bad idea. Instead, he heads towards the door while telling Iuile to follow him. When Niall exits the room, and into the second floor's center wing, he realizes that he just came out from where the ballroom should have been. He begins to peer over the handrails, and down at the foyer's first floor, to make sure that he is where he believes he is, followed by hearing the door slam shut. Fearing for the worse, Niall turns with hope that Iuile is still with him, only to fall into despair upon seeing that she is nowhere to be found, along with the door that he exited.

Full of frustration with Niall's error, King Tuathal yelled, "You should have at least held her hand before heading for the door!"

"I know", replied Niall who pounds his fists, in anger, into a wall across the handrail, near the door he exited out from used to be. He then asks King Tuathal with his fists still on the wall, and head tilting down, "Was Iuile wanting to kiss me part of your spell?"

"Of course not", replies King Tuathal. He then recalls what spell he cast before continuing, "Well, sort of. Like I stated before, I cast a spell that made her more honest. Her feelings for you were genuine because of your poor attempts to comfort her." Niall turns his head to the pouch that the king resides in, causing the royal leprechaun to say, "Don't give me that! Poor as it may be, it worked. Most women would get upset from what you had said, but she didn't, meaning that she is a smart girl with a healthy upbringing. Anyway, even if I didn't cast it, she still would have felt that way with you. Just not that forward. Though now that I think about it, that charm should wear off right about now."

This has Niall feel some relief that he said the right thing to Iuile, before turning and sitting down against the wall where the missing door was. His mood changed to anguish as he looked down to the ground while saying, "Glad to hear, but it still doesn't change the fact that I feel bad about what just happened. She's in danger again because of me, and my punishment for that is to recheck all the rooms with all the horrors that await in them. All while knowing in torment that she is going to be tortured in some way in the meantime." He continues in a low voice, "I . . . I love her." When he finished speaking, he turned to the front entrance windows to see that the double lunar eclipse had just ended.

Niall stares at the two moons in sorrow and agitation for a moment, before hearing a hissing sound, and sees a skog harpy rising up with her wings from the first floor. He then turns to the hallway to see two more, one crawling on the ground, and the second on the wall. These species of harpies are native to the northern part of Mystia, where they are very adaptive to the cold. They all have the head and torso of a woman with blue hair and wearing fur clothing on their upper bodies that they steal from other races.

Because they are unable to make their own due to them having no arms, but instead have purple wings that are shaped like a crow's. Their lower half and their backs are feathered in purple, with their talons and eyes being that of an eagle. Their mouths have a beak-like flesh that is barely noticeable, with teeth that are similar to a goliath tigerfish, but smaller.

"You killed our sister", said the one on the ground with a wrathful tone.

"You will pay for that", said the one flying with hate.

"How lovely", said Niall as he continued sarcastically, "more annoying pigeons, who love to leave presents on statues, to shoot down." He then confesses with slight anger, "It is also rather fair of what I did to your sister after this cursed mansion took my brother!"

This fuels the skog harpies with more anger, with the one on the wall screeching with vengeance, along with the others, before saying, "How dare you compare us to those filthy birds you . . . ." The harpy was quickly cut off by an arrow to the head from Niall, with one knee to the ground, who then fired two more at the others who were in shock from what happened to their sister.

After shooting the skog harpy that was flying, who fell straight to the ground level, Niall gets up to say, "Well, now that the flies have been swatted, I guess I'll head off and moon the Grim Reaper."

Feeling concerned with Niall's rationality, King Tuathal asks him, "Are you all right, Niall? You sound a bit off, and consumed with hatred."

"Well let's see", said Niall while trying to maintain his sanity, "I'm both hungry and tired, which may be causing me some agitation to the point of slight nuttiness, and possibly vengefulness, added with a seasoning of the madness that is going on." After speaking, he takes a deep breath, in an attempt to calm himself down, before saying, "Yeah, I'm definitely not thinking straight. I might be alright if I can at least get some food in my stomach."

"There's some jerky in here", said King Tuathal who pulls a piece out of Niall's pouch, "You probably forgot that you had some in here."

Niall did forget and quickly took the jerky from the king where he ate it with satisfaction, before grabbing some more until he was out. After finishing the last one, he takes a swig of water from his waterskin before saying, "Oh man, that's better. Starting to feel at peace now."

"Hopefully that will hold you up", said King Tuathal.

"Oh it will", said Niall. "I can last a few hours with that, plus I don't want to eat too much, or I'll get groggy. Anyway, I can now stay focused on what really matters, saving the girls, and not getting revenge that will obviously get me killed by that mad lunatic."

"Glad to hear that you're still maintaining your priorities", said King Tuathal as Niall began to check the closest door to him. Only for the king to say, "Wait a moment!" This stops Niall from turning the knob, and looks at his pouch where he continues, "I just thought of something. Return to where the door was, and press this pouch I'm in against it gently." King Tuathal's request puzzles Niall, but did what the royal leprechaun asks, and leans against the wall. "Just as I thought. The door didn't disappear, an illusion is cast over it to appear that there is only a wall. I can easily fix that. Though it may take a while."

CHAPTER 22

For Love or Friendship

Emotionally terrified of what is to come, has Iuile beating down the door in a mad panic until it occurs to her to use the doorknob, only to find that it has none. While falling into despair, Iuile slowly turns around and places her back towards the door, where she gently slides down to the floor with tears in her eyes. She then covers her face with her hands, and whispers to herself, "I should have known that it was too good to be true for him to kiss me. Why would anyone love me?"

It then dawns on Iuile as she removes her hands from her face, and asks herself, "Wait, why do I want him to kiss me?" Her inquiry is only answered by her emotions that tell her, *"Because I love him."* Such an answer only confuses Iuile who decides to question herself, "But why? I need to calm down and think clearly." While trying to focus, her emotions begin to constantly interfere saying, *"What is there to think about? Just love him. No different than loving Marquis DeGallo. Or Bradach. Love is love."*

From all the noise coming from Iuile's emotions, a whisper of her logic and reasoning appears, *"From the very beginning, he warned me, and even after ignoring his warning, he chased me. He risked his life for me and my friend, not as a result of caring, but for the obvious reason that he loves one of us. Would it not be possible that he does have feelings for me? He probably doesn't want to say that he is doing it due to his love for me, because he is being stubborn and shy, and what about me, who had always enjoyed his company. Not to mention the several times that he showed little interest in Eilis . . . showed little interest in . . . ."* Iuile's logic and reasoning fade away, and a realization has come to her as she says in a whisper, "I do love him!" Little did Iuile know, is that she admits her feelings for Niall at the same time that he admits his feelings for her.

Iuile begins to calm down and puts her arms on top of her knees where she hides her face behind her legs while continuing to ponder, *"That must be why I wanted him to kiss me. Because I love him. Yeah, he perceives my best friend in a negative manner, even though it's true. He also did try to comfort me . . . in a terrible way, that is. However, why haven't my feelings about Marquis DeGallo changed?"*

Her question is then followed by her emotions saying, *"Because I love Marquis DeGallo more than Niall. Yes, I despise him for wanting my father dead. But I can fix that with love. For unlike Niall, Marquis DeGallo confessed his feelings toward me. Even though he is despicable for forcing me to walk through that pool of roaches, in order to save Eilis who he tried to kill.*

"There is obviously good in him in the name of love. Not to mention that Niall decided not to kiss me." This epiphany has Iuile put her hands on the floor, with her knees laying to the side while still looking down, before saying to herself out loud, "Now that I think about it, why didn't Niall kiss me?"

"Because he does not love you like I do", said a familiar voice that caused Iuile's heart to skip a beat. Yet it did not surprise her, for she knew that he would show himself to torment her after what happened. It also does not help that her emotions are now starting to flare up, as they now feel like her soul is burning in acid. For she is now not sure whether or not Niall really does have feelings for her. Deciding to grit herself, while holding her tears back, Iuile lifts her head up and prepares for the worst to find not only Marquis DeGallo but Eilis tied to a chair with her mouth gagged.

"I can't believe you trusted in his lies towards me", said Marquis DeGallo in a tone that says that his heart had been broken, while Iuile slowly gets up with her back still pressed against the door. "The only reason I am doing this to you is because of my Dark Master." He begins to approach Iuile with a painful look on his face. "You see, I foolishly made a deal with the devil, which I eternally regret, and the only way to break this curse is true love." When he finishes speaking, he is already holding Iuile's hand, while kneeling, with innocence in his eyes.

This has Iuile blush once more from Marquis DeGallo's confession of his love, causing her to have doubts about Niall's warnings as her emotions say, *"See, see, he does love me, and Niall is wrong!"* Iuile then gazes at her friend who is tied up, as if being held for ransom, making her regain her faith in Niall. She ignores what her emotions are telling her, takes her hand away from Marquis DeGallo, and asks, "If that's the case, then why is Eilis tied up?"

"Because even though Foolish Knight is wrong about me", said Marquis DeGallo as he stood back up. "He is absolutely right about Sunflower. For her manipulative charms are driving me crazy, and if I fall for someone who does not love me, then I will be forever tormented by my Dark Master. I tried to resist, oh how I tried to resist, but she will not allow us to be together, because all she wants is my fortune so that she can selfishly spoil herself."

"That's a lie", replies Iuile, "Eilis would never do such a thing!"

"Is that so", said Marquis DeGallo as he stepped back to where Eilis was sitting. He then summons a crystal ball to appear in the palm of his hand, and softly says to it, "Sit and gaze . . . through sleepless dreams."

The Ram and Ewe's Quest for the Lost Lambs

Being mesmerized by the crystal ball has caused Iuile to approach it, as if she is enchanted by it, and gaze into the quartz where it recalls all the young men that Eilis flirted with. Young men who showered her with gifts of love for her, and yet she shows not the slightest interest in any of them. Iuile's anger toward her friend increases further when she sees her crush, Bradach, competing desperately for Eilis' attention. Followed by showing their conversation yesterday where Eilis said, "The first chance I get, I'll leave here to head for Dunban, and make something of myself." It is then followed by another conversation that had a tone altered, "Well you better, or I'll just take him for myself." It finally ends with the time Eilis tries to convince Iuile to have dinner with Einri, "It's different when the guy is rich."

The crystal ball ceases its images and disappears, followed by Marquis DeGallo saying, "You see! She is only thinking of herself, as she is even willing to abandon her family for her own, self-interest. She is attempting to succeed in her selfishness by trying to tear my feelings for you apart." He once more gets on his knees and asks while groveling, "Please, please, save me from her charm. I don't want to lose your love!"

This left Iuile speechless with disbelief at what Marquis DeGallo had told her. Yet her jealousy over Eilis' crushes is slowly consuming her. For not once did any of them ask her out, not once did any of them give her a gift of affection, not once did any of them pay her any attention. No, it was always Eilis who had taken everything she had for granted, even Bradach. The spite that is growing inside Iuile has caused her emotions to say, *"She needs to pay horribly for her foul deeds!"* Iuile glances at Eilis with malice as her friend muffles noises due to her gag, as if pleading.

Burning with hateful jealousy, Iuile looks back at Marquis DeGallo and asks him, "What do you want me to do?"

"To kill her with this dagger", said Marquis DeGallo who pulled out a kris dagger from his coat, and handed it to Iuile.

This shocked Iuile who quickly reply, "What? That's crazy!"

"It's the only way to end the cruel falseness of her love towards me", replies Marquis DeGallo who appears tormented. "When all I want is to love you, and you alone, my Angelic Princess. Please break this curse on me."

Several emotions begin to fill Iuile all at once, such as anger, malice, envy, hatred, and many others. Emotions that are telling her, *"Eilis has always been selfish and spoiled. Always stealing other people's love for her own self-interest. Ending her life would make everyone's life, including mine, better!"* This has Iuile finally decide to take the dagger and approach Eilis who begins to frantically thrash in her chair while trying to speak.

Iuile's hate and jealousy begin to fuel her as she stands in front of Eilis and confesses, "You were always getting attention, while I get shafted aside. You have taken all of them for granted, while I sat and waited to be asked. I thought maybe, just maybe, Bradach would have paid attention to me. But no, you wanted all the attention for yourself, while leaving not just me", Iuile quickly raised the dagger near her head and yelled, "BUT EVERY OTHER MAIDEN HANGING!!!"

Both girls are in tears as Iuile prepares to thrust the blade into Eilis' heart, who begins to gag due to her wanting to wail from crying but is unable to because of the cloth in her mouth. Iuile's emotions have become a thunderous rage that spreads like a spider's web, for she is now under the assumption that she will only find satisfaction, in the death of her friend. When suddenly, her logic and reasoning shout out, *"Remember what Niall said about the marquis!!!"*

This is followed by Iuile recalling the following words that Niall recently said, *"Because he is a manipulative liar who only tells you what you want to hear, in order to easily gain your trust, just so that he can misuse your trust for his own selfish gain."*

The realization that Iuile receives, has her say, "But of course, it's obvious that Bradach had never been interested in me. Otherwise, he would have ignored you." She hastefully turns around, and thrusts the dagger into Marquis DeGallo's chest, causing the marquis to scream in pain. Tears are still filling Iuile's eyes as she recalls the truth about her friend while releasing her grip on the dagger's hilt. After Marquis DeGallo takes a few steps back and falls down, Iuile confesses with honesty to her dear friend, "And yet . . . you never tried to take Bradach from me.

"I almost forgot, that out of all the selfishness you had done, you never really betrayed me since you always tried to not have anything to do with him." Iuile turns towards her friend and hugs her as she continues, "I'm so sorry for doubting you, Eilis. You are my best friend, who I always love and trust like a sister." This is followed by her emotions saying, *"Yes, of course, I do, I almost made a horrible mistake in killing my best friend."* Even still, Iuile's emotions have not quelled, as it is no longer a thunderous rage, but a whirlpool of despair, causing her to hug her friend tighter for comfort.

The moment of friendly passion did not last, due to their current situation, and Iuile begins to hastefully attempt to untie Eilis. While Iuile is desperately trying to free her friend, Marquis DeGallo says in shock, "How can you betray me for that traitor?" This causes Iuile to stop, look towards the marquis, and see that he is on his hands and knees. Even though the marquis' chest is not in Iuile's view, she can tell that the dagger is gone, and his wound healed, as he continues to say, "Just when I thought that you were the one." Those words cause Iuile to feel doubtful once again as the marquis suddenly raises his head, and stares into space for a moment before standing back up. Upon turning around to face the door with no knob, as if he is suspecting something to happen, the door itself blows open, with Niall coming through the remains.

Any doubt that Iuile possesses has been washed away upon seeing Niall, whose eyes are full of malice. Iuile walks by Marquis DeGallo and stops to call out Niall's name before the marquis yells, "I knew you had help! Don't try to hide from me any longer, King Tuathal of Gleannasi!" He then looks up to give a maniacal laugh for a moment, before returning his attention to Niall saying, "You will pay dearly for interfering with my fun you . . . ." Marquis DeGallo's words were interrupted by Niall shooting his arrow at his head once again, with Iuile following the fired projectile by turning her head with it and gasping from the result. Upon being shot once more, the marquis immediately screams out in pain, while being both shocked and annoyed, and yells out, "AGAIN WITH THE ARROW??!!"

Aggravating with rage over Niall's constant interference has Marquis DeGallo, without hesitation, immediately removes the arrow while showing no reaction to the pain, nor a wound to be found. He then grabs Iuile around her waist before stomping on the floor, causing a hidden trapdoor to open, where he jumps down into it with her. This has Iuile immensely hysterical, as she feels that she is now drowning in madness once more. For the next thing she knew, is that she in a mine cart that began to move on its own down a mining tunnel, and heading north. With Marquis DeGallo standing in the front of the cart with his arms folded, and one leg on top of the cart's front bucket.

CHAPTER 23

Through the Tunnel

"Great", said Niall with his head through the trapdoor, so that he could examine the railway, where he saw it going down into the tunnel's darkness. Even though the tunnel has light coming from the torches along both sides of the wall, he cannot make out how far it goes. He sees that there is a dead end behind him, meaning that they can only have gone one way with him questioning, "How in the world does this even work? This looks like it's part of an actual mining tunnel, it makes no sense." King Tuathal was standing right next to Niall, who brought his head up to say, "It's just like when Iuile and I fell into that hole earlier from the second floor, only to end up on the same floor!"

"It's truly a madhouse", replies King Tuathal calmly.

"You got that right, Your Majesty", said Niall as he got up and walked towards Eilis, "and it looks like the jig is up too."

When Niall finishes untying Eilis, she removes the rag in her mouth, gets up, and asks, "Who on Atlast are you talking to?"

Deciding to finally reveal himself to Eilis, King Tuathal appears before her on the chair's top rail and says, "That would be I, King Tuathal of the Little People of Gleannasi."

Eilis stares at the leprechaun king for a moment, before grabbing him and saying, "Got you!" She then continues with joy and excitement, "Now, I want my first wish to be for me and Iuile to appear at an inn in Dunban!"

This has Niall furious at Eilis for taking advantage of someone who is helping them, and he starts to reach out to grab her shoulder. Only for King Tuathal to grin and raise his hand towards Niall to stop, followed by asking Eilis, "And your second wish?"

"My second would be for riches", said Eilis, "with a mansion more magnificent than this, as my third."

"So be it", said King Tuathal, "and what about your fourth wish, my gracious lady, like say, eternal beauty." Eilis gives off a gleam in her eye for such an offer of receiving an extra wish and accepts it. Only for King Tuathal to disappear and reappear on Niall's shoulder, who laughs with the royal leprechaun, as the mischievous king explains, "Three wishes is all I grant, but if you get greedy and wish a fourth, then you'll lose them all."

Flushing due to pure embarrassment, Eilis begins to have tears descend from being deceived. She then becomes infuriated and yells, "My friend is in danger, and you dare mock me!"

"Hey now", said Niall who was trying to stop laughing, "you're the one trying to pull a fast one in an inappropriate moment. King Tuathal is trying to help us, and you go ahead and take advantage of his kindness."

"I'm trying to save us", said Eilis who sounds convincing.

"Oh really", said King Tuathal who is now irate, "I don't recall your first wish to also include brave Niall here. Now, if you truly care for your friend, you'll stop this nonsense."

"I agree", said Niall. "Now you have two options, you can either escape back to Arvann by yourself, or you can come with us to save Iuile."

Afraid to return home alone, but much more afraid of abandoning Iuile, and possibly losing her forever, Eilis tries to hold her tears back as she replies, "Sorry for not including you, Niall. I'll behave and go with you because I want to save Iuile as much as you do." She then asks King Tuathal, "However, why can't you use your magic to defeat that monster?"

Niall intervenes in King Tuathal's reply to Eilis so that he can tell the royal fairy, "I'll go scout ahead while you explain to her about the difference between your shenanigans, and his." When Niall finishes speaking, the king leaps towards a table, next to Eilis, while he heads for the trapdoor, only to feel his foot kicking something. Niall looks down due to curiosity about what he kicked and spots something underneath the couch. He squats down to examine the object and finds it to be none other than Einri's dagger. He picks it up saying, "So that's where it's been?" He then notices the inscription on the blade that reads:

> To My Darling Son,
> May This Blessed Blade
> Protect The Wielder's Life.

"That must be Einri's dagger", said Eilis hovering behind Niall, causing him to turn his head to her, and blush. Niall quickly decides to turn back and hop forward before getting up, with Eilis straightening herself up, while giggling at his bashfulness, before saying, "If I remember correctly, it was his mother's last gift before passing away seven years ago. Custom made, and blessed by an epipavus."

"If it's that dear to him", said King Tuathal, "then the poor fool gave it up in hopes of redeeming his misdeeds. But I hate to say that even though it is blessed, it won't be enough to permanently kill that cruel host.

Niall was only silent as he stared at the dagger, and pondered if Einri's past misdeeds was due to the loss of his mother. However, it also occurs to him that losing a parent is still no excuse to commit selfish, and bullying, acts. Niall also wonders, as he sheaths the blade into an empty scabbard, if what King Tuathal said about Einri purposefully parting with something this precious, is really his way of atoning for his sins. Sins that he is willing to forgive if the dagger fulfills what is written on it. Niall goes ahead and jumps through the trapdoor, where he lands on the tracks and looks up to see Eilis standing near the trapdoor, and staring back at him.

They both start to blush as Eilis presses her hands against her skirt and screams while backing away yelling, "Don't look up my dress!"

Due to embarrassment, and being respectful towards women, have caused Niall to quickly look away while saying, "It was an accident!"

"Now's not the time for that", said King Tuathal as he passed Eilis, while not looking up. He stops when he reaches the trapdoor and says to Eilis while not facing her, "Now go ahead and drop down", he then looks down while continuing, "and you be sure to catch her, Niall."

The lack of respecting Eilis' dignity, along with getting upset of being told what to do by King Tuathal and Niall, has caused her to glare at the king for a moment before walking towards the pit, where she jumps down while trying to keep her skirt closed. Niall catches her, sets her down, and waits for King Tuathal to jump down with them before walking down the railway with Niall leading. They walk without muttering a sound for what seems like hours for Eilis, who finally decides to break the long silence, and ask with curiosity, "So, who do you really like, me . . . or Iuile?"

Eilis' question causes Niall to feel a sudden drop in his chest, only to regain his composure and reply, "Why do you ask?"

"Oh, just curious", said Eilis with an innocent voice, and playing dumb. "It really is nice of you to help us, even though we barely know each other." Niall chose to be silent while getting frustrated by Eilis' words. He did not want to start trouble, given their current situation, and tried to bottle his feelings towards her. However, Niall's quietness is annoying Eilis, who does not like Niall's lack of response as she asks, "You come off as the shy type, which makes me wonder . . . ."

Having enough of Eilis' banter, Niall turns to her and asks in a furious voice, "Who do you like?"

This apparently catches Eilis off guard, as her only response is, "What?"

"Two of my cousins are constantly fighting each other because they don't want the other to have you", Niall explains with irritation and anger in his voice. "Even to the point that they accidentally got their sister, Orna, hurt during a fistfight. So how long are you going to play your little, 'game', that's ruining everyone's lives?!"

Between Niall's rage, which terrifies Eilis, and being indirectly responsible for someone being injured, due to her selfishness, is making Eilis feel utterly guilty. Only for Eilis to calm down, as she receives an epiphany, and says, "Oh, so you like Iuile."

This becomes the straw that breaks the camel's back as Niall grabs Eilis by her ear, pulls on it, and says angrily, "Don't change the subject!"

"Ow, ow", replied Eilis painfully, "okay! I get it! I'm ticking a lot of people off with my flirting! I just found that out from Iuile, before that mask jerk kidnapped her again. I promise that as soon as we get out of here, I will put some thought on who I'll date, and go out with him."

"I'll hold you to that", said Niall after releasing Eilis, who immediately covered her ear due to the pain. Niall begins to walk down the tunnel while saying, "Sorry about pulling your ear." He then stops to admit, "I . . . just became upset over what happened to Orna."

"That's all right.", replied Eilis as Niall continued to walk down the tunnel, "chances are that I had it coming." She then follows Niall from behind while becoming even more annoyed of being told what to do again. Because Eilis has always found it frustrating when a guy tries to tell her what to do, with her father being the only exception. For in her perspective, they act as if they know better than her, or that she should obey and be submissive.

"Now that I think about it", said Niall while still walking, and keeping an eye out for any traps, "why did you come here with Iuile?"

"Because she is my best friend who needed my help", replied Eilis.

Not buying Eilis' response, Niall replied, "Pull the other one."

"I'm serious", said Eilis who is starting to get upset.

"Please", said Niall after chuckling, "I find that hard to believe considering the shenanigans you'd been pulling."

"Alright, fine", said Eilis. "Though I am serious about aiding Iuile, at the same time I was hoping to get a wish to leave town."

All of a sudden Niall stops, turns to Eilis, and replies, "Now that's a lot of cow pie."

"What is that supposed to mean?" Said Eilis who continued with anger and conviction. "I'm telling you the truth! I've been wanting to leave that stink hole for a long time!"

"Oh come on", replied Niall who is starting to get annoyed, "if you really wanted to leave Arvann, you would've done it a long time ago." There was a long pause where Eilis began to show doubt in her reasoning, until Niall had enough of her games and said, "You know what, it doesn't really matter since all I was asking was a simple question." He starts to walk away while saying, "If you don't want to answer, that's fine, because it really has nothing to do with me, or the situation we are in."

"I was scared", said Eilis, whose words caused Niall to stop, and turn his head halfway. "I was scared that the same thing could have happened to my father. He was almost killed by a banshee five years ago, and if something similar happens again, he might not be so lucky again." Niall turns his body halfway around so that he can make eye contact with Eilis who continues as she begins to shed tears, "I'm helping Iuile . . . because that night . . . I thought I was going to lose my father! I'm helping her . . . because I know her pain."

Niall is only silent for a moment before replying, "Now was it really that hard to be honest?"

"Oh, shut up", replied Eilis who turned her head away from Niall, and wiped the tears from her eyes.

"Sorry", said Niall who began to rub the back of his head, as he realized that he had given an improper response. "However, we wasted enough time, and need to press on for Iuile's sake."

The lack of compassion from Niall only irritates Eilis, who decides to not retort due to him being right about wasting time and continues with their walk down the tunnel. After what feels like an eternity for Eilis, she gets an idea and asks, "Can I see your bow?"

Such an unusual request has Niall curious enough to where he decides to turn to Eilis and ask, "Why?"

"So that I can assist you in case we get into trouble", replies Eilis.

With disbelief at what he is hearing, Niall raised an eyebrow before asking, "Have you ever hunted, or even fired an arrow, before?"

"Oh it can't be that hard", replied Eilis. "Even though my clan possesses some range weaponry, for self-defense, no one other than Keegan, my sister Darcia's new husband, knows how to hunt, as we normally get our meat from our cattle and chickens. But I'm sure that never firing an arrow, or a gun, would make much of a difference."

"You need a good amount of training before you can hit something at a distance", said Niall. "Like say . . . three hundred yards.".

Eilis replies with logic and sarcasm, "And when am I ever going to shoot something at that distance in this tunnel?"

Even though Eilis has a good point, Niall could not help but feel that it was a bad idea to give her his bow. But he decides to humor her anyway, and hands her his bow, and an arrow, while saying, "Tell you what. If you can hit the tip of that stalactite", he points at the one he wants her to shoot at while continuing, "then I can trust you to watch my back with a bow."

"Sure thing", said Eilis as she took the weapon, and began to pull the string of the bow, with difficulty.

This has confused Niall as he watches Eilis putting all effort into pulling the string, with the string itself barely moving an inch. The sad attempt that he is witnessing has caused him to ask her, "What's wrong? Can't you pull it?"

While getting frustrated, due to the difficulties of pulling the bowstring, Eilis asks, "How do you pull this?"

"By-pulling-it", replies Niall with sarcasm, as he cannot help but feel that Eilis is doing this on purpose. He then casually said, "It can't be that difficult, it's only an eighty-pound pull weight."

This caused Eilis to immediately stop pulling the bowstring, turn to Niall, and say with shock, "EIGHTY! I can only carry twenty-five pounds!"

What Eilis had spoken, has dumbstruck Niall, who tries to process what she just said. He recalls his mother being able to use a bow with no problem. Then he remembers her saying that most girls are weaker than boys, and confessed to him a few years back that her bow is a fifty-pound pull weight. Even though he recollects his mother explaining to him how weak girls are, he never expects them to be this weak as Eilis begins to shed tears, while still trying to draw the bow. Because reality has kicked into her perspective, and that Iuile was right about men being stronger. It is also painful for her to now question if she can really stand a chance to survive on her own.

Feeling bad for Eilis' predicament has Niall wanting to comfort her. But doing so would waste time as he decides to casually take his bow back, with no trouble since Eilis shows no resistance, while trying to give comforting words, "To be fair, I had been training with a weaker bow as a child in order to build up strength with the one I'm currently using." To Niall's dismay, his words only cause Eilis to burst out crying. Realizing that he made things worse, Niall decides to pull out his second dagger, and hands it to Eilis saying, "Here, if something bad happens, then you can defend, or help, with this."

To Niall's relief, Eilis has managed to calm down and stare at the dagger, while whimpering, for a moment before accepting the weapon, and feeling insecure over her own weakness. Niall scratches the back of his head, for he has no idea on what to say to make her feel better, other than, "Listen, we're wasting time again. We need to keep pressing on, and not to be a mule, but your crying would make it difficult to rescue Iuile." Niall becomes pleased to see that Eilis was not offended by his words, and acknowledges, with annoyance and displeasure, that he is right as she tries to calm herself down for her friend's sake.

It did not take long for Eilis to settle down, which Niall was happy as the noise would attract unwanted attention if there were any monsters down the tunnel. They resume their walk which appears to have no end, until it slowly begins to be filled with thick spider webs around the tunnel's wall, along with a few cocoons. This has Eilis frightful enough to walk closer to Niall as she nervously says, "I hope we don't run into an arachne."

"Too late", replied Niall who sounded annoyed. This is due to him seeing a woman walking on the wall, with a spider's body, appear. She possesses a cocooned prey in her arms, that is obviously too small to be Iuile, that she tosses into one of her webs.

The arachne are a species that has the body of a spider, and the body of a woman down to the waist where the spider's face should be. With this type of arachne being known as the umbra arachne, a species that prefers the cold and the dark, such as caverns, mines, and large abandoned buildings with basements. The woman part is half the average size of a woman, wearing a ragged piece of clothing to cover herself, but the spider part is the length of an average-sized man. Her hair is violet with six visible eyes; with two of them a quarter of the size of a normal eye and on the center forehead, two that are one-eighth in size between her normal eyes, and one on each temple that cannot be seen due to her hair. With all the eyes being purely black. The spider part of the body is also black, with yellow twin crescent moons facing each other on the abdomen.

The umbra arachne walks down to the floor while saying, "Well, well, well. Someone to entertain me. Now, which one of you was making that horrible screeching noise."

The spider woman's words caused Eilis to blush from embarrassment before Niall said, "None of your concern." He then notices part of the tunnel behind the arachne is blocked by webs, making him ask the monster, "But more importantly, how in the world did you repair your webs when Marquis DeGallo passed by?"

"My dear", said the umbra arachne, "I am fast and proficient in my art. It also appears that you don't realize how long you have been walking down this tunnel."

"I don't see any art", said Niall tauntingly while ignoring what the arachne meant by, 'don't realize how long you have been walking down this tunnel', due to him not wanting to waste time. He notices, as the monster is slowly approaching them, an unusual stone on the rails that is an obvious trap, due to how the creature is purposely avoiding it. "It looks more like some idiot splashing paint over a canvas, and hoping that another idiot, who pretends that they are smart and sophisticated, will act like there is some deep meaning behind it, in order to make themselves appear smart and sophisticated."

After coming to a halt, the umbra arachne immediately gives a wrathful hiss, revealing her mandibles inside her mouth, in front of

Niall and Eilis as she gets ready for the kill. Only for Eilis to yell at Niall, "How dare you insult her magnificent work, you insolent buffoon!"

Niall was about to draw his sword before Eilis decided to quickly intervene, causing him to stare at her with a dumbstruck look on his face. With his only response being, "What?"

Deciding to just ignore Niall, Eilis turns and approaches the umbra arachne, so that she can ask her with enthusiasm, "Will you show me how you create your art?"

"Why certainly, my dear", said the umbra arachne with pride in her voice. The spider woman begins to lead Eilis towards one of her webs, while casually having Eilis (who was oblivious) avoid the stone trap.

Seeing that Eilis does not have his dagger, Niall turns to ask King Tuathal, "Shouldn't you do something . . . ." Only to fall silent, for the leprechaun king is nowhere to be found. Niall quickly turns back to Eilis and the umbra arachne, due to someone screaming, and sees that Eilis had stabbed the spider monster's cephalothorax with his dagger. Where she hid it, is something that Niall is not sure of, and feels that he should not question it as the umbra arachne screams in pain. Though in pain, the spider woman decides to strike at Eilis who dodges her grasp and is shot in the chest by Niall's arrow, where her spider body drops down and dies, with her human body leaning over.

"Well, it looks like you don't need pure strength to conquer a foe", said Niall who felt that he should compliment Eilis' actions, even though he believed that she unnecessarily endangered herself. "Since you just proved to be very daring in danger, as you are with flirting." Eilis is already approaching him, with a smile of accomplishment, as he continues, "Okay, I need you to immediately stop moving."

Eilis changes her grin to an annoyed appearance while continuing to walk towards Niall, and replies in an agitating tone, "I'm getting sick and tired of you telling me what to . . . ."

Dread has befallen Niall, who interrupts Eilis as he yells out, "I SAID DON'T MOVE!" But it is too late, for Eilis has stepped on the stone trap, causing a cage to fall above, and ensnares them. Niall glares at Eilis with scorn, while she gives an appearance of guilt, before asking her, "So . . . how many times had you gotten yourself, and others, in trouble due to your refusal to listen to someone?"

Giving only a soft laugh, Eilis only replied, "I lost count."

CHAPTER 24

Motherly Advice

With Iuile's emotions under the hysteria of madness, due to being alone once more with Marquis DeGallo, has her feeling like her entire existence is tearing itself apart. Regardless of all the horrible things that the marquis had done to her, her emotions were telling her to believe in him. Only for Iuile to suddenly remember her mother, who had always told her that she needed to control her emotions when the time came for her to use logic and reasoning. Otherwise, she will only find pain and suffering, as her emotions can betray her. So Iuile tries to control her feelings, only to find it to be difficult to do, as she is too concerned about whether or not Marquis DeGallo would spontaneously do who knows what to her at any second, and make her feel more radical than before.

To Iuile's relief, and terror, the cart comes to a screeching halt in front of a door, where Marquis DeGallo attempts to pick her up. Only for Iuile to panic and resist by slapping him, causing Marquis DeGallo to back away, and fall off the cart where he lands on his rear. Iuile had fallen herself inside the mine cart and tried to hold back her tears from the pain after knocking her head into the bucket. As Iuile recovers from the injury, she begins to notice the sound of whimpering, and slowly glances over the cart's bucket to see Marquis DeGallo crying in sorrow. This surprises Iuile, for she never expects him to show this level of emotion.

While sobering as if a loved one had died, and wishing only death, Marquis DeGallo asks, "Why? I thought you were the one, the one who would free me from this torment. Yet you are no different than the 'others' who believed in their, so-called, friends' lies."

"You asked me to kill my best friend", said Iuile in a stern tone, while horrifyingly recalls what she was about to do to Eilis.

With no hesitation, Marquis DeGallo gets on his hands and knees before replying, "Because she is an evil, and manipulative, girl, who used not only you but others."

"Even if that is the case", said Iuile who is only pretending to believe in Marquis DeGallo's words, while trying to ignore her feelings towards him, "you can't expect me to kill someone who I grew up with. You could have at least asked me to talk to Eilis so that I can tell her to stop it."

"You just don't get it", said Marquis DeGallo as he cried even harder. "She torments me, for I have developed feelings for her when I should only have feelings for you!"

What Marquis DeGallo confesses, has touched Iuile who is beginning to believe in him. Only for Iuile to recall once more what Niall said about the types who will say anything to gain their trust. She then remembers once more of her mother's words, *"You really need to control your emotions, sweetie. Otherwise, you'll ruin your life with irrational decisions."* Those words have made Iuile realize that her best choice is to finally take her mother's advice.

Yet Iuile could not do so due to Marquis DeGallo sobering while waiting for her to respond. As she needs time to rationalize her thoughts without the interference of her emotions. Though the only option going through her head is, *"What would Eilis do in this situation?"* Iuile's past experiences with her best friend's behavior towards men, allow her to know how to approach the situation.

The Ram and Ewe's Quest for the Lost Lambs

The first thing Iuile did was ducking out of Marquis DeGallo's sight in the mine cart. She then makes the sign of the clover for strength from Dominus Deus, in the hope that He can assist her in keeping her emotions in check until she is able to think things through. When Iuile finishes praying, she climbs out of the cart, kneels next to Marquis DeGallo, and comforts him by acting like she believes his feelings towards her are genuine. She did this by saying in a kind and caring tone, "What do you need me to do, my love?" Only to realize that her lie might backfire, causing her to improvise further by brushing his hair with her fingers, while adding in, "That doesn't involve killing someone, of course?"

Marquis DeGallo immediately stares into Iuile's eyes with a gleam of hope, causing him to quickly get up, and reach his hand to her while saying, "For now, I just want you to come with me."

With Iuile's heart pounding frantically due to her fear of what is to come next, followed by admiration of being loved back, has her casually takes Marquis DeGallo's hand while still pretending to care for him. When the marquis holds Iuile's hand, he helps her up and leads her to a wooden door at the end of the cavern. Upon entering through the door, Iuile realizes that they are in the dressing room that she and Eilis were in earlier, before joining the ball, where she asks, "How in the world does this tunnel lead back here?"

"Actually", replies Marquis DeGallo as he closes the door that they enter from, and continues while facing Iuile, "this tunnel is similar to a wormhole which will be difficult to explain to your . . . simple and beautiful mind." While Iuile ponders what the marquis meant by those words, he walks by her and heads towards the door, that is across from where they had entered, while continuing to answer, "Let's just say that it will lead to wherever I wish it to take me." When the marquis reaches the door, he turns to her and says, "Now I trust that you will change into something more, dignifying, while I wait outside, as I'm sure you want some . . . privacy. I would also like to inform you that the door we enter from, no longer leads back into the tunnel, for it is actually the closet."

When Marquis DeGallo leaves the room, Iuile uses this opportunity to control her emotions like her mother always advices her. Though difficult, Iuile manages to control her feelings and starts to think things rationally, as her logic and reasoning begin to recall a memory from her past. A time that is recent, and takes place in her home, in front of the fireplace, when her mother asked, *"Why not?"*

"Because I don't like him", replied Iuile while sweeping with a broom. Yet for some reason at that time, was not fully sincere, and used an excuse, *"Not to mention that I don't even know Niall."*

"All the more reason you should date him", said Mairead who was sewing a ripped pants, while sitting in a rocking chair near the window. *"I'm not asking you to marry him. I'm just asking that you should at least give him a chance and get to know him better. Unless of course, you have a certain someone in mind?"*

That certain someone, caused Iuile to stop sweeping, and blush in embarrassment before she lied, *"Of course not!"*

"Then that settles it", said Mairead. *"The last thing I want is for you to make the same mistake I almost made by putting courtship off. It's also obvious that you like Niall anyway since you preferred to ride home with him on his horse, instead of his cousins, Shamus and Shane."*

"That's because they wanted to use me as an excuse to see Eilis", replied Iuile who finally decided to tell her mother who she really loved. *"You know what, fine!"* She put the broom aside before approaching her mother, with her face fully red, and placed her hands on her mother's armchair where she face to face, with difficulty, confessed to her mother, *"I . . . like . . . Bradach."* Upon finishing her words, Iuile hastefully turns around, while covering her face, and takes a few steps away from her mother, in pure embarrassment, upon confessing to her.

Mairead on the other hand, stopped sewing when Iuile got in her face, and expected her daughter to yell at her. After hearing Iuile's confession, she gives a dumbstruck appearance and says, *"Oh Great Dominus, that same idiot who accidentally knocked you off, and spooked, Pixie to chase after your idiot friend? For goodness sake, Iuile, Niall's mother even told me that he cursed up a storm at that fool, who exactly knew that he knocked you over with no care. It also surprised her when Niall got angry as well, for apparently he rarely gets upset. You're lucky that Niall and his cousins were not too far off when it happened."*

This only angered Iuile who turned to her mother and yelled, *"I STILL LOVE HIM!"*

There was only silence in the room, with the only sound coming from Iuile's younger siblings and cousins who were playing outside. Mairead takes a deep breath before saying the cold truth which Iuile chose to ignore at that time, *"Honey, only because you love someone, does not mean they share that same love with you. And Bradach does not love you."* Those words only angered Iuile, who only became madder when her mother said, *"Not to mention that like Niall, you know nothing about him either."*

Another memory of a few years further manifested, and it involved a time when Mairead was passing on knowledge of being a woman, while they were preparing for dinner. Iuile replied to her mother with insecurity, *"But I don't like how I am feeling right now."*

"I know, sweetie", replied Mairead, *"but this is your new normality. But we'll talk more about that later. Right now I need to warn you about certain people who will try to manipulate you through your emotions. The type of people who care very little of your well-being, as their only interest, is their own."*

Iuile's memory then recalls what Niall said earlier, *"Actions speak louder than words, and he obviously does not love you."* It was also followed by, *"I mean come on, if he really loved you, he wouldn't send that cait sith to kill Mr. McBannon."*

Such recollections allowed Iuile to finally realize that Marquis DeGallo does not truly love her. For it is as Niall said, if he did love her, he would not send cait sith to kill her father, nor would he put her and her companions in danger, or try to trick her into killing Eilis. Then horror has befallen Iuile that her father could be killed at any moment, or worse, already dead. All that she has left, is hope that he is still alive long enough for her to save him. Iuile's concern for her father shifts to feeling foolish, for she is now remembering all the obvious signs that Niall always liked her. To times when he always glanced in her direction whenever they passed by, or at school, to times when he checked on her whenever she was alone either crying, injured, or in need of help.

Especially earlier, before entering this nightmare, when she was underneath the tree with Eilis. Niall had done so much for Iuile while acting shy and indifferent, which irritates her as he could have been more compassionate. Iuile also has the realization that like Einri, Niall had never shown any interest in Eilis, and therefore always had eyes on her. This epiphany makes Iuile want to scream at the top of her lungs, as she is furious upon admitting that her mother was right all along. But it also occurs to her, while grinning, that she does not need to tell her mother that she is right.

Even though Iuile is aware of the actual reality, she still does not want to be alone again with Marquis DeGallo, for fear of her emotions. As it then occurs to her that the marquis could possibly, or already have, used his powers to manipulate her emotions. Just like how he may have used his powers to add another lock when she crossed that horrible pit again. So Iuile has come to the decision that for her own safety, from her own emotions, is to trust Niall, and Niall alone, until she at least returns home. For even though Niall had never been as romantic as Marquis DeGallo, or understanding of her feelings like Roisin and Eilis. Niall has been the one risking his life for her and Eilis, tries to honestly comfort her, and most importantly, sees the marquis as he really is.

After promising herself to trust and believe in Niall, Iuile's emotions begin to calm down at a reasonable level. Feeling relief, Iuile decides to run towards the closet door to see if she is really trapped, even if it seems pointless. But she wants to see for herself, just to be sure, and opens the door. Only to find that the tunnel is still there with her saying to herself, "Wait, if the tunnel is still here, then what in the world was Marquis DeGallo talking about?"

"Down here, lass", said a voice that caused Iuile to look down, and see that it was King Tuathal. Fear has overcome Iuile, who is under the impression that she is gazing upon one of Marquis DeGallo's minions. She backs away, without breaking eye contact with the royal fairy, only to trip and fall on her rear. King Tuathal hastefully pleas, while not stepping into the room, "Don't scream! I'm here to help you. I'm King Tuathal, ruler of the Leprechauns of Gleannasi, and I'm a friend of Niall, who is with your friend, Eilis, at the moment.

"I decided to scout ahead, due to your friend bickering with Niall, and managed to catch up with you when you entered this room. It was a good thing, too, that I went on ahead because this tunnel was way longer than we thought. Anyway, I was able to keep this room attached to the tunnel with my magic, which I can only do as long as I'm inside it, where I then begin to ponder on what to do for a while, only for you to suddenly open the door." He then asks her while examining the room, "On that note, where is that scoundrel of this manor?"

After wondering for a moment whether or not King Tuathal can be trusted, Iuile turns her head to the actual exit to the room, and replies, "He left me in here by myself to change." She turns back to face King Tuathal saying, "Not to mention that Eilis starting an argument, is something that she would do."

This has King Tuathal appear very pleased as he said joyfully, "What incredible luck! Come now, I'll explain more as we head back to the others." Iuile is still not sure if she should trust King Tuathal, as he might be another trick sent by Marquis DeGallo. However, she is also aware that she does not have much of a choice, but to trust the fairy.

They begin to travel through the tunnel in the mine cart, that King Tuathal jury-mag while sitting on top of the front bucket, and facing away from Iuile. During the travel back, Iuile explains what had happened before the king showed up to rescue her. When Iuile finishes speaking, King Tuathal begins to explain to her where he was the whole time. With him ending his side of the story by saying, "I also realized that the umbra arachne would slow them down further. So I cast a nasty hex as I snuck passed her due to the fact that I did not want to lose track of you. Because only Dominus would had known what that monstrous host would have done to you if left alone for, too, long.

"As for Niall and Elise, I knew that Niall should not have any problems with that spider-beast, thanks to his accomplishments that he made this night, though the spell I cast on her was just to ensure his, and your friend's, safety." The king starts to mumble to himself, "Though I probably should have told him where I was going now that I think about it." He then continues in his normal voice, "Anyway, it is lucky for us that fool decided to leave you all alone, and thinks that this tunnel to the dressing room had closed up. I can only imagine how furious he will be when he finds out that you have left."

Starting to feel trusting with King Tuathal, Iuile asked him, "That sounds good, but wouldn't he know where we will be at?"

"Not a chance", said King Tuathal, "because he knows that he will have to wait a long time for you to change. Giving us plenty of time, thanks to this speedy cart, to easily return to the others. Then I can easily open up another door somewhere else, but only inside

The Ram and Ewe's Quest for the Lost Lambs

Diavolo Mansion. So when we reach Niall and Eilis, I'll summon a door to our location, and he'll be none the wiser."

As they ride through the tunnel, Iuile begins to recall the recent moments of King Tuathal hiding in Niall's satchel. From Niall's second rescue, to Einri's betrayal, to something that made her glow bright red to where she decides to ask the king, "Umm, did you hear my conversation with Niall in the room with the fireplace?"

"Sorry, lass", said King Tuathal with guilt. He then continues while avoiding to mention his involvement with their conversation, "Normally I would mind my own business in those situations. But I couldn't, and you shouldn't be upset with Niall, because I told him not to speak a word about my presence at the time." The royal leprechaun then remembers something, turns to face Iuile, and says to her, "I had however, heard from one of my retainers about your conversations with Niall, back in town."

This agitated Iuile who becomes embarrassed, due to the invasion of her privacy, and threateningly said, "You little cretin, how dare you spy on me. I have half a mind to . . . ."

The mine cart suddenly comes to a complete stop, with no motion affecting Iuile and King Tuathal. This is followed by the tunnel filling itself with fog and thunder as King Tuathal says with anger, "How DARE YOU talk to me like that! I, King Tuathal of the Little People of Gleannasi, have half a mind myself, to curse your entire family with plagues and misfortunes for generations, for such disrespect! For I can do things much worse than what Marquis DeGallo has done to you!"

A new level of terror has filled Iuile, a horror one receives when one crosses the line with a being of great power. Feeling absolute regret for her disrespect, Iuile said, "I'm so sorry! Please understand that I'm just a foolish maiden who felt that she had been trespassed! I'll be more respectful from now on!"

As if the whole thing was an illusion, the thunder fog disappears, with King Tuathal replying causally, "That's all I ask, lass, and fair enough with you being upset. You just need to use better tact next time." His voice becomes low as he continues with malice, "Just don't let it happen again." After having Iuile know that one should respect their elders, King Tuathal has the mine cart return to its original speed while explaining, "As I was saying earlier, from what I was told, you chatter like a woodpecker on a tree." He then mumbles to himself, "Typical for a girl her age to talk too much.

"Anyway", the king continues with Iuile who heard what the king murmur, "it's understandable that you want to talk about your problems with someone, but you need to leave a break in the conversation, in order to see if the recipient wants to give you feedback. Poor Niall knows so little about you to the point where he doesn't know the real you. Then there's you not knowing anything about him, so much so that he could have abandoned you back in the ballroom if it wasn't for Einri."

"Fair enough", replied Iuile with some offense with what King Tuathal said, and chose to be compliant with his advice, since he does have a point after everything that had happened. That, and she wishes to avoid offending the royal fairy again.

"It will also be a good way to repay him after everything he has done for you tonight", replied King Tuathal, "by just getting to properly know each other for a change." The king then notices that they are approaching a wall of webs, and stops the cart with his magic. He quickly stands up and examines the webs while saying to Iuile, "We walk from here, as it appears that Niall and Eilis have not reached the arachne yet. I'll just have to handle her myself since I am no longer in a hurry . . . ." He trails off upon seeing Iuile still sitting down while covering her face with her arms, which are on top of her knees.

"Oh my goodness!" Iuile thought to herself while being as red as a tomato, *"That would be an actual date! And what if I also decide to show him my appreciation with a kiss?!"* The thought of

showing such affection to Niall, causes her to squeal with excitement and embarrassment.

"Now's not the time for this", said King Tuathal. "We need to keep moving and meet up with Niall and Eilis. Those words made Iuile realize that he was right, for now is really not the time to feel hopeful. After taking a deep breath to calm down, Iuile gets up and climbs out of the bucket. This is unexpected to the king as he quietly says to himself, "Quickly got her act together, lass is more mature than I thought." When King Tuathal jumps off the cart, he begins to use his magic to cut through the silk. They continue to travel through the mine tunnel on foot while moving at a slow pace, and being alert of their surroundings. This is because they have no idea when or where the umbra arachne will appear, due to them not knowing that she has already been slain.

During this time, Iuile worries about losing control of her life, and asks with concern, "What would you do if things don't work out between me and Niall . . . Your Majesty?"

"If it's never meant to be, then it's never meant to be", said King Tuathal with no care in the world. "As long as you give him a chance, I'm satisfied, even if things don't work out." This gives Iuile relief that she still has free will in her life while the king continues, "You're still young and have time to find someone, just don't waste too much time by playing around, or you'll eternally regret it. There are words for women like that."

"Several words, actually", reply Iuile who is familiar with such phrases. "With crazy cat lady being one of them."

"Or a weird, perverted, old lady that lives in a cabin with a terrier at the north end of the glade", said King Tuathal who hastefully stopped. This has Iuile stopping as well, while being befuddled by the sudden halt, as the leprechaun king looks up and yells, "I know you heard me, Granny Yueng! I may not know where you are at, but I know you're watching us right now by immoral means. You old, hypocritical, ninny."

"Wait a moment", said Iuile with a geyser of hope, "Granny Yueng is watching us right now?" She then begins to say to the ceiling, "Granny Yueng! It's me, Iuile McBannon! My father is deadly ill and endanger of being killed by a cait sith! Please return to Arvann and save him, I beg of you!" Iuile stands in place, with her eyes watery, and wonders if her pleas have come through before getting herself together, and turns to King Tuathal to ask, "Do you think she heard me?"

Not wanting to disappoint Iuile, as Granny Yueng will now have to make a three-day journey back, King Tuathal replies, "I'm sure she did, lass. Let's hope that she will return to your father in time." For in case you do not know, King Tuathal is only updated on current events within his realm on a daily basis. Such as her uncle and the others already making a pointless attempt to chase after the wizardess. Anything beyond that will only reach his ears within days, or weeks. So King Tuathal decides to advise Iuile to continue their travel, and not get her more hopeful of what he already knows, as even he has his doubts on Donal's survival rate.

Upon tearing the next wall of webs, they found, to their surprise, the umbra arachne's corpse. And not too far from the monster's body, are Niall and Eilis who are still trapped in the cage, making King Tuathal ask, "By the Almighty, what happened here?"

"Ask Miss I-Don't-Need-To-Do-What-You-Say", said Niall sarcastically, while leaning forward with his face pressed between the bars of the cage, and making Eilis, who is holding the bars and blushing out of embarrassment, gives him a menacing glare. Iuile's heart begins to flutter like never before upon seeing Niall, but is too shy to speak even a single word to him as he asks King Tuathal, "We heard you yelling about the old hag. Is she around?"

"Ha", laughed King Tuathal, "she doesn't have the courage to be here. Just gazing at us in her crystal ball."

"That stupid thing where she can only communicate with those that possess their own crystal ball, or a magic mirror", said Eilis.

She then continues with mockery, "Because it's black magic to look into the past, future, or some stupid . . . ." The sudden pause from Eilis is caused upon seeing Iuile with her arms folded and appearing very displeased.

While still giving Eilis a nasty stink-eye, Iuile asks her, "You ignore a guy for telling you not to do something again, didn't you?"

"No I didn't", Eilis lied, while feeling guilty upon Iuile figuring out what had happened. "He just didn't say that there was a trap on the ground."

"This sounds very similar to the time that you didn't actually start that stampede", replied Iuile. "By, what was it? Ignoring your eldest brother's warning by letting that stray dog you found run after the herd." Iuile decides to continue in a mocking tone, "Oh please, Padraic, there's no way that a herd of cows would panic from her. How can they, when they are already used to our other dogs . . . why is she biting that calf?"

"Fine, you made your point", said Eilis with a mixture of annoyance and embarrassment. All the while rubbing her buttocks, due to recalling her mother's punishment for the damages she caused. "Now get us out of here!"

"There should be a mechanism nearby", said King Tuathal as he examined the tunnel, and spotted a hole in the wall. He asks Iuile to inspect it and leaps onto her shoulder where they both look inside it. "There it is, only big enough for a hand to reach in there."

"What about the flames that are blocking it?" Iuile questioned before continuing, "It's bad enough that I had to walk through a pool of roaches."

"Well then", said Niall as he continued sarcastically, "you can either risk injury to save us, or you can leave us here to save yourself. To which we'll just sit here, and starve long enough before I decide to go cannibal on Eilis."

Appearing as if Eilis had just woken up, she replied with confusion, "Wait, what?"

"Or", said King Tuathal while giving Niall an amused grin, "I can put the flames out with my magic, that way Iuile can pull the lever with no harm coming to her."

"That's even better", said Niall. "Dominus knows how badly Eilis would've tasted."

A nerve has stricken Eilis who replies in anger, "EXCUSE ME!!!"

CHAPTER 25

Fire and Pitchforks

When Iuile and her party exit the mine tunnel, and into one of the mansion's wings, Niall goes ahead to lead the way down the hallway towards the stairs while saying, "I recognize this area when I was first searching for you two. We're on the third floor, north wing."

This is followed by Eilis who is puzzled by their surroundings as she questions, "Third floor? This looks nothing like the third floor", she then asks the leprechaun king who was riding on Niall's shoulder, "and why didn't you send us to the first floor, King Tuathal?"

"One question at a time, lass", replies King Tuathal. "As for why I brought us into this floor, is because this isn't my type of magic. In order to get us out of that tunnel as quickly as possible, was to just pick a random spot, and hope for the best. With luck, he'll examine that tunnel before searching the mansion for us." We ought to be grateful that it sent us to the third floor, and not the fourth floor. Just one less flight of stairs to deal with before escaping."

"Wait, what do you mean by 'fourth floor'?" Ask Iuile as they enter the south wing, "Eilis and I only saw three stories when we came to this mansion. How can there be four?"

Dumbstruck that Iuile and Eilis are questioning this now, Niall asks them, "You didn't hear me mention about this earlier?"

"I thought that you made a mistake", replied Iuile.

Iuile's response has stupefied Niall to the point of asking, "Did you not even notice when we first went down the stairs, that we went down an extra flight upon reaching the second floor?"

"Yeah", said Eilis who, along with Iuile, started to feel embarrassed, "we clearly weren't paying attention."

The girls' lack of awareness has caused Niall to make a noise of annoyance as they reach the stairway. As they begin their descent, Niall says to them, "Anyway, in case you also didn't notice", Eilis begins to feel that she is being insulted, while Iuile blushes even redder, "there is also the tunnel that should not physically exist in this mansion, as it, and the room above it, should have entered the ballroom, which they didn't. Or how about falling from the second floor, into the second floor again?! This place apparently isn't normal, as I even entered a room earlier with a lake and waterfall that actually covers, at least, the entire mansion's wing!"

When Niall finishes speaking, they reach the bottom of the stairs to the second floor where King Tuathal signals them to halt on the stairway, and for them to be quiet. He whispers to them to wait, and scouts ahead to examine if the south wing's second floor is all clear. While they wait, they hear a commotion from the foyer that causes Iuile to ask in a low voice, "What is going on over there?"

"We'll find out soon enough", said King Tuathal upon returning, "because the coast is clear, let's travel through the south wing with caution." They quickly and quietly, without running, traverse the south wing to reach the balcony and the stairs of the center wing.

"That makes no sense about the structure of this mansion", Eilis whispered about their early conversation.

"All part of the host's dark powers", said King Tuathal who appeared on top of Niall's shoulder, causing Eilis to be spooked enough from his sudden appearance that she stopped for a moment before recovering herself to catch up. "Though I am more concerned of what will happen to me and my people since that devilish trickster now knows that I have been aiding you."

This makes Niall feel worried for the king and his people, causing him to ask, "What will you do once we escape?"

"I have no choice but to prepare my people for war", said King Tuathal. "But before that, there's the matter of the lassies' . . . ." The king trails off from saying 'curse', due to the ruckus, and asks with irritation, "What on Atlast is all that commotion?"

When they reach the balcony of the center wing, they look down to the foyer to find a mob of people from their own town with fire, pitchforks, swords, axes, scythes, bows with arrows, and rifles, as they thoroughly search the first floor. A group of them are trying to break open the doors to the ballroom with a wardrobe, with a few young teens circling the dead skog harpy that Niall killed earlier, with one of them poking the corpse with the butt-end of his pitchfork. King Tuathal immediately disappears, in order to avoid trouble from the townspeople, as Iuile and her party dash down the stairs, while yelling for them to stop. When they reach the bottom of the steps, Niall yells out, "There's a horde of monsters locked in there!"

Followed by Eilis yelling, "The last thing we need is for you to accidentally release them!" The townspeople trying to break through the ballroom doors stop upon hearing this, and back away from the doors after dropping the wardrobe, which crumbled to pieces.

Appearing from the mob are Mairead and a blonde-haired, bearded, man, causing Iuile to say, "Mom! What are you doing here?"

Mairead's reply was interrupted by Eilis who yelled, "Papa!" Where she then ran towards the bearded man.

Surprise to see what his daughter is wearing, Eilis' father questions, "Peachy pie? Is that really you?" When Eilis reaches him, he examines her for a moment before hugging her while saying, "It is you! I'm so glad that you're safe, thank the Almighty." They were then surrounded by Eilis' male kin, who were thankful that she was safe.

"A fairy appeared at the clinic and said that you were tricked into having it kill your father, who is safe by the way", replied Mairead while walking towards her daughter. Mairead's words give Iuile a sigh of relief that her father is safe while ignoring Eilis and her family's joyful reunion. When Mairead is standing in front of Iuile, she continues her story, "Upon hearing this, and taken care of that foul creature, I went to Lord O'Ceallachain's manor to ask him to gather a mob.

"To my surprise, he was already in the middle of doing that, as apparently his son never returned home from Killy Ri Forest. He therefore sent us over here without him. While the mob was still being gathered, with the help of your brothers, uncles, and other kin, Dermot and Aileen found out that Eilis was missing. To which I informed them that she might have gone with you to this cursed mansion, since that cait sith mentioned that you came here with friends. We ended up splitting up into two groups, one to head straight to Diavolo Mansion for you and Eilis, while the second stayed in Killy Ri, in case Einri was not with you."

When Eilis heard that Mairead informed both of the parents of her possible whereabouts and finished speaking, she asked her father, "Mama knows about this?"

"I'm afraid so", said Dermot who appeared upset for what was in store for his daughter, while twiddling his thumbs. "Last thing I heard from your mom before heading out is, 'I raised that ungrateful child better than that.'" This has Eilis utterly horrified of what is in store for her once she returns home.

Wanting to know the truth about the cause of this mad journey, Mairead asks her daughter, "Did you free willingly come here, and dragged Niall and Eilis with you?"

While glancing down, Iuile begins to fidget with her skirt, as she knows that she is in serious trouble with her mother. She also knows that she cannot lie to her mother in this situation, as Mairead will see right through it. So Iuile prepared for the worst, and honestly replied, "I did."

This shocked Mairead for a split second before asking, "Why?"

"Because Dad is deadly ill", Iuile burst out. "I thought that it was worth the risk if it was to save his life"

"Even with good intentions", replied Mairead while trying to maintain her emotions, "you should never make a deal with the devil, you foolish . . . ." She decides to pause, and take a deep breath in order to calm down before continuing, "Did you forget that Granny Yueng might be able to treat his illness?"

"But she had left for Amelon days ago, remember", replied Iuile. "It'll take too long to bring her back!"

"Against all odds", said Mairead, "your Uncle Garvan, with his eldest sons and your brother, Gearoid, dash after Granny Yueng on their horses with the hope of catching up to her. With your brother snatching Roibeard's horse, Glory, with him. They managed to find Granny Yueng's carriage broken down in Dun Mulla Wood, which forced her to go farther down east to a nearby town, Callard, to receive aid. When they finally reached her, they found that she left a trail of burnt carcasses of orcs, wolves, and a dubhar-chu running by them while dragging his buttocks on the ground.

"Gearoid brought Granny Yueng back to Arvann on Glory, while your uncle and cousins stayed behind to repair her carriage. Gearoid came by the clinic an hour before midnight to drop Granny Yueng, who is now working overtime after your father had gotten himself worked up when he found out that you were here. Anyway, I told Gearoid to go home and get a good night's rest, while I continue to stay at the clinic and care for your father. A night's rest that he is unable to have when he found out what happened to you."

"Wait", said Iuile, "what do you mean by, 'continue to stay at the clinic'? Didn't you come home with us?"

"Ohhh, I knew that you didn't notice that I never returned home with you", said Mairead with frustration. "I stayed behind to look after your father. Why do you think Roibeard and Raicheal came home with you and your siblings and stayed the night? Or that Gearoid was nowhere to be found at the clinic? Because it turns out that he left without saying anything when he found out that Garvan was heading after Granny Yueng.

"Something that I knew nothing about until after you, your siblings, and your nieces, left when Caitriona decided to inform me that Gearoid was with her husband, and why that is. I then told her to inform Roibeard about this, along with everyone else, as soon as she returned to the ranch. Because I wanted everyone to pray for their success in catching up with Granny Yueng. With the only exception is you, since you decided to go to bed early. Which apparently it turned out that you secretly left the house."

This surprised Iuile for a moment, before realizing that the reason she did not notice any of this, was because she was too distressed on her father's fate. This has led her to focus on when and how to sneak out of the house, and whether or not she should undergo such a perilous journey alone. With Roibeard and his family having dinner with them, was something that they sometimes did. Eilis on the other hand, has her right eye twitching due to the irritation that she almost got killed on multiple occasions for no reason, followed by being in serious trouble with her family, causing a sudden urge to murder a dear friend. However, she also realizes that it is divine punishment for the number of times she had almost gotten Iuile killed, or in serious trouble, due to her own shenanigans. So Eilis decides to try to let this one go and waits silently to see how Iuile will respond to her mother.

Except that Iuile is utterly speechless because she has no words to express the horrible mistake she has made, other than to say, "I . . . I didn't notice that Gearoid was missing, or that you never returned home with us."

This seems to be the final straw that made Mairead slap Iuile hard enough to leave a mark saying, "That's for being foolish, and making me devastatingly worried." Mairead slapped Iuile a second time (followed by a whistling sound coming from someone), and said with tears in her eyes, "That's for endangering your friends." As she attempts a third slap, Iuile closes her eyes with tears already in them after the first slap. Only to instead feel the warm embrace of her mother's hug. "This is for being safe, and in one piece." The warm embrace from her mother, who is holding her daughter tightly with joy, causes Iuile to break out crying, and return the affection.

The other townsfolk stood and watched with joy that everything had gone well, and no serious injury had come to anyone. When Iuile and Mairead finish hugging, one of the townsfolk says, "It's good that Niall and the girls are safe, but what about Einri? Is he in here, or back in the forest?"

"That's a good question", said Mairead who was facing the townsfolk. After wiping her eyes, she turned her attention to Iuile and asked, "Did you by any chance see Einri in the forest while you were on your way to this mansion?"

"Well . . . yes", reply Iuile who is feeling guilty, where Eilis on the other hand, begins to scream internally while keeping a straight face. "The short story is, that during all the chaos, and Einri's own cowardliness, he was teleported to Amelon, in Orge Street, as a sick joke."

To Iuile's amazement, Mairead did not appear upset. Instead, she just smiled and brushed the side of Iuile's hair while saying, "Well, hopefully, the Almighty will just allow him to get the beating he deserves, with only his life to spare." Iuile gives a soft giggle as her mother leads her towards the entrance, along with Eilis and her family, while telling her with a smile, "Next time have faith, and accept the will of Dominus Deus like your father said. Now let's join your uncles, brothers, and cousins, who are looking around the outside of the mansion. You also be sure to apologize to Gearoid, who refused to stay back and rest while you were in danger."

"Yes ma'am", replied Iuile with sincerity, for she is eternally grateful that her father is still alive and well. Yet slightly worried of what Gearoid is going to do to her when he gets his hands on her.

As Iuile and them head towards the exit, one of the townsfolk said, "Orge Street? Oh boy, Lord O'Ceallachain is going to demand someone's hide for this."

"We'll just blame it on the village idiot like we usually do", said a farmer.

"Sounds like another day in pig filth for Uilly", said another farmer.

"Rather pointless since he's starting to get used to it", said the tailor.

"Used to it", said the banker, "more like that blasted fool enjoys rolling in it."

"By the way", said Mairead with curiosity as they approached the front doors, "do you mind explaining to me why you're dressed like you're ready to be an escort to a night on the town?" Before Iuile could answer, both she and Eilis clasp the back of their neck, due to the sharp pain coming from it, followed by falling to their knees when they are only a few feet from the doors. Horrified of her daughter's torment, Mairead asks Iuile with concern, "What's wrong?!" Follow by the occurrence of the real danger, "Oh drat, we forgot about Marquis DeGallo!"

"Now you're aware of my existence", said Marquis DeGallo who is at the top of the stairs, spinning his cane with his right hand, while his other hand has him leaning on the stairway's newel cap. "Such a wonderful reunion together. Too bad the mood is ruined thanks to the Sacrificial Mark I placed on them. For you see", he stops spinning his cane and points at Iuile, followed by Eilis, saying, "I own these two, and as long as they have that mark", he then tosses his cane to his left hand, and snaps his fingers, causing both Iuile and Eilis to appear hovering next to him, "they can never leave my mansion. Even if you drag them out, the pain will be severe enough to kill them." When Marquis DeGallo finishes speaking, he begins to give a maniacal laugh.

Niall immediately draws his bow, along with the other citizens of Arvann, who either bring their bows or rifles, and take aim. Only for Mairead to instantly halt them by yelling, "Put those down! He might use my daughter and Eilis as shields!"

"Oh my", said Marquis DeGallo, "one of you has a brain. Well, no matter." He points at Niall saying, "My offer still stands, Foolish Knight. Meet me on the fifth floor. As for the rest of you maggots", his tone becomes threatening, and his appearance slightly demonic, "my minions will have you, pay, for destroying my home!" As soon as he finishes speaking, he immediately disappears with the girls, who both beg to be saved.

CHAPTER 26

The Fifth Floor

Before Marquis DeGallo appeared to kidnap Iuile and Eilis, Niall was talking to his two elder brothers (while Iuile and Eilis were talking to their own individual parents). The O'Faolan brothers do appear somewhat similar to each other, as they even possess the exact same hair color, right down to the tone. However, the difference between the brothers' appearance is obvious with attention to detail. Sadly, people not related to them manage to get Niall and his brothers, older or younger that are close to age, confused when they see them separately as they seem to look alike to them (including the assumption that one of them is their father on rare occasions).

They do, however, have different eye colors as the eldest has hazel, while the next is brown. They inform Niall that their father is leading a search party, with some of their relatives, in Killy Ri Forest, as they believe that Niall is still in the tainted place. With a second search party, who is led by Dermot, heads towards the mansion with the rest of Niall's kin. With Niall himself informing them why he was in the mansion, along with his accomplishments, minus the parts involving King Tuathal for the time being.

"Good Dominus, none of us would think that you had the courage to come here", said the eldest.

"Normally I wouldn't, Adhanh", said Niall who sounded annoyed. "But I couldn't let them get spirited away by doing nothing." His eyes wander to where Eilis is with her family, and notices that her brothers and cousins are teasing her, and smacking the back of her head when Dermot and her uncles are not looking. With Eilis herself getting angry and upset by their actions, followed by attempts to slap them herself, without her father noticing. They do so in such a manner, that it appears rather comical to anyone who is watching them.

"Or", said the second eldest with a taunting tone, "you have a crush on one of them."

The thought of his brothers teasing him for liking a girl agitates Niall to the point where he replies, "Slaine, how about you shove your kricker in a hornet's nest."

"Oh, how original", replied Slaine with sarcasm. "I'm sure some of our cousins would love to hear that one, after they finish looking around the outside of the mansion, of course."

"Knock it off, Slaine", said Adhanh. He then turns to Niall to say, "But with all seriousness, we're glad to hear that you gave that dastard a good licking for what he did to Caolan. Even if you couldn't kill him. I'm sure he is smiling in Heaven from all that you had accomplished tonight."

Niall chose to be silent, as he does not want to reply due to a certain knowledge that he received from King Tuathal. Knowledge that is not known to everyone in his town, and beyond, including his clan. For such information would be unbearable for his family to know, and is tearing him up. Niall's brothers notice that something is wrong, and attempt to ask what is bothering him. Only to be interrupted by a commotion that made the three brothers turn to where Iuile is, and realize that her mother slapped her.

"Boy, Mrs. McBannon is flaming water right now", said Slaine as they watched Iuile get slapped for the second time, causing him to whistle. "Oh yeah, flaming water."

"I'm going for; none of our business", said Niall as he knows that getting involved would make things worse.

"Don't blame her given that she endangered the entire town to rescue her and Eilis", said Adhanh as Iuile was then hugged by her mother.

The O'Faolan brothers watch in silence for a moment, before Slaine decides to say, "Would've been nice if it was Iuile and Eilis hugging after finally being safe." Upon finishing his comment, Adhanh immediately smacks the back of his brother's head, with Niall shaking his head, and rolling his eyes over his married brother blurting out pointless nonsense again.

"Toireasa would hang you for that", said Adhanh.

"No crapshoot", replies Slaine. "Why do you think I say things like that when she isn't around."

Wanting to put in his two zincs over Slaine's choice of words, Niall attempts to reply, only to go silent when a townsfolk questions Einri's whereabouts. Upon hearing Einri's fate from Iuile, Niall's brothers turn to him with Adhanh asking, "Is that true?"

"Pretty much", replied Niall. "But with all seriousness, that jackass had what's coming to him." His brothers agreed, along with other townspeople who were more curious of Niall's tale, than Iuile's. "Now that I think about it, did someone in the Killy Ri Expedition bring any type of gold?"

"Not sure about everyone", replied Slaine. "But Mr. Smyth is with them, and he always wears his golden clover pendant. Why?"

"That's good to hear", said Niall before replying to his brother's curiosity, "because there is a bastoir dullahan that almost got me in Killy Ri Forest."

This shocks his brothers, along with the other townsfolk, with Slaine saying, "Good grace of all that is holy!"

"My thoughts exactly", said Adhanh. "Dominus Deus is really with you tonight."

"That's it", said Slaine, "I'm taking church more seriously from now on."

When Slaine finishes speaking, Niall notices that Mairead, Iuile, Eilis, and her kin, are heading toward the front entrance. It then dawns on Niall who asks his brothers, "Now that I think about it, didn't anyone notice the monsters through the ballroom windows before coming in here?"

"We would if it weren't for the drapes", said Adhanh.

"Oh, crud!" Said Niall calmly as he realized something else, "We forgot about the curse that dastard placed on them!"

"Ah, crapshoot", said Slaine with annoyance, "don't you dare tell me that this isn't over yet."

The O'Faolan brothers then notice Iuile and Eilis falling to their knees in pain. After Marquis DeGallo disappears with Iuile and Eilis as his captives once more, Niall's only response is, "Well, we certainly walked into that like Uilly walked into a cave full of hungry wolves, just so he can pet them."

"I still don't understand how he survived that with only losing a pinky toe", said Adhanh.

"I still don't understand his fascination with sheep", said Slaine.

"Fifth floor?" Whisper King Tuathal who appeared on Niall's shoulder, without his brothers noticing since he is behind them. "There's no fifth floor!" Niall turns and sees that the king has taken the form of a raven. "No worries about our conversation, as no one is paying any attention to us to think twice. Nor do I want to get into another game of 'free wishes from the fairy with a side order of a flaming kricker', with your danglewangle brothers."

This was not what was on Niall's mind, who decided to ask the king in a soft voice, "Why didn't you take that form before?"

"Because that sick demon would have figured me out on the spot", whispered King Tuathal.

"Ah", is the only thing Niall said as he turned back to where Marquis DeGallo was originally standing. He then replies to King Tuathal's question about the fifth floor with another question, in his normal volume, "I wonder if that scuttle that I saw a while back is what he was talking about?"

Overhearing Niall's words while approaching him and his brothers, with the hope that he knows where their daughters are taken, Mairead asks with Dermot right behind her, "What is this scuttle you speak of?"

The raven flies off as Niall turns to her and replies, "A scuttle, an opening in the ceiling. I saw one when I was on the fourth floor, it was covered of course. I only knew what it was due to the time when Dad sent me, and these two lunkheads, to Lord O'Ceallachain's manor to help him get rid of a rodent infestation that was in his attic."

"Lunkheads, is it", said Slaine who began to crack his knuckles.

"Knock it off, Slaine", said Mairead with a strict, yet threatening, tone.

"Yes ma'am", replied Slaine who wishes to not wake a hibernating mama bear.

Satisfied that Slaine chose the correct move, Mairead turns to Niall and asks him, "Take me to this fifth floor that dastard mentioned."

"Okay, time out", said Adhanh. "What fifth floor? This mansion only has three stories, and where did that raven come from?"

"Now Mairead", said Dermot who cuts in, for he has become concerned on what Mairead is planning to do. "Donal will never forgive me if something happens to you. I, along with several others, will go with Niall while . . . ." He is immediately cut off by the ballroom doors bursting open.

"Such an excellent harvest that has to bestow upon us", said a male maru elf. "Let's take advantage of this wicked moment, for which the Great Marquis DeGallo has given us, before unlocking the doors, and murdering the deadnights out of them!"

"Ohhh, I've been waiting for some blood and guts all night!" Said a Romalian lamia.

"Not us", said a beathair. "We're not dumb enough to get into a fight when it's this close to sunrise!" She quickly dashes off towards the entrance, along with the rest of the dallions, and bursts through the front doors where they disappear into the darkness that will soon be no more.

The townspeople watch with the horde, who were dumbstruck from the abandonment of their allies, towards the entrance. They then turn and glance at each other for a moment, before the townspeople decide in unison to raise their range weaponry, and fire at the remaining monstrous creatures. The townspeople fired all their ammo that had taken the life of half the horde, before drawing their blades, or pitchforks, that are made of iron (and if not, then blades made from other metals while pulling out a piece of iron that they brought from home) when they ran out of ammunition, and clash with the horde. But before the battle collided, many of the fairies immediately backed away and made a run for it with the dallions due to their fear of iron. The departure of the dallions, followed by the fairies, drew the attention of the rest of the townsfolk who were still outside and came rushing into their neighbors' aid.

As Niall attempts to draw his sword, after putting on his iron ring that he took off earlier, Mairead grabs his arm and dragged him up the stairs. When they reach the second floor, Mairead brings Niall ahead of her and says, "Well go on, lead the way."

Stupefy by Mairead's choice to face Marquis DeGallo with just the two of them, caused Niall to reply, "But what about my brothers and . . . ."

"They'll be fine", said Mairead cutting Niall off. "We shouldn't waste any more time dealing with small fry when Iuile, and her idiot friend, are still in danger."

Facing Marquis DeGallo with just the two of them is a foolish move, even with the aid of King Tuathal, whom Niall has noticed that he is flying over them. However, Niall realizes that she is right, especially since numbers will not mean much after everything he has been through, and decides to reply, "Good point. Let's go."

While they head towards the south wing, Mairead asks, "Can you explain to me what exactly happened?" When Mairead finished her question, a mask flew into the left side of her face.

This causes Niall to turn to her and see the mask, where he then looks down the balcony and asks, "Where did that sheep mask come from?"

Upon removing and examining the mask, Mairead replies, "It's a ewe mask", she then tosses it over while saying to Niall, "and let's not lose focus."

"Right", replied Niall who continued towards the south wing, with the Columbina ewe mask falling into a gorigo's mouth, causing it to choke to death.

Mairead once again asks Niall to explain what had happened. When Niall attempts to reply, he is instantly cut off by Slaine, who yells at him while fighting the horde, "You better claim your lucky love, little brother!" This was followed by Adhanh howling like a wolf, causing Niall to walk away with a facepalm, due to the nerve that they are acting in such a manner with Iuile's mother right behind him.

"Sorry about those idiots", said Niall while thinking up ways to get back at his brothers. Mairead only stares at his brothers and shakes her head while giving a smirk of amusement. Because she knows full well that if her husband was here, and heard them, he would have dragged and pushed them down a hill in a barrel, after beating the tar out of them. When they enter the south wing, Niall says while staying alert, "Anyway, while I was hunting in the forest, Einri came out of nowhere and scared my buck . . . ."

Niall recalls everything that he is aware of, in a short summary, while not including his aid from King Tuathal, or his battles as he deems them not important for the time being. He did so while trying to figure out how to get King Tuathal to help them get through the scuttle without Mairead knowing. As he fears that Mairead might try to capture the royal highness for his wishes, like Eilis, and apparently his older brothers, tried to do. When Niall finishes his perspective of what had happened, they reach the fourth floor of the south wing.

When they walk down the hallway, Mairead asks Niall while feeling eerie due to an extra story, "What about this so-called, Sacrificial Mark?"

"I haven't seen it", Niall said honestly. "They must have had it covered." Niall recalls when Einri reached around his neck while Marquis DeGallo teased him about his freedom. Followed by when Iuile and Eilis reached for the back of their necks the moment they were in pain. "From what had happened so far, I'm betting it is behind their necks." Niall suddenly feels guilty as he continues without giving full details, "Though to be honest, I heard that they were cursed to be sacrificed earlier. I just forgot about it due to all the chaos we had been through. Sorry Mrs. McBannon, I should have remembered."

"They should have remembered it themselves", said Mairead who is not upset by Niall's confession. "Anyway, what's done is done, and even if you did remember, chances are that the results would still be the same. So there is no need to beat yourself up, Niall." This made Niall feel relieved as Mairead glanced up and asked, "Now that we got that out of the way, what is the deal with that raven circling over us?"

While Niall tries to think of an explanation, King Tuathal lands his raven form on Niall's shoulder, and appears in his true form to Mairead saying, "It is I, King Tuathal of Gleannasi."

"Oh", said Mairead who appears unfazed from seeing King Tuathal, "it's you again."

This surprised Niall who decided to ask her while removing his iron ring, "You two are already acquainted? Does that mean that you don't view them as demons?"

"Oh they're demons alright", replied Mairead as they entered the north wing. "Not those that serve the Princes of Darkness, mind you, but the kind that likes to play shenanigans. I recall Donal chased one down, in order to wish for a big house for us, a couple of decades ago. Fool fell off a cliff after a failed attempt to catch him, your liege. Only for your servant, that Donal was trying to catch, to use his magic to save him, and apologize, as he didn't mean for that to happen."

"Ah, yes", said King Tuathal, "I remember Clancy telling me about that. Still feels guilty about it. We, the Leprechauns of Gleannasi that is, like to play tricks on you. But not in a way that would endanger you. Unlike some of the other leprechaun clans who wish to do you harm for pleasure, or paranoia from losing their treasure. We're one of the clans that like to keep things lively, in a pacifist way. Unless you deserve the bad karma."

"Here it is", said Niall as he pointed towards the ceiling. He turns to his shoulder where King Tuathal resides, and asks him, "Any way to get us up there, Your Majesty?"

"Of course I do", said King Tuathal who jumped down, and cast a spell that moved the plywood that was covering the scuttle. He then creates a staircase made of magical energy, with rainbow colors, to allow them to walk up to the fifth floor.

Deciding to climb the prism stairway first, Niall leads the way with his sword ready as Mairead follows him from behind. King Tuathal decides to ride on Mairead's shoulder where she asks the royal fairy, "I gather that you have been aiding Niall this whole time?"

"That I have", replies King Tuathal, "though now is not the time to explain why."

"I understand, given the circumstances", said Mairead who began to feel terrified. "What I would like to know, is if the reason you hadn't rescued my daughter, and her idiot friend, yourself, is because he is more powerful than you."

"I'm ashamed to say that it is true", replies King Tuathal as he feels frustrated over his own weakness.

When they reach the top of the steps, they enter the same room where Iuile, Eilis, and Einri played against Marquis DeGallo. The twisted host happens to be sitting in his usual chair, and shuffling his cards saying, "Welcome to my penthouse floor. You are only allowed to play my game, by betting your souls. For it is the only way to win the girls back."

CHAPTER 27

The Stakes

"What's the game?" Mairead asks casually.

"That would be Joker", replied Marquis DeGallo, while giving a devilish smirk.

This stuns Niall, for he had no idea that Mairead would dare accept the marquis' challenge, and ask her, "What are you doing?"

"I agree", said King Tuathal who was shocked himself. "What in the world are you doing?"

"Saving my foolish daughter and her idiotic friend", replied Mairead without glancing at King Tuathal and Niall. She begins to walk toward Marquis DeGallo, while he is explaining the rules of Joker, where she then sits down across from him with a disinterested appearance in what he has to say. When Marquis DeGallo finishes speaking, she asks him, "So I'm betting my soul, for both my daughter, Iuile, and her friend, Eilis?"

"My dear", said Marquis DeGallo, "I need more than your soul if you want both of them."

After jumping off from Mairead's shoulder, and onto the table, King Tuathal asks, "Why would it matter since you'll win anyway?"

"Your trickery won't work on me", said Marquis DeGallo casually. "If you want them both, then you'll need to even the payment." He turns his attention to Niall who has already drawn his blade, and circles around the table where the marquis says to him, "Oh come now, boy. You should know by now that mortal weapons cannot kill me.

"Not to mention that you have no idea where the girls are." Marquis DeGallo snaps his fingers to make Niall's sword disappear from his hands, followed by having the scuttle close by a steel cover, instead of plywood, that is fused to the wood around it. "And that's to make sure you won't go wandering off." He begins to ask Niall in a friendly manner, "Now, will you care to join us for the other?"

"He will not", replies Mairead who cuts in.

While chuckling, Marquis DeGallo reply, "So you think you could beat me twice for both girls? Come now, let's do this in one go!" The marquis returns his attention to Niall, who stares at him with malice while clenching his fists. "Ah, I thought you look familiar. Did you lose a brother to me?" Niall's wrath intensifies, and begins to slowly approach the table while the marquis carries on mockingly, "Oh how he screams, and beg, while I toy with his life to the point where he starts to question everything", he begins to give off a cruel, and sinister, smile before continuing, "even his faith." After Niall stops in front of the table, and next to Mairead, the marquis asks as if he is doing Niall a favor, "But I'll tell you what, if you beat me, not only will I let the one you love go, but I will bring your brother back to life."

"How about I just offer this instead", said Niall as he pulled out the radiant cut jewel, and placed it on the table.

Upon seeing the jewel, both Marquis DeGallo and Mairead are stunned, as they both recognize that it is no ordinary jewel, causing Mairead to ask, "Is that what I think it is? Mystal?"

This made Niall curious about what Mairead knew about the jewel, and asked her, "What's that?"

"It's mana in its solid form", said King Tuathal who caused Niall and Mairead to turn to him. "It is normally used on staves or wands as a catalyst to cast spells, and also an amplifier to strengthen them. But those are usually smaller than this one." He continues while slowly glancing at the marquis, "Of course, I learned to use magic without it, along with this foul rat of a trickster, since he was granted the forbidden arts of sorcery."

"Oh come now, King Tuathal, you can insult better than that", replied Marquis DeGallo with a perplexed look. He then decides to ask Niall while still staring at the mystal, "It looks familiar. Where did you get this?"

"I got it from one of the stone golems that I slayed over at the ravine's entrance, by Killy Ri Forest", replied Niall as he noticed a shocking appearance from the marquis.

"Obviously", said King Tuathal. "That's why it is larger than normal, it was made to power a large golem.

"You destroyed both of my golems?!" Reply Marquis DeGallo who, for the first time to Niall, seems genuinely surprised. But his tone hastefully changes to doubt, "That's impossible, there's no way you could succeed in such an impossible feat."

"The impossible he did", said King Tuathal with a smirk on his face as he continued, "you can zip on over there to see for yourself if you like. Of course, after ceasing to exist, and having its source of fuel removed, a golem's body will slowly break apart, and in a stone golem's case, all that is left are scattered rocks."

Astonish by this interesting news has Mairead cut into the conversation, while pretending to know nothing about the fallen golems, and asks, "You mean those boulders in front of the ravine's entrance, that the others and I passed by, used to be golems?"

The idea that Niall truly defeated such dangerous creatures, has Marquis DeGallo say to himself, "Inconceivable." For never did he expect that a simple boy could ever defeat an enormous golem by himself, let alone two. He starts to mumble to himself to where Niall and the others can hear, "Though it would explain how the townsfolk in those numbers got here in one piece." He begins to ponder on how Niall did it, only to decide to find his answer later while presenting a sinister smile.

For Marquis DeGallo knows that Niall will not answer him willingly, and therefore decides to wait patiently till he acquires the 'necessity', to make him talk. "Impressive", Marquise DeGallo said with false praise. "You deserve a wonderful spoil for achieving such a great feat, and since I would like to have it back, so I can avoid unnecessary work, I'll be taking that offer for the other girl. But not for your brother's revival. Unless, of course, you offer your soul too. Now have a seat . . . ."

"Actually", said Niall who purposefully cut the marquis off, "I really don't play poker, due to the fact that I subconsciously give off tells that I don't realize until it's too late. Not to mention that I seem to have bad luck when it comes to acquiring the cards that I want. So I know for sure that I will lose. Which is why I'm letting Mrs. McBannon take that offer instead."

"You have that much faith in me, Niall?" Ask Mairead who is surprised that Niall is betting everything on her, yet relieved that he is not endangering himself.

"I really don't have much of a choice now, do I", reply Niall who continues in a whisper close to Mairead's ear, "and from what I heard, you're the only one with the necessary skills to beat him."

"Fair enough", said Mairead who sounded confident.

After settling that only Mairead will challenge Marquis DeGallo, Niall turns his attention to the marquis, and says while controlling his anger, "As for bringing Caolan back from the dead. There's no guarantee that you will keep your promise without dire consequences. Not to mention that bringing the dead back to life with the use of sorcery is blasphemous. So I'll pass you worthless cur."

"Glad to hear that you're not a fool like some of your brothers, or cousins", said Mairead who likes to ask in full detail what is going on. For she was under the impression that Caolan had met his fate on a hunting gone wrong. However, Mairead decides not to bother as she believes that it is none of her business and that she is more concerned with saving her own foolish daughter, and her idiot friend.

Though disappointed in the failed attempt of alluring Niall, Marquis DeGallo only replies, "Interesting", and decides to play along as he can entice Niall again after winning Mairead's soul. He gives a huge grin on his face as he speaks directly to Mairead, "All right, I'll allow it, you bet your soul, and this mystal, for both of the girls' souls. He then snap his fingers which causes the jewel to magically disappear.

This surprised everyone, with Niall replying angrily, "Why did you do that?"

"You haven't even won yet?!" Said King Tuathal immediately after Niall.

"Now, now", said Marquis DeGallo, "I made a special offer, which I rarely do, so don't push any luck that you have left, boy . . . . Now, let's play."

"Hold it", said Mairead. "I want to first verify some things, along with ensuring that there is no cheating."

With only the smile of a cat cornering a mouse, and waiting to see what the rodent will do before ending its life, Marquis DeGallo asks with curiosity, "And what would that be?"

Mairead turns to Niall and asks him, "How much do you trust King Tuathal?"

"As far as I know", replied Niall who is surprised that Mairead is questioning this now, "he is in debt to my ancestor, and will not abandon any of his descendants with a good soul. He also helped me plenty of times to prove his trustworthiness."

"That settles it then", said Mairead before turning to King Tuathal, "I want you to deal, and to make sure that there is no cheating."

"That I will, milady", said King Tuathal while swaying his hand and bowing.

With the assurance of having some chance of victory, Mairead returns her attention to Marquis DeGallo. The cruel host has been sitting quietly while maintaining the same grin on his face, as if he is taking pleasure in seeing a dog swimming away from a shark. Mairead is able to maintain her composure and ask him, "Are you alright with this?"

"Why certainly", reply Marquis DeGallo with a hint of cockiness, "I'll allow this peace of mind."

Marquis DeGallo's confidence worries Mairead, for she knows that his agreement without question is too good to be true. To ensure the return of her daughter and Eilis, Mairead carefully asks, "I want to be sure of our understanding that all I need to do for you to free the souls of my daughter, Iuile, and her friend, Eilis, from your clutches, and to remove their curse so that they will no longer be sacrificed, is for you to lose this game?"

"But of course, madam", replies Marquis DeGallo.

"I only have two more requests", said Mairead who, for some reason, appears relieved.

With utter politeness, and a hint of sarcasm, Marquis DeGallo asks her with some curiosity, "And what would those be?"

"The first request, is for the game to not start until I believe that I have a good hand", said Mairead. "In other words, if I fold on the first turn, then I lose nothing."

"Fair enough", replied Marquis DeGallo with sincerity. "I'll allow the handicap. Why I'll even give you a fair advantage by accepting any cards given to me, once you believe that you have a chance, and to show that I am not cheating, Foolish Knight here can look into my hand. As long as he doesn't tell you what I have, of course."

"Whatever helps you sleep at night, deary", replies Mairead who sounds as if she is saying that what Marquis DeGallo is offering, is not necessary. Such confidence amuses Marquis DeGallo as Mairead turns to Niall and asks him, "That is the second time he said Foolish Knight. Is he referring to you, or something else?"

"He's referring to me", replied Niall with slight annoyance while maintaining his composure. "Long story short, he gave me that nickname due to my sarcasm."

"Ahhh", replies Mairead who asked herself out loud, "rather curious if he did the same thing with Iuile and her idiot."

"Angelic Princess and Sunflower", replies Marquis DeGallo with a counterfeit friendly smile. "With Dunderhead being the fool I sent to Elosa."

"Right", said Mairead who cares very little from being quickly answered. "Anyway, I would like my second request to be for you to go first."

The last request comes off very odd to Niall, along with King Tuathal who raises an eyebrow. Marquis DeGallo on the other hand, does not seem too concerned, and allows it, for he sees no harm in either one. This has Niall curious to the point that he asks the marquis, "Are you really alright with such demands?"

Marquis DeGallo only chuckles before replying, "Absolutely! Of course, she is not the first one to make such requests. I even had . . . players . . . ask for one or the other. Now take your position, boy."

Such confidence, and arrogance, have Niall concerned and irate, before finally deciding to walk around the table. While trying to control his urge to strike at Marquis DeGallo, Niall asks him, "You also wouldn't mind having Iuile and Eilis present for this?"

"That is not a bad idea", said Mairead. "For all I know, you might try to stiff the deal if you lose."

As if Mairead said something idiotically funny, Marquis DeGallo begins to snicker before replying, "My dear, do you really think you can beat me when I never lost a game within centuries of my life?"

"Well then", said Mairead who sounded as if nothing was at stake, "if you don't want me to play . . ."

"No, no", said Marquis DeGallo as he tried to control himself, "I'll humor you." He whisks his hand to where both Iuile and Eilis appear, tied up and gagged, in their own individual chairs. "Now then . . . let's, play."

After seeing that Iuile and Eilis are safe, who both appear to be confused about what is going on, has brought relief to Mairead and Niall. With King Tuathal saying to Mairead, "Good luck, Mairead, cause you're going to need it." He turns his attention towards the center of the table, summons a deck of cards, and lays them out to ensure that every card is present, and individually different, before shuffling them in the air.

"Now that I think about it", said Niall as he stood behind, and to the right of, the marquis, "that maru elf mentioned that you let them, your guests I guess, out of the ballroom. Why wait till then to do that?"

While King Tuathal passes the cards, Marquis DeGallo turns by the waist to Niall, and replies as if he is amused, "Why not?"

This only confuses Niall, only for him to recall earlier when he asked the marquis on the stone golems' matter. He decides to respond while sounding unsettled, "Because you are either curious about how far I get, or just plain mad?"

"My, you are a 'clever' little man", replies Marquis DeGallo while giving a mocking appearance of him being impressed with Niall's guess, in which Niall decides to ignore his counterfeit impression.

When Mairead glances at her hand, she tossed her cards away saying that she folded and causally says as if she was talking to a group of her friends, "You know, I was known to be the best myself. I lost to no one except for one person." King Tuathal deals the hand.

Amuse by Mairead's anecdote has Marquis DeGallo reply sarcastically, "Would that be me?"

Unfazed, and not amused, by the marquis' retort, Mairead only looked at the next hand dealt to her and says, "Fold. My, someone's mother never gave him enough attention. How many siblings did you have?"

The counter-retort made Marquis DeGallo annoyed, while King Tuathal shuffled the next hand, before finally replying, "None."

"Poor dear", said Mairead in a tone that says that she felt sorry for him. "Raised in an orphanage?"

Such a question has apparently made a severe dent in Marquis DeGallo's nerves, who immediately gets up to say in a harsh tone, "I'll have you know that my parents were nobles!" During Marquis DeGallo and Mairead's quarrel, Niall has been standing quietly with his arms folded the whole time, in hopes of controlling his anger and resisting the urge to strike the marquis who is staring at Mairead with malice. For the wrath that is inside him, yearns for him to take Einri's dagger, and stab the marquis with it. Only for his conscious to remind him how pointless that is.

"Interesting use of the word, 'were'", said Mairead as she glanced at her new hand. "Fold. Anyway, like I was saying, I lost to no one except for one person, and all he asked upon winning was for me to go on a date with him. Because it was the only way that he could get me to do so, as I always refuse to date him otherwise, mostly due to the time he confesses to me that he is going to marry me someday." Mairead then turns to Iuile before continuing, "Being the fool that I was at that time, I thought that my beauty and fun were eternal, and with me and my sister being barmaids for our father's pub, made it seem like it was. With our main joy coming from collecting large winnings, from parting fools with their money.

"Whenever he had any money, he would play against me with the only winning from me, was a single date. I lost count of how many times he lost, or even how much money I won from him. It wasn't until four months of one loss after another, did your father finally beat me." Iuile becomes surprised by this, as she never knew this is how her parents got together, with Eilis turning to her friend in amazement too. "A year later that dang, wonderful fool, kept his word and married me, and I am thankful for his stubbornness. For you see, Fiadh and I both thought that we could put off marriage till we were much older, only for Donal to change my mind, for which I am eternally grateful. Otherwise, I would have ended up like your Aunt Fiadh, who is still single, and childless, because she has thrown away many chances for marriage, like I almost did."

While Mairead is giving her monologue, Marquis DeGallo is hunched over the table with his right index and middle finger touching his temple, his thumb underneath his chin, and the two remaining fingers covering his mouth with an irate look. When Mairead finishes her exposition, the marquis says with annoyance and sarcasm, "A truly lovely . . . and unnecessary lesson for your . . . 'special' girl." Niall on the other hand, somewhat agrees with the marquis, which he hates to admit, as now is not the time to give Iuile a life's lesson when her, Iuile's, and Eilis' souls are on the line. Marquis DeGallo turns to King Tuathal, who had stopped shuffling the deck due to being intrigued by Mairead's tale, to say, "And I know that you're not getting interested in her story, since you always keep tabs of what goes on in their town, gremlin."

"Gremlin, is it", said King Tuathal who broke out of his trance. "You arrogant, cocky, roach. Only because I'm aware of this, doesn't mean that I can still enjoy hearing it from the horse's mouth!" He begins to grumble curses while passing a new hand.

When Mairead picks up the cards that is dealt to her, she quickly puts the cards face down and says, "I can work with this."

This only has Marquis DeGallo give a devilish smile, as the fun will soon begin for him, and casually grab his cards. He gazes upon his hand where he sees that he possesses the ace of spades, ace of clubs, and a six of hearts. King Tuathal lays down the jack of hearts in the shared cards, before turning to Marquis DeGallo to see if he wants any cards. Marquis DeGallo ponders a bit, before giving up the six of hearts for the joker and showing no concern over it. This does not surprise Niall, because the marquis can easily discard it on the next turn. When the king asks Mairead if she wants any cards, she quickly passes without looking at her hand again.

This has Niall wondering what Mairead has before turning to Marquis DeGallo, who shows no worries about the final outcome. Niall glanced back at Mairead to see that she is giving the perfect poker face, as she showed no interest in what was at stake. When King Tuathal lays down the king of hearts, he turns to Marquis DeGallo who disposes the joker, and asks for another card that turns out to be the ace of diamonds. Niall's heart begins to beat fast with panic, for he knows that if King Tuathal lays down the ace of hearts, then Marquis DeGallo will have a four-of-a-kind. This would not bode well with Mairead, who on the other hand as Niall looks back at the shared cards on the table, might win with a royal flush if the ace of hearts is laid down. However, she must have the ten of hearts and queen of hearts in order to pull it off.

When Mairead's turn is up again, King Tuathal once more asks if she would like any cards, only to pass. This causes Marquis DeGallo to tap his fingers on the table, and ponder. Only for his eyes to widen upon receiving an epiphany, and immediately stands up to yell at King Tuathal, "ARE YOU HELPING HER CHEAT!!!"

The accusation, mixed with being yelled at, has made King Tuathal aghast and offended to the point where he replied to Marquis DeGallo, "How dare you! Of course not!"

"Don't toy with me", said Marquis DeGallo. "Given what you had laid down, it is obvious that you are giving her the royal flush!"

"I dare say", said Mairead whose interruption caused everyone to turn to her, "I guarantee that he is not helping me in any way, though I should ask if you are cheating yourself."

"Of course not", said Marquis DeGallo. "Ask the boy here, he'll tell you that my hand never changed except for what this imp had given me."

This incurs King Tuathal's wrath once more, and replies while trying to maintain his anger, "You now dare call me an IMP!!! If you weren't the Dark Prince's . . . ."

"When I was a little girl", said Mairead who caused the king to be silent and listen, along with everyone else, "my grandpa sat me on his knee and told me a story of his youth. One part of his history was the time he worked as a stevedore at a rail freight. It involved the owner, who had always assumed that his employees stole from him. Such accusation always annoyed my grandpa, for he had never stolen anything in his life. So one day, he asked one of his seniors why their boss claimed that they were a bunch of thieves. The senior replied with an amused grin, that it is because he had stolen himself when he was a stevedore at a shipyard."

There was a moment of silence as Niall, King Tuathal, and Marquis DeGallo, understood what Mairead was getting at with her philosophy. Niall decides to turn to see how Marquis DeGallo would respond, only to see that he is giving a deadpan appearance as if he is pondering on the situation, before turning to the fireplace, and staring at it. It was not long before Marquis DeGallo turned back, and sat down while appearing more confident than ever while saying, "Point taken. My apologies, but you should look at my point of view, as I don't like cheating myself."

"No, I don't", replied Mairead. "Because I don't stoop to the level of a pathetic monster who tricks people into selling their souls."

Niall is now afraid to look at Marquis DeGallo, for he knows that Mairead struck another nerve. But Niall forces himself to look, out of curiosity, and to his surprise the marquis is perfectly calm while giving a sinister grin. The only thing Niall can conclude is that Marquis DeGallo is so sure that he is going to win, that he is holding in his frustration until his victory, then he will make Mairead pay for her disrespect.

While maintaining his composure from being insulted again, King Tuathal decides to go ahead and lay down the last card, which happens to be the ace of hearts. After laying down the ace, Marquis DeGallo casually said, while maintaining his grin, "I'll pass, but just to let you know, milady, if you lay down a royal flush, then I will know for a fact that you two are cheating, and our . . . deal . . . is . . . off."

This shocks Niall as he turns to Mairead who replies, "Fair enough", before picking up her hand, and takes the ace of hearts off the table. Doing so seems pointless to Niall because Marquis DeGallo can still win with a three-of-a-kind.

When Mairead lays down the card that she is replacing the ace with, everyone's heart sink to the bottom of their feet. In a mad panic, Marquis DeGallo hastefully gets up and yells, "YOU CAN'T LAY THAT DOWN!!!"

This perplexes Mairead who replies, "But the rules did not state that I could not switch it with the shared cards, only that it cannot be dealt into the shared cards. Therefore, I win."

"But, but", said Marquis DeGallo who sounds as if he is breaking apart in a mad panic, "putting down the joker . . . means that you lose too!"

"My dear, pathetic, little man", replied Mairead. "Who said I was trying to win the game? I was simply . . . trying . . . to win . . . the bet."

Astonish of such an idiotic answer has made Marquis DeGallo regain his confidence, and laugh hysterically before saying, "You fool! You have to win the game in order to win the bet!"

"Not so fast", said King Tuathal with full excitement. "I seem to recall her saying that all she needs to do to save her daughter and her friend, is for you to lose", he begins to give a huge grin as he continues, "and lose you did!" He then burst out into laughter upon witnessing a brilliant trickery.

Realizing what the leprechaun king said is true, has made Marquis DeGallo fully terrified, as if he is in the presence of the Angel of Death himself, before saying, "No, no, no!" He begins to run towards the Demonic Fireplace, gets on his knees, and begs to it, "This doesn't count! It's a draw! I didn't lose!"

The Demonic Fireplace begins to flare upon its firebox, followed by a response in a maleficent voice, "The rules which you stated, says that whoever possesses the joker upon finishing the last round, automatically loses. That includes the shared cards as part of your possession."

"No, no, no", cries Marquis DeGallo as he continues to beg the Demonic Fireplace.

"We had a deal", said the voice from the Demonic Fireplace, "your soul, for the forbidden powers of magic that will make you a sorcerer, and to never lose in a game! In return, you will be allowed to hold onto your current soul, in exchange for the souls that you had claimed in your games after you're tired of playing with them. However, if you somehow lose in a game, then I will reclaim what I had given to you, including your own SOUL!!!"

When the Demonic Fireplace finishes speaking, an invisible force seems to pull something out of Marquis DeGallo, who then pats himself before asking, "What just happened?" He is suddenly grabbed and forcefully hurled to the ground, and punched severely into his left face by Niall, who cannot help himself anymore. The marquis' left side of his mask begins to crack more, and more, with every punch as he cries out, "Why . . . are my powers . . . not pushing . . . you back . . . ? And why . . . am I . . . bleeding . . . like this?" When Niall has enough, he stops punching Marquis DeGallo, whose blood is pouring down to his neck, filling around his left eye, and seeping through the cracks of his mask with his nose bent. It was during this time that the marquis realizes that Niall was using the broken arrowhead, from the aftermath with the stone golems, that are sticking out between his index and middle fingers.

Rage and satisfaction are what Niall is feeling, as he now believes that he is able to kill Marquis DeGallo. Only to realize that killing him with his own hands is pointless, for it will not bring his brother back. So Niall decides to release the marquis, along with dropping the arrowhead to the ground, and says, "It seems that your master has made you powerless. You'll pay for your horrible actions. But not by my hands, but by the hands of the townsfolk, who will have you lynched, you worthless cur . . . ." Niall trails off upon noticing Iuile's wooden clover, which happens to be hanging off Marquis DeGallo's inside coat pocket. He immediately grabs it, and asks with puzzlement, "Why in blazes is a pagan such as yourself, carrying this?"

As Marquis DeGallo attempts to reply, the voice from the Demonic Fireplace interrupts him to say, "I will not wait that long for his death. I was hoping to curse you once you kill him, but it seems that won't happen. Regardless, we will always claim, what is rightfully due."

Flames in the form of whips, spur out of the fireplace with attempts to grab Marquis DeGallo, who dodges and tries to escape after Niall pockets Iuile's wooden clover and jumps off of the host. With Niall himself doing his own evasion as he runs back towards Mairead and King Tuathal, who are themselves horrified by Niall's actions, followed by what the Demonic Fireplace is doing. When Niall is almost to safety, one of the flame whips manages to snatch his right ankle and drags him toward the firebox. Even though the whips are aflame, there seems to be no burning sensation, or damage, around Niall's ankle as he tries to grasp something.

Only for Mairead to decide to grab his wrist, and tries with all her might to pull him back. With Iuile and Eilis watching in horror, and helpless due to being tied up, Mairead believes that she is the only one capable of saving Niall. But Mairead's attempt to save him is failing, which is evident due to her sliding on the floor, as even King Tuathal takes hold of the fur coat on Niall's shoulder, to no avail. Because even though King Tuathal is very powerful, he knows that his magic is insignificant compared to the Princes of Darkness.

It is at this moment that Niall realizes that they are only going to be pulled into the fireplace themselves and become forever doomed. The only thing that is going through his mind, is to gaze into Iuile's eyes, where he sees that she retrieved the same agonizing pain that she had when she started her quest. A pain that only quells, upon talking to her mother earlier. With only one way to ensure that Iuile will not lose her mother, Niall decides to forcefully release his grip from Mairead and tells her and King Tuathal to get back. The mother and the king stand in shock when Niall, for no reason, decides to roll on his back and notices Einri's dagger on his belt.

Seeing Einri's dagger has Niall immediately recall the blade's inscription, and with nothing to lose, unsheathes the dagger and lifts himself in a sitting position while saying, "Almighty Deus! Please have mercy upon me, and aid me in this darkest hour!" After praying to the Almighty, Niall strikes the flame whip. The fiery whip releases Niall's ankle with a screech of pain, before withdrawing into the firebox. Upon being free, Niall quickly gets up and runs back towards Mairead and King Tuathal, who moved back to where Iuile and Eilis are still tied up, and says to himself, "Thank you, Dominus."

When Niall reaches where the others are, he turns back and sees the inevitable happen to Marquis DeGallo. For at some point when Niall was ensnared, Marquis DeGallo had been caught by one of the flame whips, and screaming in terror. The successful capture is followed by several more of the whips wrapping themselves around a leg, or waist, where they begin to drag him towards the fireplace at a slow pace. This is due to the marquis digging his fingers into the carpet, where he made ten tiny trenches while heading towards the firebox.

While Marquis DeGallo is being dragged, a portal have been opening up, and reaching its peak, within the Demonic Fireplace. The portal is also the source of where the whips appeared from and forcefully pulls the marquis into it as it slowly closes. Niall, Mairead, Iuile, Eilis, and King Tuathal, watch in horror as Marquis DeGallo begs them to save him. Except there is no avail in doing so as he passes through the portal, where it completely closed.

CHAPTER 28

The One Girl

For anyone who is wondering about Einri's fate, be relieved that he is still alive. But not well, for as he said, the thugs on Ogre Street in Amelon, beat and stripped him of his belongings after pulling him into an alley. As he wakes up from unconsciousness, facing up, he stares at the twilight sky where he hopes that the others are all right and that Niall succeeds in rescuing the girls. Especially Iuile, whose love he feels he no longer deserves. For he has now come to the realization of his misdeeds, rethinks his life, and decides to be productive in his life in a positive manner. With the only saving grace that he has, is that he has relatives in town who can help him return home as the dawn of the new day begins.

As for the aftermath of Mairead's clever plan in defeating Marquis DeGallo, everyone was speechless over what happened. Except for Niall who feels tremendous relief from avoiding eternal damnation, and looks at Einri's dagger where he says to himself, "Your betrayal is forgiven, you spoiled fool."

It is followed by King Tuathal saying, "Well then, that was convenient, and came out of nowhere. But who am I to look a gift horse in the mouth." He turns to Niall who was sheathing the dagger, "I'm also glad to see that you are safe, thanks to Einri's dagger.

"I appreciate your concern, Your Majesty", said Niall who began to recall what had transpired. Only to realize something that does not add up to where he asks King Tuathal, "Now that I think about it, why was I only snared by one of those whips when Marquise DeGallo received multiple whips upon being caught?"

"Probably because they prefer the main dish over the appetizer", replied King Tuathal.

"That does seem to be the case", said Mairead who is grateful that everyone is safe. She is also glad that her trickery worked with utter relief, before calmly asking, "Niall, untie Eilis while I untie Iuile."

"I'll go open up the entryway that the fiend had closed up", said King Tuathal.

"You are truly generous, Your Majesty", reply Mairead.

When Iuile is untied, she quickly hugs her mother while saying with tears in her eyes, "I'm so sorry, Mom . . . . I love you so much."

Feeling joy that her daughter is finally safe, has Mairead shedding tears herself as she replies, "I know, sweetie. Just don't do something this foolish again."

"A lot of good you were", said Eilis after Niall untied her.

This has caused Mairead to be annoyed by Eilis' words where she and Iuile both turn to Eilis, while still hugging each other. Mairead then asks Eilis, "What do you mean by that?"

"Well", said Eilis, "all his attempts to save us were pointless since you were the one who saved us."

Taking offense at Eilis' ungratefulness has made Niall reply with harsh sarcasm, "You're welcome you unappreciative . . . ."

"That's enough!" Said Iuile who interrupted Niall's foul mouth as she stopped hugging her mother, and walked towards Eilis while wiping the tears from her eyes. When Iuile approaches Eilis, she angrily says to her friend, "He still risked his life several times to save us. If anything, he saved us from having more trauma and torture than we can possibly imagine. As a matter of fact, the reason that I did not stab you while you were tied up, was because he warned me about what a manipulative jerk Marquis DeGallo was.

"Therefore, you owe him your life. I'm also sure that my mom obviously wouldn't have gotten here in time to save us, both physically and mentally, if it weren't for his help." She then takes a deep breath to calm herself, before continuing while trying to control her anger, "As far as I'm concerned, Niall saved us just as much, or even more so, than my mom did. So you should show some appreciation, you ungrateful brat."

During Iuile's monologue, Eilis stared at her friend with fear and shame, only to realize something, and rebuke with confidence, "True, but if he liked one of us, he would have gambled his soul. I mean, he wasn't even playing against the marquis, meaning he didn't bet his soul." When Eilis finishes speaking, she hopes to dumbfound Iuile with her epiphany.

Only to be shocked once more by the scornful look that Iuile is giving, a look that is similar to her mother whenever Eilis tries to be cleverly mischievous. Iuile closes her eyes and takes another deep breath, before opening her eyes again and reply in a calm, yet threatening, tone, "If one of us did care for him, then we wouldn't want him to suffer the same as us."

Such retort made Eilis pause for a moment before giving an uncomfortable laugh, followed by replying nervously, "Right, my mistake." Iuile then recalled what she just said about one of them caring for Niall, causing her to blush and glance at where he was standing. Only to see that Niall is looking the other way with his face blushed, and appears that he did not hear the last part of their conversation (even though he did).

"Well said, dear", said Mairead after approaching her daughter. "Though to be honest, I can only bet my soul for one of you. Whereas Niall here allowed me to use a marvelous jewel he acquired, while traveling to this wretched place, for the other. Sadly, that curse of a man immediately teleported it to Deus knows where due to his overconfidence.

"But Niall did however give me plenty of time to come up with a plan to defeat him, while he was trying to offer that same jewel. So I can vouch that Niall helped more so than I had for you two. As for which one of you for the jewel . . . . Well, you just have to ask him yourself. Later, because I just remembered about a certain curse mark, and I am curious if it is gone?"

Upon hearing this, Iuile pulls her hair back saying, "It's supposed to be behind my neck."

"Called it", said Niall.

"You want a biscuit?" Said King Tuathal sarcastically after he finished laying out the stairs.

After seeing nothing on the back of Iuile's neck, Mairead is utterly relief before replying, "There's nothing there. The curse is broken, let's go home." With joy and satisfaction of being free, Iuile turns to her mother and agrees.

They head down the stairs where Iuile starts to feel flutter, as she decides to walk next to Niall's left side, who himself follows behind her mother who is leading the way, with King Tuathal sitting on Mairead's shoulder. Eilis on the other hand, is still standing where Iuile disputed against her, as it resulted in her being dumbstruck. As they descend the stairs, Iuile said to Niall while blushing, "Thank you . . . for all you had done for me and Eilis. You risked so much for little in return, and . . . ." Iuile begins to feel insecure about finishing her sentence as they reach the bottom of the stairs, and onto the fourth floor's north wing.

The joy of being praised by Iuile, causes Niall to rub the back of his head and reply, "Don't mention it, and sorry that you saw an ugly side of me when I attacked that pain of a mule earlier."

"Oh, I'm not", said Iuile who is already familiar with that level of behavior from her father, whenever someone mistreats her or her sisters, among others. As she begins to recall the time when her father beats someone to unconsciousness for making a pass at Roisin. While Iuile and Roisin yelled for their father to stop, their older male cousins tried to pull him away from the poor fool. Iuile then remembers something that she forgot to bring up, and halts before saying to Niall, "Not to mention that you may have saved my life by savagely beating Marquis DeGallo."

This made Niall and Mairead stop and turn to Iuile with puzzlement, where they both, along with King Tuathal, take notice that Eilis has broken out of her trance, and is running in order to catch up with them. When Iuile realizes that Niall, Mairead, and King Tuathal have their attention behind her, she turns and sees Eilis heading their way. After Iuile sees her friend, her mother asks her, "How so?"

When Eilis finally reaches them, she begins to pant while Iuile replies to her mother, "You and King Tuathal may have not noticed, since you were trying to save Niall from that horrifying whip, but Marquis DeGallo tried to kill me with a dagger."

"Good, great, Deus!" Reply King Tuathal who, along with Niall and Mairead, was shocked. "I gathered that those tether whips saved you."

"They did", replied Iuile. "But the odd thing is, was that Marquis DeGallo had evaded them quite easily. Yet one of them managed to grab him as if it was in his blind spot." She turns to her friend, who has already regained her stamina, to ask her, "Isn't that right, Eilis?"

"Seems that way", replied Eilis. "I think it is because of his left mask being damaged, and covered in blood due to Niall beating him beforehand . . . ." Eilis trails off upon receiving an epiphany, and begins to feel foolish before continuing, "Which means that Niall had indirectly saved you."

There was only silence in the south wing as everyone stared at Eilis as if she had become the new village idiot. The mute is broken when Mairead decides to say, "Dominus Deus truly does work in mysterious ways."

When Mairead finishes speaking, she turns to walk away, only for Iuile to halt her to ask, "Now that I think about it, Mom, I'm surprised that your plan worked, and that everything turned out well."

"Yes, well", said Mairead, "to be honest, I thought that I was going to lose my soul too."

This surprises Iuile who immediately replies, "Wait, what?"

Mairead gave an amused smile and said to her daughter, "Sweetie, my entire plan when I accepted his game, was to at least trade places with you. You should know by now that I would give my life for you and your siblings, even my very own soul." Mairead then walks away as Iuile truly realizes, how much her mother loves her. With Niall feeling annoyed overhearing a private conversation.

They resume their trek down the south wing with Eilis walking on Niall's right side, while Iuile stays on his left. "Oh, I almost forgot", said Eilis who asked Iuile while pulling her hair back. "Do you see anything?" When Iuile replies that the Sacrificial Mark is gone, with Niall paying no attention and staring straight ahead, Eilis feels relieved and says to him honestly, "I'm sorry for being an unappreciated jerk, Niall." Upon hearing his name, Niall glances at Eilis who continues, "Thank you for all the times you saved us."

Feeling pleased that Eilis has finally decided to be thankful, Niall replies while looking straight ahead again, "Yeah, well, you're welcome since you're being grateful." His words and actions only upset Eilis, who quickly gives a pouty appearance.

"Oh no!" Said Iuile with dread as she halted once more, causing everyone else to stop and turn to her with worry. "My clover! I never got it back!"

"Clover?" Replied Niall who recalled his finding, and pulled out the wooden clover that he snatched from Marquise DeGallo. "You mean this?"

Upon seeing the wooden clover, Iuile smiled with jubilation after recognizing it as her own, and said, "Oh my goodness, yes it is! Thank you so much, Niall! Where did you find it?"

"On that dastard when I finished pummeling him", replied Niall. "I thought it was weird that he would possess something sacred."

When Iuile receives her wooden clover, she holds it upon her heart with relief, and silently thanks Dominus Deus before Eilis says to her, "Oh, now I remember. Your dad made it himself as a birthday gift."

This annoys Iuile who turns to her friend and replies, "It was a confirmation gift for confirming into Rozalinity! Your dad made one himself for your confirmation. Remember?"

When Iuile finished speaking, Eilis took a moment to recollect before feeling guilty and said, "Oh, that's right. After everything that just happened, I guess I should wear it more often."

"I would think so", said Mairead with some hope that Eilis had learned something from her ordeal. She then turns to her daughter with a smile, "I'm very glad to see that you have it back and that you hold it very dearly. Your father will be very pleased that you still love it." Mairead continues to smile as she walks away while Iuile blush. With Eilis feeling ashamed, because she now feels that she has disappointed her father. Niall on the other hand, only scratches his head before deciding to follow Mairead, along with Iuile and Eilis.

Even though the dawn of the new day reaches the island of Elosa, it has not fully reached Durigh. With the exception of the rays from the sun that can be seen in the east sky, as they can be visible through the windows of the foyer. While Mairead and the teens descend the stairs, they notice that the battle with the horde appears to have recently ended. For they see several corpses of monsters with some of the townspeople harmed, yet none of them were killed. When Mairead yells out that Marquis Savio DeGallo is no more, everyone cheers as Eilis runs toward her father, who is unharmed. When Eilis reaches her father, they were immediately surrounded by other male kin as her father decides to lift her up, and hugs her before shedding tears of joy.

When Iuile and her mother are being welcomed by their own male kin, Iuile is suddenly pulled aside by her brother, Gearoid, who immediately puts his arm around her neck. He then begins to give her a noogie saying, "C'mere you spoiled brat! You got a lot of nerve putting me through this crud after everything that I did yesterday!"

With Iuile, who acknowledges this as divine punishment, screaming, "AAAHHH!!! I DESERVE THIS!!! I DESERVE THIS!!!"

Niall walks by them with the decision to not intervene, since it is Iuile's brother, and therefore abiding by one of the golden rules of siblings: Never interfere in a siblings' quarrel, unless it is a life and death situation, or being destructive in their surroundings. As Niall is walking towards the main entrance, he notices his brothers approaching him, and says to them, "Let's go home."

Caught off guard by what Niall said, made Slaine question him with seriousness, followed by sarcasm, "So you already asked one of them out, Foolish Knight?"

"I just want to go home", said Niall who is finally showing signs of exhaustion and hunger. "I'm not in the mood to explain the meaning of that name, nor do I care if I'm sleeping in the barn for not bringing home any game. I just want to go home, and go to bed, after getting food in my stomach."

"Did you, or didn't you?" Adhanh asks with curiosity. "I mean you did help saved two cute girls. Though you may want to watch out for Shamus and Shane if you go after Eilis."

"Don't care", said Niall who has his eyes half open, "need sleep."

"Are you kidding", said King Tuathal who was hiding in Niall's satchel once more. "Now's the perfect time to ask her how you feel."

"Too tired to care", said Niall whose brothers assume that he is still talking to them.

"Blasted waste, you ignorant fool", said King Tuathal angrily.

Upon exiting the mansion, Niall, with his brothers, sees that the mob destroyed the armor golems at the front doors, along with the garden as the hedges were apparently destroyed to make an easy traverse. While Niall gazes at the mermaid fountain, he recognizes a familiar raptor standing near the fountain, along with the other mounts, and says, "Crono, is that you?"

"We found him tethered inside the ballroom", said Slaine.

"I'm surprised the horde didn't eat him", said Adhanh. "Anyway, we untied Crono after realizing it was him, and brought him out here."

"By the time we came back in", said Slaine, "you and the others came down the stairs."

"Ah", was the only thing Niall said, before deciding to approach and grab Crono's rein, climb him, and have him walk towards the gate to wait for his kin. Adhanh goes off to find their uncles and cousins who are somewhere around the mansion. While Slaine in the meantime, went off to find their mounts that were wandering with the other townspeople's horses, raptors, donkeys, pygmy woolly mammoths, oxen, a bear (owned by a merchant from the country of Rucia), and the pig from the weird uncle who took down most of the monsters after arriving late to the party (with the Rucian merchant being the second). For apparently, the mounts decided to mingle around the garden since they were not tethered.

"Are you seriously going to waste this opportunity", said King Tuathal after jumping onto Crono's head.

"Another day", said Niall who in truth, is too nervous to ask in front of everyone. He decides to reply with his excuse, "Iuile is too emotional to give a proper response at the moment, nor do I want her to feel pressure in front of everyone. The last thing that I want is for her to agree to go out with me due to pressure, only for her to regret and despise me later for it. All I want right now is some sleep, after getting some food in my belly of course." He stops his raptor in front of the gate, where he notices the horse carriages destroyed before returning his attention to King Tuathal. Niall grits it as he decides to face the truth that has been haunting him by seeking confirmation from the king through the query, "Caolan's soul is eternally condemned, right?"

"Condemned?" Said King Tuathal who appears confused for a moment, before grinning with amusement, "Is that what got you fired up this whole time, lad? Of course not! Anyone sent to Hell, but not condemned by Dominus Deus, is rescued by his angels."

Upon hearing that Caolan's soul is saved, brings Niall great joy, for the burden of despair begins to evaporate from his soul. Though he could not help but wonder how King Tuathal would have such knowledge and decided to ask the king, "Really? How do you know?"

"By mother nature, Emana, herself", replies King Tuathal. "I asked her one time during a party, as I couldn't help but be annoyed that the Almighty would abandon his children like that. Only for her to tell me otherwise. So be at peace, my lad, for your brother is with Dominus Deus in Heaven!"

Now knowing for sure of Caolan's fate, brings tranquility to Niall who replies to the leprechaun king with joy, "That's really good to know. I guess all that's left, is to find a way to convince my kin to allow me to go home separately so that I can take you home."

"I appreciate the jester", said King Tuathal, "but I can get back on my own. You truly deserve a rest after everything you have done."

"Well that's one less thing to worry about", said Niall gazing ahead. "Though I wonder if the townspeople pillage the mystal from the other golem, back at the ravine's entrance from Killy Ri Forest?" He returned his attention to King Tuathal, "I did recall you saying that's what brought them to life, meaning that there has to be at least two of them, right?"

"Actually", said King Tuathal with a cocky grin, "I had my people take care of that before catching up to you. I'm also sure they took the two from the armor golems after your townsfolk crumbled them to pieces of course. So no worries."

Something occurs to Niall who questions, "Now that I think about it, why would they break apart after having their eyes destroyed?"

This caused King Tuathal's mouth to drop for a moment before replying, "You mean to tell me, that you destroyed their eyes without knowing why it would make them disassembled?"

"Well . . . yeah", reply Niall who is now feeling foolish. "They look obviously weak, and if anything, I would at least blind them.

There was only silence between the two for a moment before King Tuathal broke out laughing while saying, "Talk about dumb luck, lad . . . and to answer your question . . . ." He manages to calm down before continuing, "Well, to simplify it, they work similar to the exhaust of any steam or coal engine, since the mystal is normally placed inside a golem. Of course in this case, if you eliminate their exhaust, then they will cease to function until they regenerate new eyes. But you removed a mystal from one of them and therefore prevented it from reassembling. By doing so, you made it cease to function altogether, and of course, my people removed the other one after you left. As for the armor golems, a few good hard whacks are enough to disassemble them for a while, due to the material and size. They can also cease to function if you remove their scroll full of incantations of how it should move and act."

"Huh, interesting to know", said Niall with satisfaction that everything worked out well, and shakes his head with a smile. "Now that I think about it", he begins to pat Crono's shoulder, "I wonder how the marquis would have reacted if he knew that the only reason I was able to defeat those golems, was because of this two-legged lizard." Crono gives a playful hiss at Niall's sarcasm.

"He may have found you less troublesome if he did", replied King Tuathal. "Though now that I think about it, a mystal of that size is still too small to fully fuel golems of that size. But of course, that fiend has the power of sorcery that may have made it possible." The royal leprechaun turns to Niall with a bow saying. "Anyway, goodbye brave Niall, and best of luck to you." From there, the King of the Leprechauns of Gleannasi disappears.

"Well", said Niall as he whipped Crono's reins, "let's go."

After causally passing through the gate, Iuile appears behind Niall and asks, "You're leaving already?"

Hearing Iuile's voice surprised Niall, as he did not expect this. Not sure of what to do, Niall decides to wing it, turn to her, and reply, "Sorry to worry you, it's just that even though we are both tired, I haven't had a decent meal since lunch yesterday."

"Oh, I'm sorry", said Iuile as she began to fidget. "I just want to thank you . . . AGAIN! I mean. I want to thank you again for everything that you had done for me and Eilis, and . . . ." She starts to blush due to being unable to finish her sentence.

Niall stands there guessing what Iuile wants to say and begins to look around to see that they are alone. After seeing that no one is close by, Niall mumbles to himself, "Better now than never." He then dismounts Crono, and asks Iuile while approaching her, "Do you want to have lunch", he then utters to himself aloud, "today is Reliday", before continuing his conversation with Iuile, "tomorrow on Luxday, after church? I would like to go out today, but it's obvious that we are going to sleep for the rest of the day, once we get home." When Niall finishes speaking, he takes a few more steps before stopping, within an arm's length from Iuile, and waits for her reply.

"I would love that", said Iuile with excitement in her voice. "Though I won't be getting any sleep till nightfall. Knowing my mom, she'll start punishing me by giving me chores as soon as I get home."

Realizing that it is too good to be true, Niall replies, "Well if you want me to . . . ."

This has Iuile cut Niall off saying, "Oh, don't get me wrong, tomorrow's fine! I'll meet you an hour before noon on the main road in front of my ranch." Iuile begins to blush even redder because she has a feeling that she might have made things worse.

"I'll see you then", said Niall whose words made Iuile smile with joy. She softly bites her bottom lip while hoping for something to happen, only to decide to return to her family. When Niall, out of the heat of the moment, decides to grab her arm and pull her towards him to where their bodies are pressing against each other. Niall stares into Iuile's eyes with yearning as he begins to say to her, "I'd fallen for you the moment I saw your heavenly blue eyes, gracefully brown hair that flows beautifully with the wind, and your freckly face that sparkles like the stars in the night sky." The genuine passion that Niall had spoken, has Iuile in complete awe, for her heart is beating rapidly with the anticipation of what is to come next. It was not until the sun finally showed itself, did they kiss.

Finis Fabula

In memory of my Papa (Grandfather).

May he bring laughter and joy, in the Kingdom of God.

Along with his wife, and my Grandmother.

May she bring her sweetness and compassion,

in the Kingdom of God.

Printed in the USA
CPSIA information can be obtained
at www.ICGtesting.com
LVHW021546231124
797434LV00003B/66